[rupture]
on the right knee

00351 919 697 977

44 0203 195 2444

WALKING ON MADEIRA

0044 0203 195 2442

8am - 8pm

Mais Clinic   R. João de Deus 12C
              9050 - 027 Funchal

WALKING ON MADEIRA

60 MOUNTAIN AND LEVADA ROUTES ON MADEIRA AND PORTO SANTO

by Paddy Dillon

CICERONE

JUNIPER HOUSE, MURLEY MOSS,
OXENHOLME ROAD, KENDAL, CUMBRIA LA9 7RL
www.cicerone.co.uk

© Paddy Dillon 2018
Third edition 2018
ISBN: 978 1 85284 855 2
Reprinted 2021 (with updates)

Second edition 2009
First edition 2002

Printed in Singapore by KHL Printing on responsibly sourced paper
A catalogue record for this book is available from the British Library.
All photographs are by the author unless otherwise stated.

MIX
Paper from
responsible sources
FSC® C004791

Updates to this Guide

While every effort is made by our authors to ensure the accuracy of guidebooks
as they go to print, changes can occur during the lifetime of an edition. Any
updates that we know of for this guide will be on the Cicerone website (www.
cicerone.co.uk/855/updates), so please check before planning your trip. We
also advise that you check information about such things as transport,
accommodation and shops locally. Even rights of way can be altered over
time. We are always grateful for information about any discrepancies between
a guidebook and the facts on the ground, sent by email to updates@cicerone.
co.uk or by post to Cicerone, Juniper House, Murley Moss, Oxenholme Road,
Kendal, LA9 7RL.

Register your book: To sign up to receive free updates, special offers and
GPX files where available, register your book at www.cicerone.co.uk.

Front cover: Madeira's highest mountains as seen from Eira do Ribeiro (Walk 37)

CONTENTS

Ponta do São Lourenço (Walk 6)

Map key

═══════════	road
▬▬▬▬▬	route on road (various colours)
━━━━━━━	route (various colours)
●●●●●●●●●●●●	alternative route (various colours)
- - - - - - - - - -	other tracks or paths
▥▥▥▥▥▥▥▥▥▥	tunnel
⬭	river/reservoir
⬚⬚⬚⬚⬚⬚⬚⬚⬚	airport
Ⓢ Ⓕ ⑤Ⓕ	start point/finish point/start-finish point
ⒶⓈ ⒶⒻ	alternative start/alternative finish
▨	town/village
■	building
▲	peak
🄿	parking
●	water feature
→	direction arrow
→	route direction arrow
•	other feature
♱	church

```
0          1          2          3
|━━━━━━━━━━━━━━━━━━━━━━━━━━━━━━| km
```

The above scale applies to all the routes in the book.

Contour Key

▨	800-1000m	▨	1800-2000m
▨	600-800m	▨	1600-1800m
▨	400-600m	▨	1400-1600m
▨	200-400m	▨	1200-1400m
▨	0-200m	▨	1000-1200m

PREFACE

Madeira has undergone many changes since the first publication of *Walking in Madeira* and most are for the good. A tortuous road system once made it difficult to reach the start of many walks, but now a splendid network of road tunnels enables quick and easy access to many formerly remote places. Bus companies have adapted and altered their schedules, with more frequent services, more destinations and rapid access through the new tunnels.

While a handful of bars and restaurants have closed, many more have opened and there are more places offering accommodation around the islands in places that are popular with walkers. No longer should anyone feel confined to Funchal or the 'Hotel Zone', as they can walk from one hotel to another on long-distance routes. Walkers have not been forgotten as the island authorities have waymarked and signposted some splendid walking routes, improved and restored others, provided safety fencing and opened completely new trails.

All these changes meant that *Walking in Madeira* was ready for a complete overhaul. For the second edition, all the routes were walked again and the route descriptions brought up to date. New routes were added and all the relevant facilities were checked. More and more walkers are seeking longer and more sustained routes across Madeira. Some routes are now structured so that they serve as day walks, and can also be linked end-to-end to create splendid long-distance walks. Improved full-colour mapping, more information and more photographs should allow walkers to get more enjoyment out of their visit to Madeira. For the third edition, following severe flood and fire damage, repair work was inspected, routes and facilities were checked, and changes were made where necessary.

Paddy Dillon

Looking towards Pico Ruivo from Cabeço Furado (Walk 13)

INTRODUCTION

Madeira features very steep and rugged mountain slopes

Madeira and Porto Santo rise steep, rocky and remote in the Atlantic Ocean off the coast of Europe and Africa. The nearest island groups are the distant Azores and Canary Islands. All these islands enjoy a subtropical climate that many walkers find acceptable throughout the year. A compact and mountainous island, Madeira is criss-crossed by old paths and tracks, and is remarkably scenic and accessible. Water is conveyed round the island in charming flower-fringed channels called *levadas*, which offer anything from gentle strolls to extremely exposed cliff walks. Richly wooded valleys, rocky slopes, cultivated terraces and impressive cliff coasts can be explored, along with one of the best *laurisilva* forests in the world. This book describes a rich and varied selection of 60 walks to suit all abilities, covering the whole of Madeira and Porto Santo, as well as a cruise to the Ilhas Desertas.

LOCATION

Madeira is a small island of 750km² (290 square miles). It lies at 32°46'N/17°03'W in the subtropical Atlantic Ocean, about 600km (370 miles) from Morocco in North Africa, and about 950km (590 miles) from Portugal, to which it belongs. Its closest neighbours are Porto Santo, about 40km (25 miles) away to the north-east, and the Ilhas Desertas, about 20km (12½ miles) south-east of Madeira at their closest point. Madeira is loosely associated with the Azores and Canaries, since they all lie along the same huge complex of fracture zones in the Earth's crust, but they are far from view.

GEOLOGY

Madeira is essentially a volcanic island, although volcanic activity has long ceased. Basalt from deep within the earth spewed onto the ocean floor around 130 million years ago. Gradually, enough material built up for land to appear above the water, so that Madeira raised itself from the ocean about 2.5 million years ago. Some corals established themselves round the fringe of the island as it grew, and these are preserved as fossils in very limited areas.

The overwhelming bulk of the island is made up of ash and basalt lava flows shot through with dolerite dykes. It is thought that volcanic activity ceased around 25,000 years ago and the rock is now heavily weathered. Porto Santo is older and more weathered than Madeira. Although mostly basalt, Porto Santo features a central band of calcareous sandstone that produces a fertile soil in the middle of the island that has eroded to form a magnificent golden beach.

HISTORY

The true story of Madeira's 'discovery' may never be known, but early records agree it was a densely-wooded uninhabited island. The many fanciful tales of Madeira's discovery don't tie in easily with historical documentation. Some early maps show the island and there is a suspicion that the Phoenicians may have been the first to set eyes on Madeira, whereas others say the Genoans discovered it. Some records state that the Spanish were in the habit of stopping off at Porto Santo on trips between Spain and the Canary Islands. A strange story relates how an Englishman, Walter Machim, along with his wife and a companion, were marooned on Madeira and thus became the first temporary settlers.

Reliable records date from 1418, when Prince Henry 'The Navigator' of Portugal patronised voyages to seek new territories. João Gonçalves Zarco and Tristão Vaz Teixeira were leading one of these voyages around Africa in 1419, when they were blown off-course onto Porto Santo. While checking out possibilities for settling the island, they also discovered Madeira. In 1425 great fires were started to clear Madeira's native woodlands and open up sunny slopes for settlement and cultivation. In 1452 slaves were drafted in to work the land and dig a network of irrigation channels,

Thick layers of volcanic ash and lava flows criss-crossed with basalt dykes on Porto Santo (Walk 60)

Charming thatched houses at Queimadas (Walk 25)

or levadas. Christopher Columbus is said to have visited Madeira and Porto Santo in 1478, convinced that by sailing ever-westwards he would find India.

Madeira and Porto Santo, being remote from Portugal, were open to attack by pirates from Europe and Africa. The islands suffered several raids, resulting in the destruction of property, looting and the capture and killing of inhabitants. Fortifications were constructed, including a wall around Funchal in 1542, but most island communities were unprotected. In calmer times good trade links were developed, along with agriculture, and Madeira became known for producing fine wines. By 1662, following a marriage between Charles II of England and Catherine of Braganza, English merchants settled on Madeira and took key positions in the wine

trade. English troops were stationed in Madeira in 1807 as Napoleon conquered more and more territory. In more settled times, during the 1850s, cholera wiped out thousands of islanders, while disease destroyed their vines. Banana cultivation developed, with the 'dwarf banana' proving the most suitable type for Madeira's climate.

Tourism has developed since 1890, with the climate making it a favourite winter destination for rich Europeans. Although Portugal was neutral in the War years, it suffered under a dictatorship and many Madeirans emigrated to other parts of Europe, or to Angola, Brazil and Venezuela. Madeira has been an autonomous region since 1976 and, following Portugal's entry into the EU, vast sums of money were applied to its infrastructure. As elsewhere in Europe,

LEVADAS

Early in the 15th century, short and simple water channels were dug to divert streams out of valleys onto sunny slopes where areas had been cleared for cultivation. These channels were known as *levadas*, from the Portuguese verb *levar*, meaning 'to take along, or carry'. The main crop was sugar, and water power was also needed to drive mills.

As the population grew and more areas were cleared for cultivation, more streams were diverted into a growing network of levadas. These were generally cut by farmers, or paid for by landowners who employed labourers. In the 19th century, following the collapse of the wine industry, state funds were used to build levadas. With better tools and engineering skills, long tunnels were cut to transport water from the wetter northern side of Madeira to the drier southern side. There were disputes when state-funded levadas tapped into water supplies used by older levadas. In 1962, above Jangão, people protesting against a state-funded levada were confronted by police, resulting in a teenage girl being shot dead.

In general, the higher levadas collect water for use in hydro-electric power stations, but there is no waste, as the outflowing water is then used for irrigating crops. Water is of course also treated for human consumption.

As the levadas need constant maintenance, they are equipped with paths that have long been used by walkers. However, not all levadas are the same, and while some are easy to follow, others cross sheer cliffs, where the narrow and uneven paths are very dangerous: a slip or trip can result in death or serious injury. The intricate network of very narrow levadas that ultimately take water into fields and terraces, isn't really suitable for walking.

Anyone walking through the hotel zone in Funchal, or visiting tourist offices, will be assailed by advertising for 'levada walks'. These can be a good option for cautious first-time visitors: if you wish to join one, they usually supply a local guide and arrange pick-ups, which can be useful, especially in places where transport is limited. However, only a few easy levadas are offered, so anyone wishing to explore further will have to make their own arrangements.

sources of money have dried up, leaving some projects unfinished. Tourism continues to boom and walking is an important pursuit for many visitors.

A lively way to appreciate Madeira's history and heritage is to visit the Madeira Story Centre on Rua Dom Carlos I in Funchal, www.madeirastorycentre.com/en.

LANDSCAPE

Madeira's landscape is one of exceptional beauty and ruggedness. The first thing visitors notice is the steep slopes. Between the airport and Funchal these slopes are well-settled and dotted with white buildings. However, there are also plenty of trees and shrubs along with a splendid array of colourful flowers. Bananas and palms jostle with bird-of-paradise flowers and amaryllis, while further uphill there are stands of pine and eucalyptus. Exploring beyond Funchal, quiet wooded valleys feature exceptionally steep and rugged slopes, with bare mountains at a higher level. The steepness of the slopes is always apparent, and anyone exploring on foot needs to find routes with acceptable gradients.

On the northern side of Madeira there are damp and green *laurisilva* forests. Water is abundant and in many places it is drawn off along levada channels, through awesome rock tunnels beneath the mountains, to generate power, keep domestic supplies running and to irrigate cultivation terraces on the drier southern slopes of the island. Old roads, tracks and paths twist and turn so much that they present ever-changing views, while the network of new tunnels offer no views at all!

Variety is one of the great charms of the island, and there is plenty of variety beside the levadas, through the wooded valleys, over the mountain tops and along the rugged coastline. Old paths and mule tracks have been hacked from bare rock and constructed by hand to reach all parts of the island.

TREES AND FLOWERS

The moment Madeira rose from the ocean, terrestrial plants strived to gain a root-hold. Maybe lichens and mosses eked out an existence in tiny crevices, sometimes thriving, then overwhelmed by later lava flows. A variety of plants, including flowers and trees, will have become established later. The first seeds to reach the islands could have arrived

Walkers follow the wooded Levada da Serra, seen here with a fringe of agapanthus which binds the earth banks (Walk 3)

A delightful display of 'angel's trumpets' grow from a bush and are commonly seen early in the year

Madeira is blessed with lovely flowers including the 'bird-of-paradise', Madeira's national flower

Agapanthus was imported from African deserts and its tough root mass is used to bind steep earthern banks

after floating on the ocean currents, borne on the wind or deposited in bird droppings. No one can know for sure. When Madeira was first discovered it was referred to as a well-forested island. Unusually, most of the trees were *laurisilva* species, once common in the tropics millions of years ago but now much less common. Porto Santo was famous for its primeval 'dragon trees' (more recent specimens can be seen in gardens on the islands).

Madeira has one of the largest *laurisilva* forests in the world, featuring the mighty til tree, bay tree and Madeira mahogany. There are delightful lily of the valley trees and intriguing wax myrtles, or candleberry trees. The *laurisilva* is also termed 'cloud forest' as it draws moisture from mist or fine drizzle, condensing it and dripping it onto the ground, keeping Madeira well supplied with water. This is especially the case on the densely-forested northern slopes. The 'cloud forest' is rich in ferns, mosses and liverworts, some of them endemic to Madeira, or known only from fossil records elsewhere in the world.

The mountains are covered in gnarled tree heather and tall bilberry. Those who trample heather and bilberry moors in Britain are surprised to find it grows so tall and dense on Madeira that it blocks the sunlight! Large areas are covered in ubiquitous bracken, especially the plateau of Paúl da Serra. Sadly, frequent first fires have ravaged many fine forests, leaving the burnt slopes to be colonised by invasive broom.

Porto Santo was almost rendered uninhabitable when rabbits were introduced, stripping the island of vegetation. Much of the island's plant life has been lost and some badly-eroded areas have had to be reforested.

The bird-of-paradise flower is Madeira's national flower, while the 'Pride of Madeira' and amaryllis are popular. Entire books have been written on the endemic flora of Madeira; 200 species are indigenous to Madeira, the Azores, Canaries and Cape Verde islands, while 120 of these are endemic in Madeira.

Add to this the number of plants that have been introduced, growing in gardens or under cultivation, and the species count becomes bewildering. Notable non-native plants include the soil-binding agapanthus and hydrangeas that flourish beside many levadas. Non-native trees on Madeira include the invasive eucalyptus, mimosa and acacia, and efforts have been made to stop them spreading into the *laurisilva*. Vines grow on some lower, sunny slopes and there are plantations of 'dwarf bananas'. All kinds of fruit and vegetables are grown on terraces hacked from the mountainsides. Long-established gardens and parks are planted with exotic trees, shrubs and flowers. In some of the parks, trees and shrubs are labelled to help visitors identify them in the wild.

To delve deeply into Madeira's wonderfully extensive and complex flora, visit the many botanical gardens around Funchal and elsewhere, or try the following books: *Madeira: Plants and Flowers of Madeira*, by António da Costa and Luis de O Franquinho; *Endemic Flora of Madeira*, by Roberto Jardim and David Francisco; *Parks and Gardens of Funchal*, by Raimundo Quintal and Margarida Pitta Groz.

BIRDS

Creatures could only reach the 'new' volcanic islands of Madeira and Porto Santo unaided if they could fly, and such creatures included insects, bats and birds. While the species count is low, and some species are becoming alarmingly scarce, some birds are endemic to the islands. The long-toed pigeon lives in the most secluded parts of the *laurisilva* and is notoriously difficult to spot. Other birds include the tiny firecrest, smallest of Madeira's birds, as well as Madeiran varieties of chaffinch, grey wagtail, pipit and rock sparrow. The Madeiran storm petrel spends most of its time far out to sea and is rarely spotted, while other rare petrels choose remote and inaccessible cliffs as nesting sites. Specific bird-watching trips are available but if planning to do your own thing a useful book is *Where to Watch Birds in the Madeira Archipelago*, by Claudia Delgado. A useful website is Madeira Birdwatching, www.madeirabirds.com.

ANIMALS

Apart from lizards, which may have arrived clinging to driftwood and now often over-run sunny spots, most land animals were brought to Madeira by settlers. The introduction of animals to these islands created problems, such as the plague of rabbits that stripped Porto Santo bare, or the goats that over-grazed the Ilhas Desertas. Madeira has such steep and dangerous cliffs that free-range farm animals are rarely seen. Cattle, sheep, goats and pigs tend to be confined indoors or kept on short tethers outdoors, while farmers cut and carry huge bundles of vegetation for fodder and bedding.

Among the invertebrates there are delightful butterflies and honey bees, while small millipedes are seen almost everywhere.

The sea around the islands teems with large mammals, including several whale species, half a dozen species of dolphin and rare monk seals. There was once a thriving whaling industry operating out of Caniçal, where the Museu de Baleia, or whaling museum, echoes with the epic tale of 'Moby Dick'.

Madeira's 'crocodiles' – the busloads of slow walkers sent out by the hotels every morning – are not dangerous, but should be avoided if at all possible! Try and cover as much distance as you can along popular levadas before they emerge. They travel very slowly and it is almost impossible to overtake them on the narrow paths.

Fires are unfortunately common and very destructive

PARQUE NATURAL DA MADEIRA

Much of the central and high ground in Madeira is designated as a vast 'Parque Natural' (www.pnm.pt). It includes virtually all the uncultivated and uninhabited wild areas and especially the lush, dense *laurisilva* forest. The few buildings in the park are generally owned by the government, including the occasional 'Posto Florestal' or Forestry Post. Walkers should cause as little disturbance to the wildlife as possible.

Of prime importance is the conservation of the remaining *laurisilva* forest as a living ecosystem. Special areas include Fanal with its huge and ancient til trees, and the Parque Ecológico do Funchal, where native trees are being replanted, but as fast as progress is made, it is destroyed by forest fires. The bare, arid and rocky Ponta de São Lourenço is also protected. Its flowers are being conserved and badly-eroded slopes are being stabilised and re-vegetated.

The Ilhas Desertas are rich in bird-life and contain a breeding colony of monk seals, so the land and the sea bordering it are protected. A marine reserve has been established east of Funchal, the Reserva Natural Parcial do Garajau.

FUNCHAL AND MONTE

Funchal is the biggest settlement in Madeira so familiarise yourself with it straight away. Pick up a free town plan from the tourist information office and carry it with you always. The town comes in three parts which are, from west to east, the Hotel Zone (*Zona Hotelera*), Town Centre (*Centro*), and Old Town (*Zona Velha*). If you are based in the

Funchal is the largest settlement in Madeira and the buildings are stacked steeply above the sea

Hotel Zone and walk into town you will pass the Parque de Santa Catarina and Jardim Municipal. Exotic trees and flowers can be studied free of charge at both. Other popular gardens around Funchal may charge an entry fee.

All facilities are available, but anything that can't be obtained here has to be sought in mainland Europe! Throughout the town centre, shops sell wine, embroidery and Madeiran souvenirs. The centre is always busy and bustling, with flower-sellers on the streets, but there are also quiet pedestrian streets and charming squares. The Madeira Wine Company at Avenida Arriaga 28, www.madeirawinecompany.com, is worth a visit.

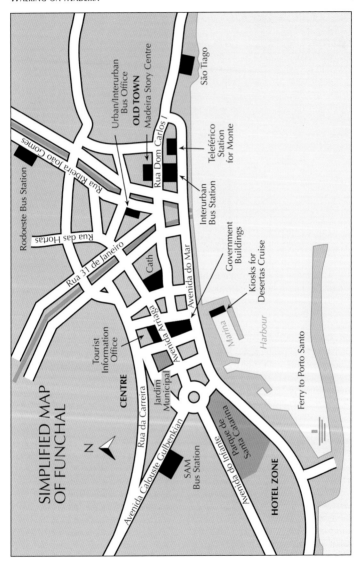

SIMPLIFIED MAP OF FUNCHAL

N

Rodoeste Bus Station

Rua Ribeira João Gomes

Rua das Hortas

Rua 31 de Janeiro

Urban/Interurban Bus Office

OLD TOWN

Madeira Story Centre

São Tiago

Teleférico Station for Monte

Rua Dom Carlos I

Interurban Bus Station

Cath

Avenida do Mar

Government Buildings

Kiosks for Desertas Cruise

Tourist Information Office

CENTRE

Rua da Carreira

Avenida Arriaga

Jardim Municipal

Marina

Harbour

Avenida Calouste Gulbenkian

SAM Bus Station

Avenida do Infante de Parque de Santa Catarina

HOTEL ZONE

Ferry to Porto Santo

Madeira is a rugged island rising from the Atlantic Ocean

There are plenty of churches, ranging from the central Cathedral, or Sé, to the secluded English Church. Museums focus on topics as diverse as history, natural history, contemporary art, sacred art, photography, electricity and sugar! Start with the Madeira Story Centre on Rua Dom Carlos I, www. madeirastorycentre.com/en. The fort on the Avenida do Mar is the seat of the Regional Government of Madeira.

The main coastal road, and the narrow streets running parallel, lead to the Old Town, where the fort of São Tiago can be seen. The Old Town is very atmospheric, with its narrow streets, crumbling buildings and relaxed air.

Walking up the steep roads to Monte is very tiring; instead you can go there cheaply by bus, or use the much more expensive *teleférico* from the coast. Attractions include a fine church above a shady square, and the Jardim Tropical Monte Palace. The most unusual and expensive way back to Funchal is to be pulled down a steep road in a wicker basket, or 'toboggan'.

Staying in Funchal

If your accommodation base is in Funchal, build up your knowledge of the place before and after each day's walk. Even if you choose a quieter base, you are likely to need to change buses in the city. All the bus companies on Madeira are based in the town, so it makes sense to spend an hour or so discovering where the bus stations and important bus stops are located. Time can be wasted, and buses missed, when walkers are wandering around aimlessly looking for this information at the last minute. Make it a priority!

Free town plans will be available from your hotel or from any place displaying tourist literature. There is no need to purchase a detailed town plan, although they are available. Most visitors are interested only in the narrow coastal strip between the Hotel Zone, Town Centre and Old Town. Shops and services are generally located in that strip, but you may wish to explore further inland, bearing in mind that there are some very steep and tiring roads.

Many visitors opt to stay in the Hotel Zone, obtaining a package deal that includes all meals. Others may take self-catering apartments or may be looking for a selection of fine restaurants serving evening meals. There are far too many restaurants to list, but visitors need to decide whether they want a cosmopolitan choice, or local fare. Tourists will frequently swap notes, but for decent local specialities, talk to local people. Generally speaking, if a menu comes in many languages, then prices are likely to be high. The restaurants favoured by Madeirans are down-to-earth establishments. Beware the taxi driver who knows 'just the place you're looking for' as it will be miles from anywhere, and you'll be stuck there until he comes back!

GETTING TO MADEIRA

Flights

Madeira is very well served by charter and scheduled flights. Most visitors choose a package deal, so their flight, accommodation, meals and maybe even car hire are all included. This is fine for a first-time visit, but such an arrangement would limit anyone wishing to explore more extensively. Flight-only deals are possible, using the national

carrier, Air Portugal (www.flytap.com), other national carriers such as British Airways (www.britishairways.com), or budget operators such as Easyjet (www.easyjet.com) and Jet2 (www.jet2.com). Shop around as prices vary enormously. To fly to Porto Santo it is usually necessary to fly to Madeira first, then take a 15-minute 'hop' to the island. See www.aeroportomadeira.pt/en/fnc/home.

Ferries

There are no ferries from mainland Europe to Madeira. Cruise ships regularly berth at Funchal, but never give passengers enough time ashore for a decent walk.

GETTING AROUND MADEIRA

Car hire

Cars can be hired at the airport or delivered to you, but hiring a car is not always recommended and doing so can actually spoil a walking holiday. Despite recent improvements, there are still many narrow, steep, tortuous roads with blind bends and the danger of rockfalls. While a car is essential for walks on the plateau of Paúl da Serra, most of the walks in this guidebook are linear, in deference to the steepness of the terrain. Arriving by car means returning to the car afterwards, which can be inconvenient and frustrating.

Bus services

Madeira has a comprehensive and remarkably cheap bus network, providing vital lifelines to the most distant villages. Buses were used extensively to research the walking routes in this guide.

Buses serve most parts of Madeira at regular intervals

It is well worth visiting the various bus offices or their kiosks to pick up more information. Study timetables a day or two in advance of your walks and always be aware of your options. Some services are fast and frequent while others may be slow and irregular. Service numbers are quoted in this guide, but they can and do change, so always seek the most up-to-date timetables.

Fares can be paid as you get on the bus, but at bus stations and kiosks you can buy tickets before boarding. Bus stops are marked by a sign reading 'Bus' or 'Paragem', but sometimes the stop is indicated by yellow lines painted on the road. If in doubt about the location of a bus stop, ask a local person for help and advice. If in doubt whether an approaching bus is yours or not, give a hand signal anyway. If it is yours, then at least you stopped it in time. If it is a private coach, it

won't stop, and if it is the wrong bus, just apologise for stopping it and politely ask the driver for advice.

Horários do Funchal – urban

Funchal is particularly well served by Horários do Funchal buses, which are yellow with a white stripe (www. horariosdofunchal.pt). Visit the office inside the Centro Commercial Anadia to pick up a free 'urbanos' timetable and route map. In this guide these services are referred to as 'urban bus'.

The company operates information kiosks and kiosks dispensing pre-paid 'Giro' tickets. Departures are from stops all around Funchal but are especially concentrated on or near the busy coastal Avenida do Mar. Refer to the 'urbanos' map to locate your stop, then watch for the route numbers displayed on the buses.

Horários do Funchal – interurban

The far-flung suburbs of Funchal are also covered by Horários do Funchal buses – but they are grey and white with a yellow stripe. Services run to Camacha and Santo da Serra, to Monte and Poiso, then down to Faial, Santana and São Jorge, as well as to Curral das Freiras. Visit the office at the Centro Commercial Anadia to pick up a free 'interurbanos' timetable and route map. In this guide these services are referred to as 'interurban bus', and they operate from a small bus station with a nearby kiosk, just off the Rua Dom Carlos I in Funchal, near the teleférico station.

Sociedade de Automóveis da Madeira

This company's buses are mostly white, though older buses are green and white

Earth steps on a forested slope above Queimadas (Walk 25)

(www.sam.pt). It might be the first bus company that visitors experience, as they operate the Aerobus service between the airport and Funchal. Services cover towns and villages east of Funchal to Machico, Caniçal and Ponta de São Lourenço. Buses also climb from Machico to Santo da Serra and reach Porto da Cruz and Faial. In this guide these services are referred to as 'SAM bus'.

The company operates two bus stations, one on the Avenida Calouste Gulbenkian on the west side of Funchal and the other at Machico. Go to either station for timetables.

Rodoeste

The Rodoeste bus company serves the whole western half of Madeira (www.rodoeste.pt). Bus colours are white with grey and red stripes, though older buses are grey and white with a red stripe. The most regular services run to Jardim da Serra and Ribeira Brava, decreasing in frequency as they extend further west and north. In this guide these services are referred to as 'Rodoeste bus'.

There is a bus station on the Rua Ribeira de João Gomes on the east side of Funchal, as well as roadside kiosks, and another kiosk at Ribeira Brava. Visit any of these for timetables, or go to the Rodoeste office at Rua do Esmeraldo 50 in Funchal.

Taxis

Hire a taxi to move faster than a bus, or to reach a remote or awkward location. Taxi drivers operate meters on short runs, or work to an 'official' table of fares for long-distance runs, but it may be possible to negotiate a fare. Taxi drivers sometimes tout for trade, pulling up alongside walkers on roads, or those who are waiting at bus stops. Before dismissing them, listen to what they are offering. If they are a long way from home and travelling empty, they sometimes offer bargain fares that are well worth considering.

Taxis are nearly always yellow Mercedes with a blue stripe and a number, though some are minibuses suitable for small groups. If you see a taxi in a remote location, simply flag down the driver. Even if the car is full a message could be relayed to another driver.

Many taxis will provide drop-off and pick-up services at either end of linear walks but may apply a 'day rate' for the service. Some offer mini-tours with a commentary if required.

The Levada Nova approaches the lower part of Tábua (Walk 56)

ACCOMMODATION

Accommodation in Madeira is mostly concentrated around the 'Hotel Zone' to the west of Funchal and a large hotel complex at Garajau, but there is plenty more around the island. Walkers looking for small and simple places to stay will find several options at a range of prices. Check your favourite accommodation booking websites to discover what is available for your dates, comparing locations, prices and facilities.

There are remarkably cheap pensions in the centre of Funchal, as well as an English B&B at Trejuno, halfway up to Monte at Livramento. Mountainside lodgings include the Pousada dos Vinháticos and Hotel Encumeada above Serra de Água. Most towns and several villages offer small hotels and pensions, so there are great opportunities for long-distance walks from one place to another. Campsites are very limited and wild camping is technically forbidden, though it does take place.

PORTO SANTO

Three walks are offered on the island of Porto Santo for those who want to visit somewhere close, but quite different, to Madeira. The island is small and often seems bleak and barren, but it looks very fresh in spring and has all sorts of hidden places well worth seeking out. The three walks could be covered in one energetic weekend, or sampled bit by bit throughout a week. A long, golden, sandy beach is one of the highlights of Porto Santo, and each of the three walks can be extended along it for a very pleasant finish.

Windmills are common on the island of Porto Santo

Flights

Very short flights operate between Madeira and Porto Santo. These can be booked online through Sevenair (fly.sevenair.com), through a tour operator, or simply by turning up at the airport without booking, though this could involve a long wait until a seat is available. Flights take only 15 minutes.

Ferry

The Porto Santo Line ferry, the Lobo Marinho, runs most days between Madeira and Porto Santo, taking about 2hr 30min per crossing. Day trips do not allow enough time ashore for a decent walk, though it might be possible to rush up and down Pico Castelo. Either book through a tour operator, or book directly with the ferry company, www.portosantoline.pt.

Moinho bus

Moinho operates a bus service on Porto Santo, as well as hiring cars and offering a bus tour around the island. Obtain a timetable from the kiosk in Vila Baleira and study it carefully as services are quite limited.

Taxis

Taxis can be hired in Vila Baleira, conveying walkers quickly and cheaply anywhere on Porto Santo.

Accommodation

A few hotels are available on Porto Santo, notably in Vila Baleira and at Cabeço da Ponta. There is also a campsite. While it is possible to organise travel and accommodation separately, good deals are available if you book a ferry crossing with the Porto Santo

Line and let them organise accommodation in one of the hotels at the same time. Assistance can also be sought from the Tourist Information Office, tel 291–985244.

CURRENCY

The Euro is the currency of Madeira. Large denomination Euro notes are difficult to use for small purchases, so avoid the €500 and €200 notes altogether, and the €100 notes if you can. Many accommodation providers will accept major credit and debit cards. The availability of banks and ATMs in particular areas is given within the walk descriptions.

LANGUAGE

Madeira's language is Portuguese and if you speak any Portuguese you will notice that Madeirans have their own accent and colloquialisms. Learn a few key phrases to negotiate a bus journey, ask for basic directions or order food and drink, but many Madeirans have a good grasp of English. Don't be afraid to practise the language; as so many islanders speak English, you can pick up words very quickly as someone can always explain things to you. No matter how bad you think you sound, be assured that the islanders have heard much worse.

Some Portuguese place-names are highly descriptive and it is worth checking common ones in the language notes and topographical glossary in Appendix B.

FOOD AND DRINK

Food and drink are abundantly available around Madeira and the locations of bars and restaurants are given for each of

One of a number of stone shelters near Pico Ruivo (Walk 25)

the walking routes. Some bars are very small and supply only a small range of refreshments, but they are always likely to serve bottled beer, wine, soft drinks, coffee and water. Restaurants vary enormously, with some catering very much for an international clientele, while others are very definitely pitched at local people. No matter what is on the menu, it is likely to be good and wholesome, and even if unfamiliar, is unlikely to upset anyone's stomach. If you have special dietary requirements, or allergies to certain things, such as seafood, nuts or gluten, then feel free to ask questions about items on the menu.

Two similar-sounding, traditional Madeiran dishes could cause confusion – *espada*, or black scabbard fish, and *espetada*, or spicy skewered beef. Try them both and they may well become firm favourites. Be warned that traditional Madeiran bread, *bolo do caco*, can contain considerable quantities of meat! Other typical food and drink items are listed in the language notes in Appendix B.

Ordinary tap water is perfectly safe and drinkable everywhere in Madeira. The water comes from occasional rainfall, or is condensed from the mist by the *laurisilva* 'cloud forest', filtering through great thicknesses of volcanic ash before being drawn off along levadas to water treatment plants, and from there into the domestic supply. It really couldn't be cleaner, but if you prefer to buy bottled water, that too is available. On Porto Santo the tap water comes from a desalination plant. Again, it is perfectly safe to drink, but some people dislike the taste and prefer to buy bottled water.

WEATHER

Madeira is generally hot and humid, but not excessively so, and is an all-year-round destination. That said, the summer

Clouds often form across the mountains during the day

months can be too hot and winter brings more rain and a slight risk of snow in the mountains. A typical day on Madeira starts sunny and clear, then during the afternoon clouds begin to form which may completely blanket the mountains. In the evening the cloud may break up, but not before the mist has dampened the 'cloud forest' on the high mountains. Some places look arid, but on the whole Madeira is remarkably green and well-watered. Porto Santo is hotter, drier and browner, except in spring when it turns wonderfully green and flowery.

The greater the altitude, the more likely there is to be cool air, mist and light rain, but it is seldom so severe that it forces walkers to retreat, and often it is sunny and clear all day long. However, Madeira is a subtropical island and, depending on the direction of the wind and the amount of moisture it carries, there can occasionally be prolonged or torrential rain, causing rivers and levadas to flood, which can result in rockfalls and landslides. Torrential rain and flooding in February 2010 killed 49 people, injured many more and left many homeless. Water also soaks deep in the bedrock, enabling many rivers to flow throughout the year. Porto Santo is lower and has less rain, so sea-water has to be desalinated, while the Ilhas Desertas have no permanent running water at all.

TOURIST INFORMATION

The main Tourist Information Office in Madeira is located centrally at Avenida Arriaga 16 in Funchal. It is usually open from 0900 to 2000 Monday to Friday and 0900 to 1800 at weekends. English-speaking staff can assist with queries about accommodation, transport, tours and visitor attractions (tel 291–211902, www.visitmadeira.pt/en-gb). Small tourist information offices are found throughout Madeira and a list with contact details can be found in Appendix C.

HEALTH ISSUES

There are no nasty diseases in Madeira, or, at least, nothing you couldn't contract in Britain. There are no venomous creatures apart from occasional bees and wasps, and having a mosquito in your bedroom is annoying, rather than dangerous. However, Madeira's weather is generally hot and humid, which can cause excessive sweating, leading to

The first part of the Levada da Serra is covered, while later parts can be exposed as it crosses sheer cliffs (Walk 14)

distressing conditions such as prickly heat, dehydration and sunstroke. The sun can be very strong indeed on clear days, so it is sensible to wear long-sleeved, light-coloured clothing, and cover exposed skin adequately with sunscreen.

The health service on Madeira is good, as any ex-pat will happily confirm. There are two hospitals in Funchal and dozens of health centres and pharmacies scattered around Madeira, with a health centre and pharmacies also on Porto Santo. Treatment for EU citizens is free, but obtain and carry a European Health Insurance Card and consider taking out adequate insurance cover. Arrangements for UK travellers are subject to change in the wake of Brexit.

EMERGENCIES

Don't over-exert yourself on very steep and rocky slopes when it is hot and humid; this will leave you tired and weary when faced with a steep and rocky descent, when accidents are more likely to happen. On many paths in Madeira, there are places where one slip, trip or stumble could result in serious injury or death, so always watch where you are putting your feet. Never attempt a rocky scramble or follow an exposed path without having the proven ability to do so and a good head for heights.

Be alert to the danger of landslips and rock-falls, especially during wet and windy weather. Check the weather forecast and wear appropriate clothing. Walking in full sun requires the use of a sun hat and sunscreen, and plenty of water needs to be carried. It is a good rule to walk in the sun, but rest in the shade. Never start a fire, and if you witness an out-of-control fire, keep well away and report it immediately (tel 112).

Carry a first-aid kit to deal with any cuts or grazes along the way. Madeira has no specific mountain rescue service. If you need assistance the Ambulance, Fire Service or Police could be involved in your rescue. All three services are contacted via the same emergency telephone number – 112.

MAPS OF MADEIRA

Maps of a quality similar to Ordnance Survey Landranger and Explorer maps of Britain are not available in Madeira. The Portuguese 'Serviço Cartogràfico do Exército' produces the 1:25,000 'Carta Militar', or military maps of Madeira. These are grossly out-of-date, but remain a good reference for walkers. Nine sheets cover Madeira, but they aren't sold on the island and so must be obtained before you go. The 'Instituto Geogràfico e Cadastral' produces the 1:50,000 'Ilha da Madeira' on two sheets, but this is also grossly out-of-date. The 1:50,000 Kompass map of Madeira is fairly up-to-date and uses a grid system. The 'Madeira Mapa de Estradas e Percursos Pedestres Recomendados' is a useful road map with detailed military map extracts of Madeira's 'official' waymarked walks.

Order your maps well in advance from British suppliers such as: Stanfords (7 Mercer Walk, London WC2H 9FA, tel 0207 836 1321, www.stanfords. co.uk), The Map Shop (15 High Street, Upton-upon-Severn WR8 0HJ, tel 01684 593146, www.themapshop.co.uk) or Cordee (www.cordee.co.uk).

Many walking routes have been signposted and waymarked

MAKING MULTI-DAY TRIPS

Walkers who hire cars on Madeira are quickly frustrated when they realise that most of the best walks on the island are linear. The steep and rugged mountainsides of Madeira do not easily support circular walks. There are some circular walks in this guidebook, but the ascents and descents are sometimes formidable so most of the walks are linear, and most of them start and finish on bus routes. Appendix A details the start and finish points of all the walks covered in this book. The end of one walk is frequently the start of another walk, giving you the opportunity to keep walking, day after day, week after week, as long as you can spot the opportunities.

The walking routes in this guidebook are presented as a series of single-day walks, but they are also loosely grouped into areas for convenience. Within these areas, if you look carefully

at the overview maps, you will see that some routes cross other routes, or have stretches that run in common. Once you have spotted this, it is a simple matter to chop and change between routes, to extend a route or choose a different destination, in the sure and certain knowledge that you have all the information to complete the walk, and know what facilities and services are available on the way.

The main issue for a long-distance walker on Madeira is to know in advance whether food, drink and accommodation are available along a route. This information is in the route descriptions. There is nothing to stop adventurous walkers altering and adapting routes to walk from hotel to hotel, from one end of Madeira to the other. Wild camping isn't permitted on Madeira, but it takes place regardless. There is no need to feel confined to the Hotel Zone in Funchal. Break free and walk from place to place.

The Levada do Rei rushes downstream beside a waterworks near the start of Walk 27 at Quebradas

USING THIS GUIDE

The walks

Madeira is a place of steep and rocky slopes, and many of the walks in this guide run downhill rather than uphill. Some routes are roller-coasters with several ascents and descents. Cautious walkers should start with easy levada walks before tackling strenuous mountain walks.

This guide begins with easy, popular, shaded levada walks that are handy for Funchal. These 'starter' routes have good bus services and useful facilities along the way, so are suitable for less experienced walkers.

More levada walks follow in eastern Madeira, as well as rugged coastal walks, taking walkers into steeper, rockier and more exposed locations. Old roads to Porto da Cruz and Santana offer insights into how people travelled long ago. Mountainous levadas are followed higher above Funchal and some of these

cross particularly exposed cliffs. Always read the route descriptions carefully and don't tackle anything beyond your ability. You cannot suffer from vertigo, or be in any way clumsy or unsteady on your feet on any of the exposed routes.

Walks in the central mountains take in rugged ridges and the highest peaks, sometimes on steep and rugged slopes and sometimes deep in the *laurisilva* forests. Some levada routes cross mountainous terrain, where there are some particularly exposed cliffs. Some of the levadas feature long, dark, narrow tunnels where a torch (and even a spare torch) is essential. Buses giving access to and from the walks are always mentioned, but there are no buses over the plateau of Paúl da Serra, so a car or taxi must be used for access.

Rugged levada walks can be followed down from Paúl da Serra towards Ribeira Brava and Porto Moniz in the extreme north-west of Madeira. The long levada that runs from Ponta do Pargo to

Calheta, then on to Ponta do Sol, can be followed for days through one of the quietest parts of Madeira. This could be linked with more levadas to provide an even longer route. In fact, most of the walks in this guide can be linked with other walks, so that anyone who wants to walk long-distance from place to place has all the information they need.

Three walks explore almost the whole of Porto Santo, and there is a final chapter covering a short cruise to the Ilhas Desertas, where walking opportunities are very limited, but where it is possible to spot some of the rarest of Madeiran wildlife.

There are plenty of splendid opportunities to explore Madeira and Porto Santo on foot, either by searching for your own routes, using this guide or by

A flight of stone steps leads to the gap of Boca das Torrinhas (Walk 30)

joining a guided walking group for a day, or a guided walking holiday for a week or more.

Some of the routes in this guide-book are fully signposted, waymarked and equipped with mapboards. They are 'official' walking routes on Madeira and Porto Santo. They are signposted 'PR', followed by a number. 'PR' stands for *pequeño recorrido* or 'short tour'. Sometimes they might be closed: this can be checked by visiting www. visitmadeira.pt, clicking 'what to do', and then 'walks'. Reasons for closures are not always given, and some walkers ignore route closures if the damage to the path is only minor.

Route description and maps

Step-by-step route descriptions are provided for all of the walks. Any shops, bars and restaurants along the way are mentioned; otherwise you need to be self-sufficient in remote locations and carry food and drink for the day. Always read the route descriptions carefully, carrying appropriate maps and equipment – not forgetting a torch if there are tunnels – and the most up-to-date bus timetables to get to and from the starting and finishing points. Take particular note of any stretches that are exposed, remembering that one slip, trip or stumble could result in serious injury or death.

This guide uses strip maps, concentrating on features close to the walking routes. Features shown in bold in the route description can be found on the accompanying route map. Sometimes, two, three or four routes are shown on the same map, and these are colour-coded to distinguish between them.

An old cobbled road offers an early ascent to Cabo Aéreo (Walk 28)

Colour is used only to distinguish between different routes and not to signify difficulty or any other feature. Walkers can quickly see how to link one route with another, something that walkers are increasingly doing as they strive to enjoy longer walks across Madeira.

Walk times

The timings in this guidebook are only a rough estimate. Some walkers go faster than others and no-one is ever going to match the stated times all the time. Giving precise timings on routes where all kinds of things can affect progress is difficult, but walkers need some sort of guidance if they are hoping to catch a bus late in the day. Take note of the timings and assess your progress. If you keep beating the stated times, then you probably always will, and you might safely plan to walk longer and further each day. If you keep falling well short, then you probably always will, and you should work out how much extra time you need in order to compensate. Pencil notes into the margins and refer to them!

The timings are purely walking times and do not take any account of time spent resting, stopping for lunch, or taking more than a few snaps with the camera along the way. Any time spent motionless, maybe contemplating an exposed cliff or levada walk, must be taken into account, so that by the end of the day you might find another two or three hours need to be added.

1 EASTERN MADEIRA

Penha d'Águia as seen from a viewpoint at Portela (Walk 9)

The eastern part of Madeira is very easy to get around for anyone based in Funchal or Machico. The walks in this section include some of the most popular levada walks on the island, as well as two stunning coastal walks and a convoluted route that offers the chance to explore a fine *laurisilva* forest. It is unlikely that you will have any of these walks to yourself, and in the case of the popular Levada dos Tornos, you could end up stuck at the end of a long 'crocodile' of walkers.

If visiting Madeira for the first time and staying in Funchal, then most of these walks are served by regular buses. Use urban and interurban buses from Funchal to reach different parts of the Levada dos Tornos and Levada da Serra. The main bus company for eastern Madeira is SAM, and they serve all the other walking routes. Always remember to check bus timetables carefully, preferably the day before you walk.

Funchal and Machico were the first two urban settlements on Madeira. They have plenty of facilities and there are regular bus links between them. Funchal has the largest range of accommodation on Madeira, much of it lying west of town in the Hotel Zone. Those who want more peace and quiet can stay in Machico.

Cautious walkers, unsure of their ability, should sample some of the easier levada walks before attempting the more rugged coastal walks. The latter require a sure foot and a head for heights, and anyone lacking these attributes will have difficulty when they begin to explore the more mountainous parts of Madeira. First-time visitors might prefer level levada walks until they feel more comfortable with the heat and humidity, and understand how the buses work. Keen walkers, however, will easily spot opportunities to link walks together in this region to create longer routes.

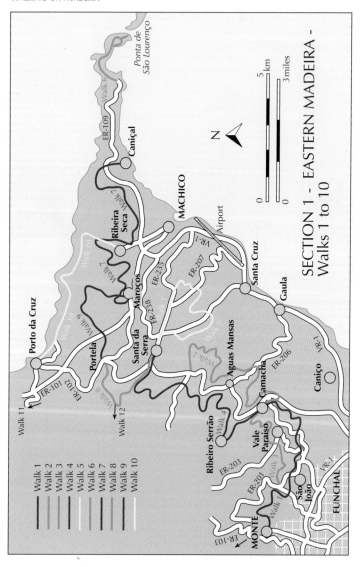

SECTION 1 - EASTERN MADEIRA -
Walks 1 to 10

WALK 1

Levada dos Tornos: Monte to Camacha

Start	Monte, above Funchal
Finish	Camacha
Distance	15.5km (9¾ miles)
Total ascent	330m (1080ft)
Total descent	130m (425ft)
Time	5hr
Terrain	Apart from short ascents and descents at the start and finish, mostly level walking on wooded or cultivated slopes, with one avoidable tunnel.
Maps	Carta Militar 9
Refreshments	Snack bars and/or cafés at Monte and Babosas, around Lombo da Quinta and Nogueira. Plenty of choice at Camacha.
Transport	Urban buses 20, 21 and 48 serve Monte. Teleférico from Funchal to Monte. Urban bus 22 serves Babosas. Teleférico from Jardim Botânico to Babosas. Urban bus 29 serves Curral Romeiros. Urban bus 47 serves Hortensia Gardens and Jasmin Tea House. Interurban bus 110 serves Nogueira. Interurban bus 129, 77, 85 and 110 serve Camacha. Taxis at Monte and Camacha.

The popular Levada dos Tornos carries water from north to south through Madeira. The northern parts are largely confined to tunnels, but the southern part runs in the open and the general altitude is around 600m (1970ft). The levada path is about 27km (16¾ miles) long. Strong walkers could cover it in a day, but most take two days, detouring into the basket-making centre of Camacha. There are two options between Babosas and Curral dos Romeiros – left and right. Left is only for those who are sure-footed and have a very good head for heights.

Start at the bus stop at **Monte** where a cobbled square at 550m (1805ft) is shaded by tall plane trees. ▶ Head for a candle-lit shrine and a drinking fountain dating from the 16th century. Climb 172 steps built from small stones to reach the imposing church of **Nossa Senhora do Monte**. Enjoy views over Funchal then walk straight down steps to the Belomonte

Restaurant, café, souvenir stalls and toilets.

*The church of Nossa
Senhora do Monte
and its stone steps*

Restaurante Snack Bar. Wicker 'toboggans'
are stacked ready to whisk people down to
Funchal. Follow a level, cobbled road,
Largo das Babosas,

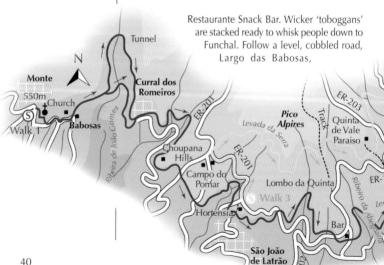

signposted for Babosas. Pass the Jardim Tropical Monte Palace (montepalace.com) and continue past a teleférico station. ▶

Walk gently down to **Babosas**, reaching the Pátio

Map continues on page 54

Café do Monte and toilets.

41

das Babosas café, urban bus 22 and a ticket kiosk for another teleférico to the Jardim Botânico da Madeira. This shady spot has tall plane trees and views over a steep, wooded valley. Follow a cobbled track, the Caminho Rev Padre Eugénio Borgonovo, down towards the teleférico station, but pass below it. The valley ahead was devastated by a forest fire in 2016 and the track was repaired in 2017–19. Walk down the track and avoid a turning on the right, which is for the Levada do Bom Sucesso. Further down the track at another junction, either turn left up a path for the **Levada dos Tornos,** or turn right to continue down the track instead. Both routes re-join at **Curral dos Romeiros**.

The left-hand (exposed) option

The rugged path on the left is awkward as it climbs beside a rocky cutting. Eventually, the Levada dos Tornos emerges from a tunnel. Follow the water downstream to pass a stone arch. The levada has a narrow parapet and exposed, unfenced stretches, and needs great care. ◄ Houses are reached at **Curral dos Romeiros** clinging to a steep slope, where it is necessary to go down steps to reach a crossroads in the village.

Views stretch across the valley to Babosas and down to the harbour at Funchal.

The right-hand (easy) option

The easy track on the right zigzags downhill and crosses an arched bridge over a bouldery river. It then climbs a slope zigzagging past regenerating trees to reach **Curral dos Romeiros**. Walk up a road and go straight through a crossroads. ◄

Urban bus 29.

The road gives way to a stone-paved path, then watch for a sign pointing left up a flight of concrete steps. Walk up these and turn right along the Levada dos Tornos. The levada is covered at first, but the water channel is soon revealed. After leaving the village, the next valley is wooded, while agapanthus flanks the path. Following a forest fire, eucalyptus is dominant, as well as mimosa.

After looping round small valleys, the levada passes beneath a road and enters the **Choupana Hills** resort. Stay on the path as the facilities are private. Some houses were destroyed by fire, along with the resort's hotel and bar/restaurant. Go through a gate in a fence and cross a steep road

Walkers follow the Levada dos Tornos from Choupana towards the popular Hortensia Tea Gardens

near Quinta do Pomar, then pass a couple of houses and a water intake. ▶

Cross another steep road later, pass eucalyptus and a small farm, then make tight turns to cross a couple of streams. The path later runs beneath a road. ▶ Then a concrete road is reached near the delightful **Hortensia Gardens** tea house. Follow the levada further with views of Funchal and the Ilhas Desertas. Walk through woods and cross the **ER-201** road on a bend at Lombo da Quinta. Eucalyptus and pines flank the path. There is access to the Jasmin Tea House if required, then there is a break in the trees. Walk into a quiet wooded valley, then out of it, and later the levada reaches a bend on the busy **ER-102** road, so cross carefully. ▶

Infrequent urban bus 94.

Urban bus 47.

Urban bus 36A.

43

A water regulating building on the Levada dos Tornos

Pass a water intake and keep left of a large workshop building. Cross a road and turn left to continue along the levada. ◀ Apple trees give way to dense eucalyptus and mimosa.

The Bar 1 Maio is uphill.

You will reach a tunnel entrance – either walk through it or over it. To go through, use a torch, noting that the path is narrow and the roof is low. The latter half drips and is wet before the tunnel exit. To go over, climb earth steps and cross a wooded slope. Follow a concrete road to a tarmac road at **Pinheirinho**. ◀ Turn left up the road, then right down the Estrada do Pinheirinho. Turn left along a narrow concrete access path to reach a house set back from the road. Walk down concrete steps and turn left down a steep path on a wooded slope to reach the levada near the tunnel exit.

Urban bus 37 and Bar Levada dos Tornos.

Continue through woods to a road called the Rua do Pomar and turn right. The levada almost immediately drifts away to the left and is less wooded. Chestnut and oak are seen while traversing the valley, and there is a knot of canes and a footbridge at the valley head. Turn left up the Vereda da Nogueira among the scattered houses of **Nogueira**. Turn right up a tarmac road, passing the Pastelaria Candeeiro snack bar.

Interurban bus 110.

Walk straight up through a housing estate, avoiding turnings to right and left. ◀ There are bus stops, if an early finish is needed; otherwise walk to a road junction facing the large disused industrial building. Turn left up the **ER-205** road, then right along the Travessa João Claudio Nobrega. Walk straight downhill from a crossroads along the Caminho Fonte Concelos. The road winds down through **Ribeirinha**, passing a number of houses and passing beneath an elevated main road. Follow the minor road uphill, and note a sign on the right marking the continuation of the Levada dos Tornos. Take this turn if continuing directly with Walk 2, otherwise stay on the road.

The road climbs over a wooded rise. Turn left to along the Caminho Fonte Concelos, which later swings left and climbs steeply among tall trees. Cross a busy road and climb straight past a modern church to reach a fine square in the centre of **Camacha**.

CAMACHA

A monument on the square declares that the first game of football played on Portuguese territory took place here in 1875. Just off the square is a fine basket factory well worth a visit. There is accommodation, as well as shops, bars, restaurants and a bank with ATM. Interurban buses 129, 85 and 110 link Camacha with Funchal while bus 77 links with Funchal and Santo da Serra.

If the Levada da Serra is broken at Camacha, have a look inside the basket-making factory in the village

WALK 2
Levada dos Tornos: Camacha to Quatro Estradas

Start	Camacha
Finish	Quatro Estradas on the ER-102
Distance	17km (10½ miles)
Total ascent	150m (490ft)
Total descent	100m (330ft)
Time	5hr 30min
Terrain	Apart from short descents and ascents at the start and finish, mostly level walking on wooded or cultivated slopes. Some short exposed stretches, short sections of rugged terrain and some tunnels (two with limited headroom and one where you'll need a torch).
Maps	Carta Militar 6 and 9
Refreshments	Plenty of choice at Camacha. Basic bar at Quatro Estradas.
Transport	Interurban buses 129, 85 and 110 link Camacha with Funchal while bus 77 links Quatro Estradas with Funchal and Santo da Serra. Taxis at Camacha.

The second and less popular half of the Levada dos Tornos runs from Camacha into a series of well-wooded valleys. It ultimately reaches a dead-end, although it could be extended along the Levada Nova with reference to Walk 5. To finish, follow roads up to Quatro Estradas, with a view to catching the bus that links Santo da Serra with Funchal.

For map, see Walk 1.

◀ Head downhill from the modern church in **Camacha** to cross a busy road and continue straight down a quiet road, the Caminho Fonte Concelos. Turn right at a junction, then right again to cross a wooded rise before dropping down towards **Ribeirinha**. Watch for a sign on the left, where a path leads down a slope of pines to the **Levada dos Tornos**. Turn left to follow the levada path.

Cross a steep road, then cross another steep road at some houses. Continue through woods and along a concrete path to reach more houses and a short tunnel, where the water from the levada runs through a pipeline. The path is

good, but the tunnel roof is low. Emerge to follow the pipeline past a couple of houses on the side of a wide valley below Camacha. There are views in places, but other parts are well-wooded. Cross a footbridge and follow the pipeline through another **tunnel**, with good headroom.

Low headroom on the levada near Eiras de Dentro

Don't trip over concrete blocks supporting the pipeline as it runs towards the head of the valley, and the path may be wet and slippery as it narrows. Pass a water intake building then cross a levada footbridge over the **Ribeira do Porto Novo**, whose overspill may form a slender waterfall. Pass a weeping wall and turn round a densely wooded spur below **Eiras de Dentro** to enter a side valley. Watch for rocks overhanging the path, turn round the valley, then walk past chestnut and pine trees. Go under a little bridge to reach another short tunnel. There is a good path and good headroom, then a brambly corner. The next tunnel is curved, so a torch is useful, though the path is good and there is good headroom. ▶

The tunnel can be avoided by taking a path down beside a cliff, but climb steps on the left to return to the levada.

Later, there are some short exposed stretches, as well as views back across the valley to Camacha. Pass a mixture of trees and shrubs before crossing a steep and narrow road at **Pico da Gaula**. Follow a concrete path with street lights alongside and cross another steep and narrow road. ▶

Agapanthus and tall pines grow alongside the levada.

47

Pass by a water intake and small reservoir; the path is broad as it turns round **Lombo Grande**. Cross the **ER-206** road.

Continue walking into denser woods then cross a narrow road where there are a few buildings at **Fonte dos Almocreves**. The levada passes pines to reach the head of a little valley where there are chestnuts and willows. The valley is mostly cultivated and, on leaving it, you will cross a steep concrete road. Turn into the next little valley, which is also cultivated, with a view down to the airport. Go through a short tunnel under a road, where the path is uneven and headroom is limited. Follow the levada onwards, passing a house and stands of pine and eucalyptus. ◄ Enter another little valley where the vegetation is tangled and willow grows at the head of the valley.

There are a few chestnuts here, and some of the pines later have charred trunks.

After turning round a tiny valley with a few houses and terraces at **Eiras Velhas**, pass a derelict house. ◄ The path then narrows and drops below the levada for a short while and the view down the valley reveals the Ilhas Desertas. Take care when you reach a narrow concrete parapet along a rocky edge. Avoid it by going down steps, then follow the path back up to the levada. Head into a steep-walled, well-wooded gorge, and cross a levada footbridge over the

Masses of agapanthus grow beside the levada.

The Levada dos Tornos near Ribeira do Eixo

48

Ribeira dos Vinháticos. There is another rocky edge to negotiate. Cross a track and turn into a side valley, while admiring terraces in the main valley. Willows grow at the head of
the side valley, then pines and eucalyptus. The path becomes
concrete and has street lights, leading past houses to cross a
concrete road at **Ribeira do Eixo**.

Follow the levada past nurseries, taking in loops before
passing a circular reservoir and crossing a road. After a short
walk, cross another road, then turn round a blunt nose on a
hillside into a little valley. ▸

Tall pines, mimosa
and eucalyptus
grow on the hillside,
and tall mimosa
in the valley.

On leaving the valley turn a corner, with a view down
to the airport and the Ilhas Desertas beyond. Walk past
pines and chestnuts before gaining another view, with more
mimosa and tall eucalyptus, and agapanthus alongside.
There is a rocky stretch before another turn into the next little
valley, where willows grow around the valley head. On leaving the valley the mixed woodlands include laurels. Cross
a steep tarmac road and pass a house below **Ribeira João
Gonçalves**.

Head into the next little valley, where there are views of
small farm buildings. The head of the valley is a jungle, but
later there is a view down the main valley, drained by the
Ribeira de Santa Cruz. To leave the Levada dos Tornos, reach
a signposted path junction and turn left up an old, cobbled
track. This becomes a concrete road, passing a house, then is
cobbled again on the way up to a junction. Walk straight up
a tarmac road, the Rua Mary Jane Wilson, passing a junction
with the Caminho da Pedreira, to reach a fairly busy junction
with the **ER-102** road at **Quatro Estradas** at 750m (2460ft).
There is a very basic bar off to the left in the direction of
Camacha.

WALK 3
Levada da Serra: Campo do Pomar to Camacha

Start	ER-201 road above São João de Latrão
Finish	Camacha
Distance	10km (6¼ miles)
Total ascent	120m (395ft)
Total descent	100m (330ft)
Time	3hr 15min
Terrain	The levada path is clear, level and easy to follow; generally well wooded with some cultivated areas.
Maps	Carta Militar 6 and 9
Refreshments	Bar at Achadinha. Plenty of choice at Camacha.
Transport	Urban bus 47 to São João. Interurban bus 111 serves Achadinha. Interurban bus 129, 85 and 110 link Camacha with Funchal while bus 77 links with Funchal and Santo da Serra. Taxis at Camacha.

The Levada da Serra do Faial can be walked in a day but most walkers break halfway and head for Camacha. The full length of the well-wooded levada path measures 23km (14¼ miles) and rises from 750m (2460ft) above the Estádio da Madeira, to 800m (2690ft) above Camacha. The levada itself was drained many years ago and in recent years a water pipeline has been buried beneath the path.

For map, see Walk 1.

◀ No bus runs to the start of the levada, so use urban bus 47 to reach a point at 630m (2065ft) on the **ER-201** road above São João de Latrão. When the bus turns downhill, continue walking along the bendy high road to pass the stadium, Estádio da Madeira. Turn right at a crossroads up the steep, cobbled and well-wooded Caminho do Pico do Infante. After a bendy stretch, turn right along a path at 750m (2460ft). The way isn't signposted, so watch for little manholes and the concrete edge of the **Levada da Serra**.

There is no water in the narrow channel and the slopes are covered in eucalyptus, chestnut, laurel and pine. Later the levada path passes mostly eucalyptus, which grew on the slopes of **Pico Alpires** after a fire, though a few charred chestnuts survive.

The ground cover is bracken and brambles, with aga-panthus beside the path. There is a view of Funchal before a ruined stone building is passed. Walk round a valley above **Lombo da Quinta**, noting a few habitations below the path and a view of the Ilhas Desertas. Leaving the valley, cross a cobbled track and pass a short tunnel at the same time. There is no need to enter the tunnel.

The de-watered Levada da Serra and its wide path

Walk through dense woodlands and pass the **Ribeiro de Abegoaria**. Swing round a bend where there are tall pines, oaks and laurels covered in ivy. Pass a gateway on the left, then cross a track leading up into the old estate of **Quinta de Vale Paraiso**. Views from this point take in the Ilhas Desertas. The track beside the levada runs though lovely mature wood-lands. Cross the **ER-203** road near a house called Casa do Reviver. ▶

Infrequent interurban bus 112 to Funchal.

The levada path is flanked by trees, with a few houses above and below, and tangled terraces. Swing round to cross a bridge, later crossing a steep road, the Caminho Ribeira Grande. A house called Quinta Proteas is just uphill. Continue along the wooded path, noting pines growing in the valley, though there are other well-established trees, including oaks with scorched trunks. ▶ Pass close to a mas-sive concrete buttress that holds a sports ground in place. The

The higher parts of the valley feature rampant bracken and gorse.

path is pleasantly wooded and crosses a narrow road called the Caminho da Madeira above the **Casais de Alem**.

There are plenty of eucalyptus trees, though oaks also grow alongside the levada, as well as banks of gorse. Camacha is seen, but the levada describes great loops and the village doesn't get any closer. A slope covered in pines gives way to denser woods. Later, drop down steps onto a road and turn left to reach **Achadinha**. ◄

Snack Bar Moisés and interurban bus 111.

Walk straight through a crossroads signposted 'Levada da Serra – Faial'. A concrete road passes a few houses, with the levada to the left. A rugged track and clear path lead into lovely mixed woods. A track leads past houses and reaches a crossroads with the Caminho Municipal da Portela. Either continue straight to Santo da Serra via Walk 4, or turn right and follow the road down to **Camacha**.

WALK 4

Levada da Serra: Camacha to Santo da Serra

Start	Camacha
Finish	Santo da Serra
Distance	19.5km (12 miles)
Total ascent	120m (395ft)
Total descent	140m (460ft)
Time	6hr 15min
Terrain	The levada path is clear, level and easy to follow; generally well-wooded with some cultivated areas; one short tunnel.
Maps	Carta Militar 6 and 9
Refreshments	Plenty of choice at Camacha. Bar at Rochão. Two bars at Ribeira Serrão. Plenty of choice at Santo da Serra.
Transport	Interurban buses 129, 85 and 110 link Camacha with Funchal while bus 77 links Santo da Serra with Camacha and Funchal. SAM Bus 20 links Santo da Serra with Machico and Funchal. Taxis at Camacha and Santo da Serra.

The second part of the Levada da Serra do Faial runs from Camacha to Santo da Serra. Apart from the initial climb from Camacha, the levada rises gradually from 800m to 820m (2625ft to 2690ft). A road is used at Ribeira Serrão, but for the most part the levada runs round quiet, often well-wooded valleys. At the end, either drop to Santo da Serra or continue along the Levada da Portela.

▶ Leave **Camacha** by walking up the road signposted for Santo da Serra. Turn left at the Super Mercado Vila da Camacha and follow the quiet Caminho Municipal da Portela uphill. Turn right at a crossroads to follow the **Levada da Serra**. The track onwards is wooded, with street lights alongside, crossing a stream and traversing the other side of a valley, where there are more houses and the **Bar Flôr do Rochão**. Follow the road up to a staggered crossroads, turning right and quickly left down past a bus shelter. ▶ Walk down the road a short way to see a tunnel mouth on the left. The Levada da Serra is buried beneath the road for 3km (2 miles). Eucalyptus and oak grow beside the road, though later there is more terracing and cultivation, with plenty of houses

For first half of map, see Walk 1.

Infrequent interurban bus 112.

Another well-wooded stretch of the Levada da Serra, with a regular line of oak trees planted alongside

53

stacked on the sunny slopes. The road eventually swings round to the right and crosses a bridge over the **Ribeira do Porto Novo** at Ribeiro Serrão, passing the Rústico Bar and Snack Bar Ponte Pau. Keep to the road and pass through a cutting surmounted by a small bridge at Cancela, then swing into a couple of side valleys. When the road begins to run downhill, turn left along another road, Azinhaga do Ribeiro Serrão. It quickly leads onto a track and the levada is seen again at a junction, on the left.

The path crosses a slope of pine and eucalyptus, though a line of oaks march beside it. Enter a pleasant little valley and cross an aqueduct bridge and a concrete road. ◄ There is another wooded stretch, and the path crosses over a vigorous levada. The path makes a pronounced left bend in the trees and crosses a dirt road. Keep following the clear track alongside. Pass above **Curral Velho**, as the levada runs to the head of the wooded valley. There are oaks beside the track,

The oaks are a trademark for the route, while the slopes carry plenty of broom.

but following a fire, broom is now dominant. Cross a stout aqueduct bridge over the **Ribeiro dos Vinháticos** and walk on top of a massive stone buttress. There are denser woodlands around a derelict building, then vigorous growths of hydrangeas beside the levada, while the next valley is richly wooded. ▸

Cross a concrete bridge and walk through a short tunnel, then continue along the levada path. Cross an aqueduct bridge in the next valley and note how the water is drawn off along a lower levada. Keep following the track to pass through a gate, with no water in sight. The area is covered in straggly eucalyptus before the **ER-202** road is reached beside a vehicle compound. ▸

A signpost points back to Camacha and ahead towards Portela. Follow a clear track beside a stout fence surrounding a former piggery. There are eucalyptus trees, but the trademark line of oaks and hydrangeas still march beside the levada. ▸ Eucalyptus trees have been felled near the Ribeira da Serra de Agua, where a metal footbridge and an older stone bridge are crossed. Stands of laurel and tree heather are seen, some of them hoary with lichens. The levada passes a junction and makes a series of loops through rampant vegetation, then reaches a broad and clear dirt road at **Lombo das Faias**. The levada is abandoned here but can be followed to Portela by referring to Walk 8.

To finish at Santo da Serra, turn right and follow the dirt road down through wonderfully mixed woods. There are a couple of houses to the left on leaving the woods, then a minor road swings left and right to drop down to the main **ER-102** road. Turn right and follow the road carefully round a right-hand bend. There are bus stops here; otherwise turn left along the ER-207 road as signposted for **Santo da Serra**.

Views down the valley frame the Ilhas Desertas.

Leave early by following the road down to Quatro Estradas for buses to Santo da Serra or Funchal.

There are fine views across the eastern parts of Madeira, with pleasant loops and laurel trees further along.

SANTO ANTÓNIO DA SERRA

Commonly abbreviated to Santo da Serra, this long and straggly village has a whitewashed church at its centre and offers accommodation, shops, bars, restaurants and an ATM, as well as a popular park and nearby golf course. Interurban bus 77 runs to Camacha and Funchal, while SAM Bus 20 runs to Machico and Funchal.

WALK 5
Levada Nova from Santo da Serra

Start/finish	Santo da Serra
Distance	13.5km (8½ miles)
Total ascent/descent	180m (590ft)
Time	4hr
Terrain	A steep road and path down into a valley, followed by a level, easy, well-wooded levada. The road-walk up to Santo da Serra starts steep and gradually levels out.
Maps	Carta Militar 6
Refreshments	Plenty of choice at Santo da Serra. Basic bar at Capela dos Cardais.
Transport	Interurban bus 77 links Funchal with Quatro Estradas and Santo da Serra. SAM Bus 20 links Santo da Serra with Machico and Funchal. Taxis at Santo da Serra.

The Levada Nova offers a pleasant walk across wooded and cultivated slopes high above Santa Cruz and the airport. Buses don't cross the levada, but it can be reached easily from Santo da Serra. The levada path runs at a general level of 500m (1640ft), but access to it involves walking downhill first, then later finishing with a road-walk back up to Santo da Serra.

Santo da Serra, at 680m (2230ft), has a roundabout at its lower end. Walk through it, then turn right along the minor road, Caminho do Poiso. Follow this past a few houses until there is a cobbled road called the Travessa do Poiso dropping to the right. Walk down this road, reaching a signposted junction near a house. Turn right, then left, to pick up and follow flights of stone steps down a steep and well-wooded slope. The **Levada Nova** is reached, and while the route turns left to follow it, turning right first soon reveals a couple of waterfalls on the **Ribeira de Santa Cruz**, where the levada draws its water.

The levada is followed downstream through a wonderfully wild and wooded valley. It can be wet in places with a slippery path. There is a rocky stretch and a view of a little waterfall, then a cultivated slope is crossed. After picking a route along another rocky edge, pass a water intake and cross a steep concrete road at **Moinhos da Serra**. ▶

An earth path is flanked by agapanthus and mimosa as the levada curves round a small valley. Cross a step-footbridge in tall mixed woods and cross another steep concrete road, passing a water intake and a house above **Achada da Morena**. Swing round into the next valley, crossing another step-footbridge. Agapanthus and brambles flank the path on leaving the valley, with mimosa below. Turn round the slope and enter another valley, crossing another step-footbridge. Mimosa and eucalyptus flourish on leaving the valley. Continue towards the head of the main valley, crossing a short exposed rocky slope. The Ribeira do Moreno is spanned by a step-footbridge.

Cross a short, exposed, rocky stretch while leaving the valley, passing tangled eucalyptus in a little side-valley Turn round a slope bearing burnt tree trunks, with mimosa and eucalyptus. Enter another little side-valley full of eucalyptus and cross another step-footbridge, then a stretch of the levada is buried. Pass a big wall below a couple of houses, then head back into woods. Mimosa, then agapanthus and brambles flank the path.

Agapanthus flanks the path and the trees are mostly tall eucalyptus.

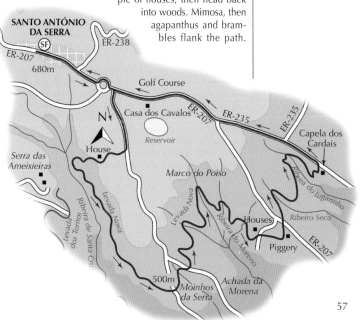

57

A rocky stretch towards the end of the Levada Nova

Cross a cobbled road, then soon afterwards, cross a concrete track and the **ER-207** road.

The levada squeezes between walls and enters the valley of the **Ribeiro Seco**. Eucalyptus grows at the head of the valley, where a final step-footbridge is crossed. Mimosa grows as the levada leaves the valley. Walk round the valley of the **Ribeiro do Lugarinho** where mixed woodlands give way to pine, which in turn gives way to more mimosa and eucalyptus. The levada makes a couple of tight turns, reaching a road and steps above the white **Capela dos Cardais**. ◀ To omit the final road-walk arrange to be met by car or taxi at the chapel, where there is a makeshift bar.

There is a view of the Ponta de São Lourenço.

To finish on foot, follow the road up a steep, wooded slope. Turn left along the **ER-235**, then turn right along the ER-207, passing a large **golf course** and the Quinta do São Jorge (a horse-riding centre with a classic car showroom and a bar/restaurant). Pass the golf course entrance and later go straight through the roundabout to finish back in **Santo da Serra**. ▶

For facilities, refer to Walk 4.

WALK 6
Baia d'Abra and Ponta de São Lourenço

Start/finish	ER-214 road at Baia d'Abra
Distance	7.5km (4¾ miles)
Total ascent/descent	450m (1475ft)
Time	2hr 30min
Terrain	Good paths and numerous steps cross steep slopes and traverse cliff edges. Several stretches have safety fencing.
Maps	Carta Militar 7
Refreshments	Possible snack van at the Baia d'Abra. Bars and restaurants back along the road in Caniçal.
Transport	SAM bus 113 serves Baia d'Abra from Funchal, Porto da Cruz, Machico and Caniçal.

The Ponta de São Lourenço is the shattered, battered easternmost point of Madeira, a place of sheer cliffs, rocky coves and jagged edges. The area is protected on account of its wild flowers, while bird-watchers hope to spot the rare Berthelot's pipit. The further east the walk proceeds, the more remarkable the scenery, but there is no way across the rocky gap of Boqueirão.

Start from the road-end **car park at Baia d'Abra**. There is a view of a lighthouse on Ilhéu do Farol, as well as a pierced headland beneath the furthest point reached on this walk. The Ilhas Desertas lie far out to sea. A signpost names the trail as the PR8 to Cais do Sardinha. Walkers should stay on the marked paths, as the area has been extensively re-vege-tated, but the soil is fragile. ▶

Rocky areas teem with lizards on sunny days.

59

Walk down 114 stone steps and cross a footbridge then climb broad wooden steps and later pass through a tumbled wall. The stony path is quite obvious and stone steps run down to a gap where there are remarkable cliff views and stacks of rock at Pedra Furada, all protected by fencing. ◄ Follow the path up 260 stone steps on a rocky slope, then head down a rugged path and more stone steps to another gap in the cliffs, where the towering rock of **Ilhéu do Guincho** is framed by the rocky arms of a dramatic cove, with colourful, contorted, banded cliffs. The distant island of Porto Santo can be seen. The path climbs and roughly contours round a slope and reaches a remarkably narrow and exposed rocky ridge at **Estreito**. The path is fenced on one or both sides and views are exceptional. ◄ Drop from the ridge to reach a path junction on a gentler slope, where there is a noticeboard.

Note how varied the rock is, with crumbling pumice, knobbly breccia and tough lava.

Look left while following the ridge for complex cliff views.

Keep left and follow the path across an easy slope, reaching yet another gap featuring great views. A network of paths becomes available, but pass above the solitary palm-shaded house of **Casa do Sardinha**. ◄

An early 20th-century residence reached by boat from a nearby quay, this is now used as a centre for the Reserva Natural da Ponta de São Lourenço.

A junction is reached above the house, where a clear path runs uphill. It features more than 200 log steps, separated by almost as many crumbling steps carved into pumice.

A hilltop boasts twin summits at 150m (490ft). There is a splendid view across the yawning gulf of **Boqueirão**, which cannot be crossed. The Ilhéu do Farol and its lighthouse can be seen, as well as the Ilhas Desertas, Porto Santo and much of eastern Madeira.

Descend and keep left at path junctions, heading down a bouldery slope to

A path crosses steep slopes, followed out onto the rugged Ponta de São Lourenço and back again

reach a footbridge and a spur path leading to a quay at **Cais do Sardinha**. Cross the footbridge and climb to a higher junction, then turn left. All that remains is to retrace steps back to the road-end, enjoying all those wonderful views in reverse.

WALK 7
Levada do Caniçal: Maroços to Caniçal

Start	Maroços
Finish	Caniçal tunnel or Caniçal
Distance	11.5km (to the tunnel) or 18km (to Caniçal) (7¼ or 11¼ miles)
Total ascent	50m (165ft)
Total descent	210m (690ft)
Time	4hr or 6hr 30min
Terrain	The level levada crosses steep wooded or cultivated slopes. The path is good, but narrow and more exposed above Caniçal. One long tunnel to walk through, if you continue to Caniçal.
Maps	Carta Militar 6 and 7
Refreshments	Bar on the levada above Ribeira Seca. Bar near the Caniçal tunnel. Plenty of choice at Caniçal.
Transport	SAM Bus 156 serves Maroços from Funchal and Machico. SAM Bus 113 serves the Caniçal tunnel and Caniçal from Funchal and Machico.

The Levada do Caniçal offers a pleasant route through the Machico valley at around 220m (720ft). Fruit and vegetables grow on the sunny, south-facing slopes, but the levada also runs into shady, well-wooded side-valleys. Either finish at the Caniçal tunnel, or walk through the tunnel and enjoy a rather more exposed stretch of the levada to finish in the coastal village of Caniçal.

Listen to people talking, children and music playing, dogs barking and cockerels crowing. Few valleys are as populated and lively as this!

Start in the valley village of **Maroços** and walk up the steep Caminho do Lombo do Talho. Just before the road bends left there is a pedestrian crossing. To the right of the crossing, a concrete ramp leaves the road and a concrete path follows the **Levada do Caniçal**. The levada runs alongside the Machico valley and is almost level, but the water is seen to flow very gently ahead.

◄ The broad concrete path beside the levada gives way to a narrower earth path heading into a side-valley, passing small houses and cultivation terraces. Cross the Ribeira das

Cales at the head of the valley, then look down on Maroços while turning a pronounced bend. Note the flight of steps called the Vereda do Lombo da Roçada, part of the PR5 trail described in Walk 9.

The path is concrete as it passes houses then it becomes earth as it passes through a narrow side-valley where a mossy cliff drips water. Leave the little valley for a fine view down the main valley to Pico do Facho, which rises between Machico and Caniçal. ▶ The path becomes concrete and crosses the Vereda do Cabecinho then swings into another side-valley drained by the Ribeira Grande. All kinds of fruit and vegetables grow on the terraces. Turn round the head of the valley and follow an earth path, rocky in places, with mimosa growing alongside pine and eucalyptus.

One by one, the Ilhas Desertas sail into view out at sea.

The Levada do Caniçal on a steep slope before the Caniçal tunnel, where the walk can be cut short

Turn round another little valley and meander past small houses. Another rocky stretch leads past a cave and through a short tunnel. Emerge with a view of Machico and continue walking. There is no real sense of exposure, despite over-hanging rock where the levada has been cut. Turn left round a corner at a water intake building to see a big valley drained by the **Ribeira Seca**. Several little side-valleys are negotiated while walking round this valley. The first little valley is under cultivation, while the next is dense with mimosa trees. The valley of the Ribeira da Nóia is long and cultivated, with only small huts and terraces and no habitations in view. Overlook the bustle of the main valley while crossing the concrete Caminho da Nóia beside the Snack Bar O Jacaré.

Turn round into another little valley, passing Vivenda João de Gois, then turn a rocky corner and cross the Vereda dos Loureiros on the way into the next valley. The head of the valley, where the Ribeira Seca is crossed, is cultivated, but also features plenty of mimosa. Only a few huts are seen on the terraces around the head of the valley. Walk past a rocky cut, then notice a dirt road down to the right, called the Vereda da Boca do Risco. ◀

The Bar Boca do Risco and buses are at the bottom of this road, which is used on Walk 10.

Stay on the levada path to continue, with rock over-hanging the channel later, though again there is no real sense of exposure. A pronounced left bend takes the path

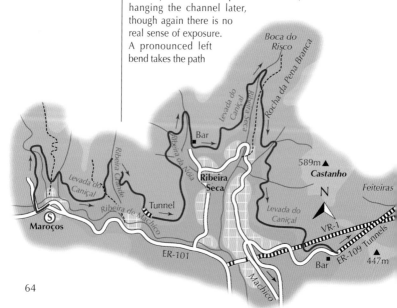

into a side-valley where more mimosa grows. Turn round the head of the valley and traverse another rocky cut. Meander in and out of folds on the steep slopes of **Castanho**, stepping up and down to cross a road, where the levada runs through a culvert. There are views down to Machico but also wooded areas with mimosa, pine and eucalyptus.

The Levada do Caniçal above the village of Caniçal

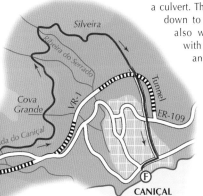

Bus stop nearby with the Snack Bar Levada Nova down the road.

Cross a wooded slope and pass a few houses, to reach the **ER-109** road at the mouth of a tunnel. ◄

To follow the levada to Caniçal, walk through the tunnel using a path on the left side where the water runs through a pipe. The tunnel has lighting and runs 800m (875yds) through the Pico de Nossa Senhora, though most traffic now uses the deeper VR-1 road tunnel. Emerge to follow the levada away from the road, but beware of rock-falls from a quarry at **Feiteiras**. The path is less trodden and clings to a cliff that some might find unnerving, but it often has a fence alongside and gets better later. There are odd mimosa trees, prickly pears and malfurada bushes. Turn round a rocky corner for views of Caniçal and the Ponta de São Lourenço, as well as sprawling industrial sites.

The path is easy to follow simply by keeping the levada in view. Cross a hillside, then cross a red-earth track near a small farm and enter dense woods of mimosa, pine, oak and eucalyptus. Turn round a little valley where the levada spans the **Ribeira do Serrado**, and later cross two tracks. Afterwards, the levada suddenly turns right and rushes downhill. Follow it, but later switch to a dirt road running parallel at **Silveira**. Join a tarmac road at a cemetery and continue down past a covered reservoir. A road called the Rua das Feiteirinhas leads down to a crossroads and the Chicago Café. Either catch a bus here, or walk further downhill along the Estrada da Banda d'Além, turning right to finish in the centre of **Caniçal**. The bus stop is opposite the Centro Cívico.

CANIÇAL

This former fishing village is now flanked by industrial sites, but has a sandy beach. There is a bank with ATM, post office, shops, bars and restaurants. SAM bus 113 serves Machico, Porto da Cruz and Funchal. Taxis are also available. The Museu de Baleia, or whaling museum, is well worth visiting.

WALK 8

Levada da Portela: Santo da Serra to Portela

Start	ER-102/ER-207 junction at Santo da Serra
Finish	ER-102/ER-212 junction at Portela
Distance	7km (4¼ miles)
Total ascent	150m (490ft)
Total descent	160m (525ft)
Time	2hr 30min
Terrain	Paths and tracks are generally easy and clear. The higher parts are well-wooded. A steep descent with steps towards the end.
Maps	Carta Militar 6
Refreshments	Two bar/restaurants at Portela.
Transport	Interurban bus 77 serves Santo da Serra from Funchal. SAM bus 20 serves Santo da Serra from Machico. SAM bus 53 serves Portela from Funchal, Machico and Faial. Taxis at Santo da Serra.

The Levada da Portela takes a convoluted, but fairly level route across a well-wooded slope around 830m (2725ft). The descent comes in a series of abrupt drops, with the water racing down to Portela faster than walkers can follow it, ending at a fine roadside viewpoint.

This route could be started at **Santo da Serra**, but the road-walk can be limited by starting at the junction of the ER-102 and ER-207 roads outside the village. Follow the road sign-posted for Portela, turning carefully round a left-hand bend. A minor road leaves on the left, runs up round a sharp bend and later passes a couple of houses. Continue up a broad dirt road into mixed woodland. The road bends as it climbs at **Lombo das Faias**.

Watch for a levada doubling back sharply on the right. This is the Levada da Serra, around 820m (2690ft). Follow it a short way round a corner to reach a flat area beside a water tower. Pointers for Portela and Ribeiro Frio are painted on the tower. ▶ The path is easy at first, but the parapet beside the levada becomes very narrow across a rocky outcrop, so

This is a popular place for walkers to take a break. A curiously contorted cedar stands beside the levada and dense laurisilva forest blocks the sunlight.

use a path running below for a while. There are fallen trees in places. The rest of the path is broad and clear, flanked by more tall cedars. There is a pronounced left bend passing a tiny tunnel then the levada describes little curves as it crosses the wooded slopes of **Lombo do Vento**.

Cross a broad track then cross a bouldery stream-bed at **Ribeira do Passa-Remos**. Reach a junction of paths around 830m (2725ft) where signposts point in all directions (including ahead to Ribeiro

A gnarled cedar beside the Levada da Portela

Frio; see Walk 12). Turn right down a clear path with a long flight of log steps, signposted as the PR10 to Portela, with the Levada da Portela running parallel. ▸ The path switches from side to side, landing on a dirt road at a toilet block, garden and picnic site at the **Posto Florestal Lamaceiros**.

The channel is narrow and steep, so the water races down it.

Follow the dirt road gently downhill, with the levada channel on the left. When the levada crosses to the right, either follow it through woods and drop steeply later, or stay on the dirt road for a more gradual descent. The levada meets the dirt road again at a junction.

Turn left along a track signposted as the PR10 trail for Portela. The track runs beside a tall fence surrounding the **Herdade Lombo das Faias**. Don't follow the levada where it runs through a very narrow cut, but cross over the channel later at a corner. ▸ Woods obscure views as the levada runs across a slope around 700m (2300ft). Suddenly, the water rushes downhill from a ruined building, and the path has nearly 200 log steps flanked by hydrangeas and agapanthus, passing a stand of mimosa and tall cedars.

There are good views of Penha d'Águia, Porto da Cruz and the coast, as well as up to Pico do Areeiro and Pico Ruivo.

Land on the **ER-102** road at a notice-board and turn left down the road. A broad, paved area features a pillar-like shrine and a viewpoint. Walk down the road to another viewpoint at **Portela**, at 605m (1985ft). An impressive flight of concrete steps avoids a road-walk down to a bus shelter opposite the Restaurante Portela à Vista.

PORTELA

A fine view takes in Penha d'Águia, Porto da Cruz and the north coast, as well as the high peaks of Madeira. The Restaurante Miradouro da Portela and Restaurante Portela à Vista offer food and drink. SAM bus 53 serves Portela from Funchal and Machico. There may be taxis. Portela is the starting point for Walk 9 along the Vereda das Funduras to Maroços and Walk 12 along the Levada do Furado to Ribeiro Frio.

WALK 9
Vereda das Funduras: Portela to Maroços

Start	ER-102/ER-212 junction at Portela
Finish	Maroços
Distance	9km (5½ miles)
Total ascent	150m (490ft)
Total descent	580m (1900ft)
Time	4hr
Terrain	A broad and easy forest road, followed by a narrow, convoluted forest path. A steep descent on paths, tracks and steps ends on cultivated terraces.
Maps	Carta Militar 6
Refreshments	Two bar/restaurants at Portela.
Transport	SAM bus 53 serves Portela from Funchal, Machico and Faial. SAM Bus 156 serves Maroços from Funchal and Machico.

The waymarked PR5 trail, or Vereda das Funduras, explores an area of lush *laurisilva* forest high above the Machico valley. Access is from Portela, using a forest road running parallel to the Levada da Portela. Later, the forest road is left in favour of a narrow path, becoming like a jungle trek. In the end, a steep descent leads down from the forest to finish on cultivated terraces at Maroços.

The Miradouro da Portela Restaurante and Restaurante Portela à Vista offer food and drink at the start and there is a fine roadside viewpoint.

The forested crest offers occasional views from coast to coast.

Start the junction of the ER-102/ER-212 roads at **Portela**, at 605m (1985ft). ◄ Follow the road beside the Miradouro da Portela Restaurante, signposted as the PR5 for Maroços, passing a noticeboard beside the Caminho das Funduras. Follow the road round a bend and turn left. Stay level to pass another notice, avoiding a path dropping steep and grassy on the left. A track runs gently downhill across a steep slope of mixed forest, with the narrow concrete channel of the **Levada da Portela** alongside. The levada runs through a tunnel, but stay on the track to find where it emerges on the other side of a ridge. Keep straight ahead at a track junction, still with the levada alongside. ◄

Watch for a path heading off to the right, signposted 'Serra das Funduras Percurso Pedonal'. This leads into dense *laurisilva*, but don't worry about how remote it suddenly seems, since there is only one path. Roughly contour across a steep slope, or

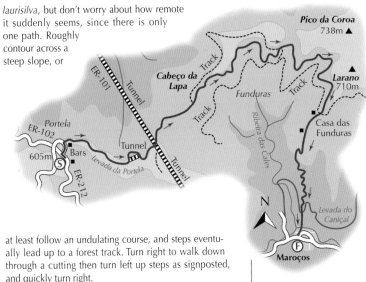

at least follow an undulating course, and steps eventually lead up to a forest track. Turn right to walk down through a cutting then turn left up steps as signposted, and quickly turn right.

The path crosses another slope of dense *laurisilva*, undulating more as it passes lush ferns and tree ferns, with mosses and liverworts in wet areas. There are more pines later then the path suddenly lands on a forest track at the Casa das Funduras. ▸

Enjoy fine views across the forested head of the Machico valley to the high peaks of Madeira.

The Casa das Funduras marks the start of a long and steep descent to Maroços

Walk straight downhill from the building as signposted for Maroços, using a narrow path with 245 log steps. When a track is reached, turn right down to a junction with another track, then turn left as signposted further downhill. Turn left at another junction, then later right as signposted at a lower junction. Keep right at a junction where there is a tall cedar. Further downhill, pass a small reservoir and a few huts, reaching a house. Begin walking down several hundred steps on the Vereda do Lombo da Roçada. 465 steps lead down to the Levada do Caniçal (described in Walk 7), then after a very short concrete road, squeeze between houses and go down another 225 steps to reach a road beside the Ribeira de Machico. There is a notice about the PR5 trail, but to finish the walk cross a bridge over the river, turn right and walk up to bus stops in **Maroços**.

WALK 10

North Coast: Porto da Cruz to Ribeira Seca

Start	Porto da Cruz
Finish	Bar Boca do Risco, Ribeira Seca
Distance	10km (6¼ miles)
Total ascent	400m (1310ft)
Total descent	250m (820ft)
Time	4hr
Terrain	Paths and roads climb steeply. A well-wooded path crosses a steep slope, becoming rocky and exposed, then wooded again. An easy valley path leads down to a road at the end.
Maps	Carta Militar 6
Refreshments	Bars and restaurants at Porto da Cruz. Small bar at Larano. Bar at Ribeira Seca.
Transport	SAM bus 53 serves Porto da Cruz from Funchal and Machico. Interurban buses 56, 103 and 138 serve a tunnel above Porto da Cruz from Funchal, but study timetables carefully as not all of them pass this way. SAM bus 113 links Ribeira Seca with Machico. Taxis at Porto da Cruz.

A fine cliff path heads east from Porto da Cruz on the north coast of Madeira, but it takes time to reach the best parts. Winding paths and roads climb steeply and the first stages of the cliff path are well-wooded. The cliffs themselves are revealed quite suddenly and, while fenced, vertigo sufferers might be unnerved. Beware of rock-falls, especially after rain. Head inland from Boca do Risco to end at Ribeira Seca.

PORTO DA CRUZ

An interesting little coastal settlement with a landmark church and a sugar factory built in 1927. Facilities include a bank with ATM, post office, bars and restaurants.

Start at the church in the centre of **Porto da Cruz** and walk down to the sea wall. To the left is the sheer cliff face of Penha d'Águia (Walk 11), while to the right a broad dirt road runs along the foot of a cliff. Walk to a water treatment works and cross a metal footbridge, the Pont da Maia, over a river. Climb a long flight of concrete steps and cross a road, picking up a narrow cobbled path to climb higher. Continue along a level terrace beside a short levada, or use a slightly

Looking towards Larano, where steep climbing is involved

73

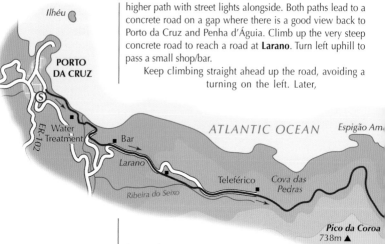

higher path with street lights alongside. Both paths lead to a concrete road on a gap where there is a good view back to Porto da Cruz and Penha d'Águia. Climb up the very steep concrete road to reach a road at **Larano**. Turn left uphill to pass a small shop/bar.

Keep climbing straight ahead up the road, avoiding a turning on the left. Later, the road turns left, while to the right a flight of concrete steps leads up to a levada with a level concrete path. Follow it alongside the wooded valley of **Ribeira do Seixo**. ◀ Turn left before reaching the end of the levada, up a flight of concrete steps to the right of a house. Around 185 steps reach a concrete road above. Turn right and walk up the road, suddenly reaching a gap overlooking the sea. A teleférico drops 350m (1150ft) at **Cova das Pedras**, allowing access for farmers to remote cultivation terraces.

Look back to see Madeira's highest mountains in the distance.

◀ Pass a mapboard and continue along a track which ends suddenly, giving way to a path across a slope of pine, laurel and heather. The path later narrows, so climb a short rocky ramp to continue.

There is another fine view back to Penha d'Águia.

The path wriggles in and out of small gullies on a steep, wooded slope, and generally runs around 350m (1150ft) above the sea. Look back along the coast to Porto da Cruz. There is little ground cover, though pine, mimosa and eucalyptus grow on the slope. Heather flanks the path before it turns round a significant point at **Espigão Amarelo**.

Enjoy views back to Porto da Cruz and ahead to the Ponta de São Lourenço and the distant island of Porto Santo.

◀ The path has several stretches of safety fencing alongside as it suddenly enters a huge bare hollow that some might find unnerving. Steep slopes of grass and crumbling rock drop to the sea. Only a few small trees or clumps of heather are dotted across the slopes, and the path is narrow in places. Beware of rock-falls, pass a pool and take particular care passing a rock-wall below **Pico da Coroa**. Follow the path past a little pinnacle of rock to reach dense heather, laurel, mimosa, and masses of brambles and bracken, where the sense of exposure lessens.

There are a couple of open areas, but also patches of *laurisilva* woodland so dense that it is quite dark inside. The path is broad and stony as it turns round a rocky headland. Go through another dense patch of vegetation, turn another headland and follow the path through gorse before rising gently to the signposted gap of **Boca do Risco** at 350m (1150ft).

Parts of the cliff path are fenced or run through woodland

Enjoy the last of the cliff-coast views before following a path inland and downhill. Although the valley seems well-wooded, the stony path often crosses grassy slopes and keeps away from denser stands of trees. Heather and laurel increase in size on the way down, and there is a small-holding where there may be a few animals. The path is known as the Vereda da Boca do Risco. Continue descending easily, though it is rockier in a rugged side-valley. Trees give way to more cultivated slopes and there are little sheds below.

Cross the **Levada do Caniçal** at around 220m (720ft) (Walk 7). A dirt road descends and there are street lights all the way down to **Ribeira Seca**. At the bottom, go down a flight of steps to reach the road at the Bar Boca do Risco. If a SAM bus 113 isn't due for a while, or at all, then follow the road onwards, passing a couple more bars on the way to the ER-109 road, where there are regular buses linking Caniçal and Machico.

MACHICO

A bustling coastal town with an intriguing history, Machico is supposedly named after an Englishman called Walter Machim. During the early settlement of Madeira this was the main base for Cristão Vaz Teixeira. The cobbled streets are delightful and old buildings stand beside new ones, with everything cosy and compact. The bus station is outside the town centre and a cobbled beach can be reached by following a paved path beside a river, which is full of croaking frogs in spring. A full range of services is available, including banks with ATMs, a post office, hotels, shops, bars, restaurants and taxis. The Tourist Information Office is in an old fort near the beach (tel 291–962289).

2 FUNCHAL TO SANTANA

View of Pico do Areeiro and Torres from Feteiras de Cima (Walk 15)

In this part of Madeira, the rugged uplands rise above steep, forested slopes. The valleys are deep and steep-sided. Levadas have been cut across precipitous slopes, sometimes tunnelling through rock to avoid cliff faces. Obviously, walkers need to tread carefully and ensure that they choose walks that are within their ability. The peak of Penha d'Águia might only be a 'little hill' by Madeiran standards, but it is surrounded on almost all sides by cliff faces and its paths are very steep.

Despite the nature of the terrain, Madeira's early settlers hacked and slashed their way through forests, constructing stone-paved highways from coast to coast. Two of these old roads, or *Caminhos Velha*, can be traced from Poiso to the rugged north coast – one leading to Porto da Cruz and the other leading to Santana. The northern slopes of Madeira are well-watered and covered in lush green vegetation.

On the southern side of the high crest, the ground is more arid and the urban sprawl of Funchal needs all the water it can get. Some of the oldest levadas on the island were constructed to carry water into town. Four levadas are followed downstream, including two from Poço da Neve to the high suburbs of Funchal and two more at a lower level that feature exceedingly steep and exposed sections that are quite unsuitable for anyone who suffers from vertigo or clumsy feet.

Funchal is an obvious base for these walks, and there are interurban buses running back and forth between Funchal, Santana and Porto da Cruz. Those who wish to experience the quieter parts of Madeira should base themselves in Santana. Those looking to create long-distance walks will find good links with routes in eastern Madeira, at Monte, Santo da Serra and Porto da Cruz, as well as links with other mountain paths from Curral das Freiras, Pico do Areeiro and Santana.

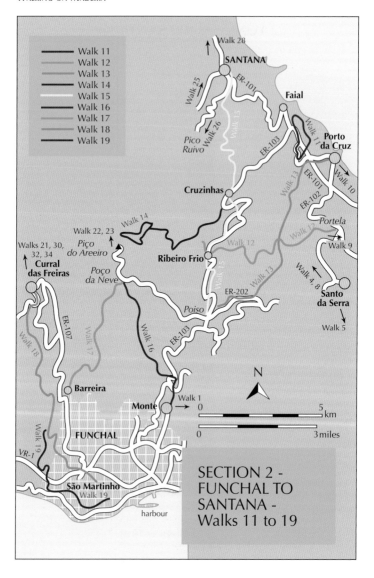

Walk 11
Walk 12
Walk 13
Walk 14
Walk 15
Walk 16
Walk 17
Walk 18
Walk 19

Walk 28

SANTANA

Faial

Walk 25

Walk 26

Pico Ruivo

ER-101

Walk 15

ER-103

Walk 11

Porto da Cruz

Cruzinhas

Walk 13

ER-101

Walk 10

ER-102

Portela

Walk 9

Walk 14

Walk 22, 23

Piço do Areeiro

Poço da Neve

Walks 21, 30, 32, 34

Curral das Freiras

Ribeiro Frio

Walk 12

Walk 13

ER-107

Walk 18

Walk 17

Walk 16

ER-103

ER-202

Poiso

Walk 4, 8

Santo da Serra

Walk 5

N

Barreira

Monte

Walk 1

0   5 km

0   3 miles

FUNCHAL

Walk 19

VR-1

São Martinho

Walk 19

harbour

SECTION 2 – FUNCHAL TO SANTANA – Walks 11 to 19

WALK 11

Vereda da Penha d'Águia

Start/finish	Between Moinhos and Faial
Distance	5.5km (3½ miles)
Total ascent/descent	550m (1805ft)
Time	3hr
Terrain	Steep and narrow steps and paths may be rocky, crumbling or overgrown in places. Densely forested on top. The final stage is along a road.
Maps	Carta Militar 6
Refreshments	Bar/restaurant near the ascent. Bars at Cruz after the descent. Bar at Moinhos.
Transport	SAM buses 53 an 156 run from Funchal and Machico to Cruz and Moinhos. Interurban buses 56, 103 and 138 serve Moinhos from Funchal and Santana.

Penha d'Águia looks inaccessible from all sides. The seaward cliffs are vertical and cliffs appear to be wrapped all the way round the landward sides. In fact, a narrow path reaches the summit from the north-west, and a steep zigzag path descends roughly south-west to Cruz. This walk is not really suitable in wet weather as the paths can become treacherously slippery.

Start on the **ER-101** road below Moinhos, at a bus stop just before the bridge spanning the Riberia de São Roque. A path called the Caminho do Passe climbs some 400 uneven steps, directly from the bus stop. The steps are made of concrete or stone, zigzagging steeply uphill with street lights alongside. ▶ The path levels out, then drops down 90 concrete steps, passing between two buildings to land on a road. Follow the road gently downhill. Either walk to the Restaurante Galé, then turn right up steps, or turn right beforehand up the concrete road called Caminho Agricola da Penha d'Àguia. Both options meet within a few minutes.

Continue up concrete steps as signposted. Aim for a white-walled, red-roofed building on the hillside, and keep left of it. The path is rugged but is always clear and in much better shape than it used to be. Watch for brambles and

There is a sheer cliff above, and a few pines and malfurada bushes on the slope.

Views stretch from
the sea to Faial and
the high mountains.

There is no view of the
sea but the mountains
rising inland look
impressive.

squeeze past clumps of heather and malfurada. Steps have
been installed but there is also bare rock in places. ◀

Climb above old terraces to enter pine forest, where the
path is narrow and crumbling on a steep slope with annoying brambles. Climb more easily, but still steeply up a slope
of pines. A gap is reached on the crest of the hill, where a
left turn is made. The crest is well defined, undulating gently
past pine, mimosa and eucalyptus. Views to the right reveal
a sheer cliff. The path is narrow but easy, with some wooden
steps. There is a tiny clearing on top of **Penha d'Águia**, with
most of the space taken by a tall trig point at 589m (1932ft).
There are small pines, laurels, heather, gorse, brambles and
bilberry around the clearing. ◀

A narrow path continues along the crest, descending
with a view through the trees to the Ponta de São Lourenço
and the distant island of Porto Santo. Squeeze past gorse and
heather and note how pines are crowded out by eucalyptus.
The path is narrow and crumbling, leading to a clearing on a
gap. An old winch cable stretches downhill, marking the line
of descent along a steep, narrow, crumbling, zigzag path.
Take great care all the way down. Don't be tempted to take a
shortcut or leave the path.

Things get better while passing a few
mimosa trees. The path is less steep
and there are fine coastal views.
Although the road can be seen
below, care is still needed on the
path. When the gradient eases on
a crest, watch out on the left to
drop down to a narrow levada on a cultivated
terrace. Turn

80

Looking up towards Pico do Areeiro from the road-walk back to Moinhos on the descent from Cruz

right to follow it across the hillside to reach the ER-102 road at **Cruz**. ▶

A signpost points back for the 'Vereda da Penha d'Águia' if the route is ever considered in reverse.

Either turn left and walk down the road to Porto da Cruz, linking with Walk 10 for a longer trek, or turn right to walk back to where the walk started. Taking the latter, the winding road eventually joins the main **ER-101** road. Walking down through **Moinhos** leads past a bar and back to the bus stop where the walk started.

Snack Bar Adega da Cruz and Katrepas Bar.

WALK 12

Levada do Furado: Portela to Ribeiro Frio

Start	ER-102/ER-212 junction at Portela
Finish	Ribeiro Frio
Distance	11km (6¾ miles); 14km (8¾ miles) if you continue to Balcões.
Total ascent	190m (625ft)
Total descent	10m (30ft)
Time	4hr
Terrain	Paths, tracks and steps are used on the ascent. There are a few short tunnels and some parts are exposed, rocky and slippery. Most is well-wooded. The path towards the end is clear, level and easy.
Maps	Carta Militar 6
Refreshments	Two bar/restaurants at Portela and two more at Ribeiro Frio.
Transport	SAM bus 53 serves Portela from Funchal and Machico. Interurban buses 56, 103 and 138 serve Ribeiro Frio from Funchal and Santana.

For facilities, see Walk 8.

Start at 605m (1985ft) at **Portela**. ◀ Climb concrete steps from the bus shelter and follow the **ER-102** road uphill towards Santo da Serra. A broad, paved area features a pillar-like

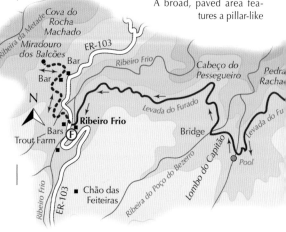

The Levada do Furado was cut in the 1820s across a very steep slope of *laurisilva* forest, linking with the Levada da Portela and Levada da Serra. There are sheer cliffs along the way, though the dense forest masks the exposure, and there are a few short tunnels. Maps often show the levada wrongly, which roughly follows the 850m (2790ft) contour to Ribeiro Frio. The walk described here is the PR10 trail, which uses the levada path to link the Portela viewpoint and Ribeiro Frio.

shrine and a viewpoint. Continue a little further up the road to reach a notice and signpost for the PR10 trail. Climb almost 200 log steps beside the **Levada da Portela**. The water races through a narrow channel and is followed upstream past tall cedars and a stand of mimosa, and is flanked by hydrangeas and agapanthus. The path is on the left of the levada as it climbs a wooded slope, but switches to the right after passing a ruined building. A gentler path leads onwards from around 700m (2300ft), reaching an open corner.

▶ The levada cannot be followed through a narrow cut so follow a broad path running parallel. Walk beside a tall fence surrounding the **Herdade Lombo das Faias** to reach a track junction with several signposts. Turn right as

There is a good view of Penha d'Águia and Porto da Cruz, as well as to Pico do Areeiro and Pico Ruivo.

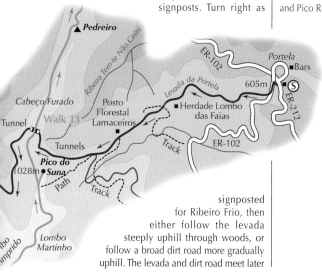

signposted for Ribeiro Frio, then either follow the levada steeply uphill through woods, or follow a broad dirt road more gradually uphill. The levada and dirt road meet later and run at a gentle gradient to a toilet block, garden and a picnic site at the **Posto Florestal Lamaceiros**.

Stay on the right of the track and follow the levada steeply uphill from the toilet block. The path climbs beside the levada at first, then a sunken path to the left is used while the water, running parallel, is out of sight. A long flight of log steps climbs to a junction of paths around 830m (2725ft) where signposts point in all directions. Turn right for Ribeiro Frio, passing a water tower just round a corner, where the **Levada do Furado** is followed upstream.

> Trees often obscure the fact that the levada clings to a very steep and rocky slope.

The levada channel slices through mossy rock and runs through dense laurisilva. ◄ Marvel at the engineering of the watercourse, which includes a few small tunnels – most for walking through but a couple for walking past. In the middle of this series is a fine view down the valley to Porto da Cruz. The levada parapet is narrow and exposed, often with fencing alongside, and there may be rock overhanging the channel. The last of the tunnels is more like a narrow rocky chasm cut through the spur of **Cabeço Furado**, though part of it is roofed. ◄

> Walk 13 crosses over the tunnel roof and can be reached using paths on either side of the tunnel.

The path is broad and well-wooded then becomes rough and uneven, turning left round a pronounced rocky corner into the valley of **Pedra Rachada**, where there are well-established laurels and tree heather. The valley head is moist and dripping; then the path becomes broad and easy on the way to another dripping valley head. Watch for the path dipping below the levada parapet where the channel has been cut across these wet areas. After turning left round another pronounced corner, the levada runs through narrow rock cuttings where walkers must step on slabs placed across the channel.

> There is a deep green pool in the second valley.

Follow the path into a couple of damp, mossy, fern-clad valleys, where the path dips below the parapet to cross streambeds. ◄ The path is narrow as it curves round the **Lombo do Capitão**, but it becomes easy and well wooded. Cross a wide bridge over the **Ribeira do Poço do Bezerro**. The path is broad and well-wooded as it leaves the valley and there is a pronounced swing into the next valley. The path narrows and has a fence alongside. After passing a weeping wall, swing round a rocky corner at **Cabeço do Pessegueiro**. ◄

> The surroundings remain forested, but there are a couple of fine views of the highest peaks on Madeira.

The path is rough and rocky, passing through a rocky notch and often equipped with fencing. After another rugged stretch, things get easier and hydrangeas grow alongside. An old mill is seen across the river before a bridge is crossed. A

A view of Torres and Pico Ruivo, seen from the Levada do Furado as it approaches Ribeiro Frio

notice-board explains about the PR10 trail, then a path leads up to the road at **Ribeiro Frio**, around 870m (2855ft).

RIBEIRO FRIO

The Restaurante Ribeiro Frio and Victor's Bar are immediately to hand, while a souvenir shop lies across the road. The Posto Aquicola trout farm is just up the road, across the river. An interesting garden can be explored across the road from the trout farm, where plants have name tags to assist identification.

Extension to Balcões

It is well worth seeking the continuation of the levada, across the road, which offers a pleasant and easy extension to the popular **Miradouro dos Balcões**. The path is well signposted, turns round a well-wooded valley, passes through a rock cutting to reach a small bar, then goes through another rocky cutting. A paved path on the right later leads to a rocky promontory, which is a perch for a splendid viewpoint. Look down the Metade valley to Penha d'Águia and up the valley to Pico do Areeiro, Pico do Gato, Torres, Pico Ruivo and Achada do Teixeira. There is also a view of the generating station at Fajã da Nogueira (start of Walk 14). The walk to Balcões and back to Ribeiro Frio is almost level and measures 3km (2 miles).

WALK 13

Caminho Velha: Poiso to Porto da Cruz

Start	ER-103/ER-202 junction at Poiso
Finish	Porto da Cruz
Distance	13km (8 miles)
Total ascent	100m (330ft)
Total descent	1500m (4920ft)
Time	4hr
Terrain	Paths give way to a good track on increasingly forested slopes. Steep and narrow paths later. Road-walking towards the end.
Maps	Carta Militar 6
Refreshments	Bar/restaurant at Poiso. Bars at Cruz. Bars and restaurants at Porto da Cruz.
Transport	Interurban buses 56, 103 and 138 serve Poiso from Funchal or Santana, as well as a tunnel at Maçapez. SAM buses 53 and 156 serve Cruz and Porto da Cruz from Funchal and Machico.

The old road, or *Caminho Velha*, can still be followed from a high crest at Poiso down to the sea at Porto da Cruz. This route includes fine views of the mountains from easy paths then descends through dark and dense *laurisilva* forest where views are limited. The final stages involve tracks and roads dropping down past cultivation terraces and tiny farms to reach the coast.

Start high on the **ER-103** road near the Casa de Abrigo restaurant at **Poiso**. Turn right at a flowery junction at an altitude of 1412m (4633ft). Follow the **ER-202** road, signposted for Santo da Serra. The road climbs gently and turns left, overlooking the south coast. When it bends right, watch for a grassy track on the left. This rises between pines, heather and gorse, to cross a gentle rise and heads back down towards the road.

There is no need to touch the road, but continue along a clear path through

Feiteira
de Cin

Cova do
Tambor

ER-103

Poiso

forest, parallel to the road, to reach a broad, grassy area used as a picnic site. Make a very easy ascent of **Pico das Cruzes**, at 1378m (4521ft), for views stretching from Madeira's highest peaks all the way down to the coast. Cross the road and pick up a narrow path running roughly parallel, then cross the road again near **Terreiros**.

Watch carefully, leaving a clear earth path to follow a grassy path across the heather-dotted slopes of **João do Prado**. Keep left at all junctions, and the path is always clear underfoot, running along **Lombo Comprido**, where views stretch from the high mountains to the rugged peninsula of Ponta de São Lourenço. The path later turns sharp right and drops down to a broad track. Turn left to follow it down across increasingly well-wooded slopes.

Keep left at junctions with other tracks until a wooded gap is

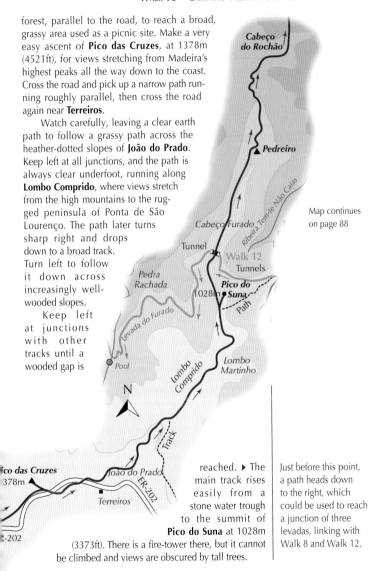

Map continues on page 88

reached. ▸ The main track rises easily from a stone water trough to the summit of **Pico do Suna** at 1028m (3373ft). There is a fire-tower there, but it cannot be climbed and views are obscured by tall trees.

Just before this point, a path heads down to the right, which could be used to reach a junction of three levadas, linking with Walk 8 and Walk 12.

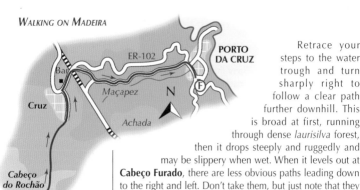

Retrace your steps to the water trough and turn sharply right to follow a clear path further downhill. This is broad at first, running through dense *laurisilva* forest, then it drops steeply and ruggedly and may be slippery when wet. When it levels out at **Cabeço Furado**, there are less obvious paths leading down to the right and left. Don't take them, but just note that they lead to the Levada do Furado, which runs through a tunnel directly beneath the path (see Walk 12).

The path continues easily, but becomes quite narrow as it traverses the steep and well vegetated slopes around 750m (2460ft). ◀ Watch for brambles as the path undulates and runs through a rocky notch. Faial can be seen down through the valley. Zigzag down from the forested peak of **Pedreiro** while views take in Porto da Cruz for a while.

A fire opened up views across the valley to the high mountains, but these are being lost as the vegetation recovers.

Tall eucalyptus forest limits the views further downhill even when the path follows the crest of **Cabeço do Rochão**. There are a few pines on the slopes, but there was a blaze in the past and eucalyptus grew afterwards. The path is plain and obvious as it zigzags further downhill, and is paved with cobbles before it reaches a narrow tarmac road. However, it

View of Pico do Areeiro and Torres from Pico das Cruzes

is possible to be drawn to the left, along a path favoured by mountain bikers, which leads down to a forest track. If this happens, simply turn right along the track. Follow the road straight ahead and downhill, reaching the main ER-102 road, around 240m (790ft), at **Cruz**. ▸

Katrepas Bar and Snack Bar Adega da Cruz.

The walk could be ended at this point, or continued by turning right to head down to Porto da Cruz. Avoid the main road by walking down the Caminho do Massapêz. Buses can be picked up at a bus shelter near a tunnel mouth, otherwise keep following the old road parallel to a main road down to **Porto da Cruz**. ▸

For facilities, see Walk 10.

WALK 14
Fajã da Nogueira and Levada da Serra

Start/finish	Fajã da Nogueira or bridge below Cruzinhas
Distance	9.5km or 18km (6 or 11¼ miles)
Total ascent/descent	390m or 640m (1280ft or 2100ft)
Time	4hr or 7hr
Terrain	Broad and clear tracks at the start and finish, on steep and wooded slopes. A narrow and exposed levada walk includes several small tunnels. A head for heights and steady feet are essential.
Maps	Carta Militar 6
Refreshments	None closer than a small bar at Cruzinhas.
Transport	Interurban buses 56, 103 and 138 serve the bridge over the Ribeira da Metade below Cruzinhas from Funchal and Santana.
Note	The longer distances and higher ascent/descent apply when you start/finish at the bridge below Cruzinhas.

Fajã da Nogueira can be reached by following a broad dirt road into the Metade valley. It is a long way to walk there and back, but it can be approached with care by ordinary hire cars. Starting from the generating station, a clear track leads up through laurisilva to the Levada da Serra, which offers an exciting and exposed walk round the head of the valley, including a series of tunnels. Note that this walk requires a good head for heights and very careful placement of feet.

89

There are glimpses of the peak of Torres high above the head of the valley.

Whether approaching on foot or by car, start from a bridge over the **Ribeira da Metade** below Cruzinhas, on the ER-103 road. The Central Fajã da Nogueira is signposted from bridge and the tarmac immediately gives way to a broad dirt road. Follow it onwards and gently uphill through the well-wooded valley, passing a few cultivated plots along the way. ◄ The road bends and climbs round the **Cova do Rocha Machado**.

You will walk around a lengthy side-valley at **Chão das Faias**, where you'll pass a building and a tunnel mouth. Cross a concrete bridge over a bouldery river and follow the dirt road to the generating station at **Fajã da Nogueira**, crossing another concrete bridge. If you drive to the generating station, park off the road.

These are the oldest discovered on the island. Admire them, but note how much damage they have suffered over the centuries.

The peaks of Torres and Pico do Gato (traversed on Walk 23) can be seen briefly from the generating station. The last part of the road is tarmac and serves a few houses, but turn right up a stony track before reaching them. The track climbs in easy loops on a well-wooded slope. Watch carefully on the left to spot two enormous til trees. ◄

Turn right at a junction of tracks and climb past more big old tils. The track leads to the **Levada da Serra**, around 970m (3180ft), which is covered with slabs to the right and earth to the left. The route turns left, but it is worth turning right first to enjoy a fine view down the Metade valley then return to the same point to continue. After walking along a covered stretch, there is an open stretch where the water is followed downstream. The path is wide at first, then passes through two little **tunnels** before more care and attention is needed, as a single slip or trip could result in serious injury or death, and this continues to be the case for as long as the levada is being followed.

Turn round an exposed ravine and go through another little **tunnel**. The next **tunnel** is curious and bendy, with a 'window' part-way through. The parapet path has both fenced and unfenced sections as it slices across a cliff face. Go through a short and low **tunnel**, which has a 'window' part-way through. The levada channel is covered and the path is uneven as it crosses an open slope. Go through another bendy **tunnel**, which has a low entrance and exit, with a couple of 'windows' along its length. The levada is quite bendy afterwards. Walk along the parapet path then walk below it for a while.

There is no need to enter the next **tunnel**, as a

The Levada da Serra clings to cliffs and steep wooded slopes

rugged path runs round the rock face instead. Tree heather grows on the slopes and a fenced path runs below the levada parapet. Enter the next bendy **tunnel**, which has two 'windows' and a double arch at its exit. Step up onto the parapet path, then step down to enter yet another bendy **tunnel**, which is quite low and has another 'window'. The path leads round a rocky gully that is both unfenced and exposed, but there are short lengths of fencing later. There is also a pinnacle of rock above the levada. Walk on and off the parapet as required, passing big til trees. Look for Pico do Gato above the head of the valley.

Cross a bouldery ravine, then turn an exposed corner. The path is mostly fenced and runs beside the parapet to cross a stone-arched bridge over the Ribeira da Fajã da Nogueira at the head of the valley.

Walk along or off the parapet as required, with or without fencing alongside. Curve round an undercut cliff that drips with water, where the levada is unfenced but covered with slabs. Go through a little **tunnel** after which the path is mostly fenced. There is another slab-covered stretch and good views down through the valley. Go down concrete steps into a tunnel that has two 'windows'. Go through a short, tall **tunnel** and continue walking on and off the parapet, where the path has fenced and unfenced sections, until another **tunnel** is reached.

Instead of entering this last tunnel go down some crude stone steps on the left, then zigzag down a slope of tall tils. Turn left at a track junction and walk down to the Ribeira da Fajã da Nogueira. Cross the river using a metal footbridge. The track drifts away from the river and climbs with less woodland alongside, reaching the junction of tracks passed earlier in the day. Turn right to walk downhill, passing the two enormous til trees, to return to the generating station at **Fajã da Nogueira**.

If a car was used, then simply drive back down through the valley towards Cruzinhas. If walking, maybe someone

A wet, slippery and exposed stretch of the Levada da Serra

will offer you a lift. If there is any length of time to wait for a bus back at the bridge over the Ribeira da Metade, it may be worth walking up to **Cruzinhas** for a break at the little Bar das Cruzinhas.

WALK 15
Caminho Velha: Poiso to Santana

Start	ER-103/ER-202 junction at Poiso
Finish	Santana
Distance	18.5km (11½ miles)
Total ascent	630m (2065ft)
Total descent	1630m (5350ft)
Time	7hr
Terrain	Forested and cultivated ridges and valleys. Steep cobbled paths and tracks can be slippery when wet. Some road walking at intervals.
Maps	Carta Militar 3 and 6
Refreshments	Bar/restaurants at Poiso and Ribeiro Frio. Bars at Achada do Cedro Gordo and Cruzinhas. Plenty of choice at Santana.
Transport	Interurban buses 56, 103 and 138 serve Poiso, Ribeiro Frio, Achada do Cedro Gordo, Cruzinhas, Lombo Galego and Santana from Funchal.

The modern mountain road between Funchal and Santana is remarkably convoluted. The old road, or *Caminho Velha*, was more direct, but featured steeper gradients and tight zigzags. Much of the old road can still be followed between Poiso and Santana, but start early and expect to finish late as a series of steep-sided valleys need to be crossed along the way. Buses serve the middle of the route, so there is no need to walk the whole route at once.

Start high on the ER-103 road at the Casa de Abrigo do Poiso restaurant at **Poiso**. Walk straight through a flowery crossroads at an altitude of 1412m (4633ft). Follow the road downhill in the direction of Ribeiro Frio, but turn left down a cobbled track. This is the *Caminho Velha*, flanked by tall

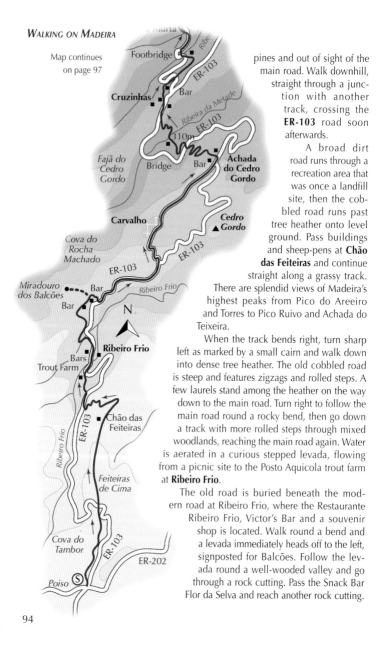

Map continues
on page 97

pines and out of sight of the main road. Walk downhill, straight through a junction with another track, crossing the **ER-103** road soon afterwards.

A broad dirt road runs through a recreation area that was once a landfill site, then the cobbled road runs past tree heather onto level ground. Pass buildings and sheep-pens at **Chão das Feiteiras** and continue straight along a grassy track. There are splendid views of Madeira's highest peaks from Pico do Areeiro and Torres to Pico Ruivo and Achada do Teixeira.

When the track bends right, turn sharp left as marked by a small cairn and walk down into dense tree heather. The old cobbled road is steep and features zigzags and rolled steps. A few laurels stand among the heather on the way down to the main road. Turn right to follow the main road round a rocky bend, then go down a track with more rolled steps through mixed woodlands, reaching the main road again. Water is aerated in a curious stepped levada, flowing from a picnic site to the Posto Aquicola trout farm at **Ribeiro Frio**.

The old road is buried beneath the modern road at Ribeiro Frio, where the Restaurante Ribeiro Frio, Victor's Bar and a souvenir shop is located. Walk round a bend and a levada immediately heads off to the left, signposted for Balcões. Follow the levada round a well-wooded valley and go through a rock cutting. Pass the Snack Bar Flor da Selva and reach another rock cutting.

94

Either go through the cutting and follow the path to the Miradouro dos Balcões, returning afterwards, or simply turn right to follow a concrete path called the Vereda do Ribeiro Frio. This runs down steps to return to the ER-103 road beside the Restaurante Snack Bar Faísca. The Jardim do Vale tea-room is nearby.

Looking back to Ribeiro Frio and Pico do Areeiro

Turn left and the road rises gently away from Ribeiro Frio. Mimosa grows above the road and there is a fine view back to Pico do Areeiro. The road descends and rises, passing a picnic site on a bend. Follow the road down past a bus shelter and turn left down the Rua de São João. Walk down this road, through the village of **Carvalho**, enjoying a fine view of the high peaks above the Metade valley. All kinds of fruit and vegetables grow in small plots. Reach a church, Bar Zeca, bus stop and the main road at **Achada do Cedro Gordo**, at 610m (2000ft).

Walk straight ahead then turn left along a concrete road. This serves a house, then the old cobbled road runs down-hill. Step to the right as it becomes quite steep and partly vegetated as it zigzags down a well-wooded slope. Some parts are wet and slippery, subject to rock-fall and landslip. Cross the ER-103 road to continue downhill. Turn right down a concrete road and right again at a house to go down a

A road bridge and an older footbridge cross the Ribeira Seca

grassy path called the Caminho Municipal da Fajã do Cedro Gordo de Baixo. Join a road, passing a former mill to cross a substantial arched bridge over the Ribeira da Metade, around 310m (1015ft).

Zigzag up a narrow road on the other side of the valley, looking down to the rugged hill of Penha d'Águia. Just before road runs downhill, turn sharp left up 14 concrete steps to a cobbled path, the Caminho Antigo da Fajã Grande, which is the old road again. Cross a tarmac road and climb 14 more concrete steps and continue up a concrete path laid on top of the old cobbled road. Turn right up the main road, but quickly leave it on the left to follow a short stretch of old road into the tiny village of **Cruzinhas**, around 420m (1380ft). ◄

Bar das Cruzinhas and interurban bus 56.

The old road is immediately below the one signposted for Fajã da Murta, and is more direct, though the modern road has the bar alongside. The steep concrete road has steps down the middle as well as street lights. Grass-grown cobbles lead further downhill then the road is concrete as it crosses the tarmac road. Go down steps and continue along a path. When this joins a concrete road, swing left to walk down to a tarmac road deeper in the valley. Follow the road down round a bend, then either cross the road bridge over the **Ribeira Seca**, or cross an old footbridge hidden among old houses around 260m (855ft). Pico do Areeiro is seen one last time at the head of the valley.

Follow the road up through **Fajã da Murta**, round a bend and across a bridge. Go round another bend, but don't cross the next bridge. Instead, climb chunky concrete steps with street lights alongside and cross an old bridge in a steep-sided valley. Continue up a cobbled and concrete track with a view of Penha d'Águia. Nearby slopes are well cultivated and dotted with houses. Join the tarmac road and climb round a bend then go straight up a broad flight of 28 concrete steps at the next bend. Walk up a cobbled track, the Vereda da Eirinha, then climb 28 concrete steps back onto the tarmac road.

Just before a **footbridge** spans the road, turn sharp left up a concrete road with street lights alongside, the Caminho do Pico do Lombo Galego. The road turns right and later rises and falls gently, then rises and falls to the tarmac road again. Climb round a bend to cross a bridge over the Ribeira do Lombo Galego, where there is a derelict mill. Follow the road uphill but, before it begins to fall gently, turn left up a steep concrete road, the Caminho Velho do Lombo Galego – Cova da Roda.

Keep zigzagging up the clearest concrete track, above all the houses at **Lombo Galego**, before patches of the old cobbled road show through the concrete. Only a few storage sheds stand on the last

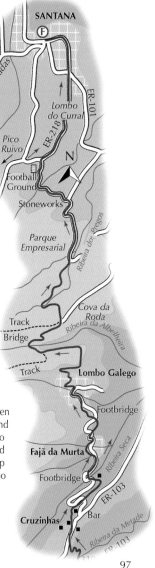

cultivated terraces before a fine view of Penha d'Águia and Porto da Cruz. Views are lost as the track swings left round a corner into a valley dominated by eucalyptus trees. When the track suddenly swings left up through a rocky cutting, don't follow it, but keep right along a grassy track. This is the old road but its cobbles are only rarely seen. The track leads down to an old grass-grown bridge over the **Ribeira da Albelheira**, where there may be rock pools.

Zigzag up from the bridge among mixed woodlands, and the grassy track becomes a broad dirt road leading to a crossroads and a house at **Cova da Roda**. Views from this point, around 690m (2265ft), stretch from Poiso down to Penha d'Águia. A cobbled track uphill is signposted for Pico das Pedras (see Walk 26). A tarmac road runs downhill, leaving only a track running straight ahead for Santana.

Follow the cobbled track past a cultivated area and continue through forest on gentle gradients to reach a junction with a tarmac road. Turn left to follow the road uphill a little, then downhill. ◀ Follow the road steeply down through forest, turning left before climbing past a **stoneworks**. Continue along the road to pass a **football ground** then keep right at a junction beside the Auto Chapinha building. Walk downhill and keep left to pass a fruit depot. There is a bar on the left later, followed by a bar on the right. Further down, a cemetery stands on the right. Reach a junction with the **ER-101** road, where there are bar/restaurants. Either turn left or head straight downhill to reach the main part of **Santana**.

The Parque Empresarial is off to the left but isn't visited.

SANTANA

Santana sprawls, but the centre is well defined. The Hotel Colmo is central, while other hotels lie further afield. Services include banks with ATMs, a post office, shops, bars and restaurants. Several tiny thatched houses are dotted around the village, mostly painted red and white, and one of them serves as the Tourist Information Centre (tel 291 575162). Interurban buses 56, 103 and 138 serve nearby São Jorge and distant Funchal. There are two departure points for buses, so study the timetables at both stops to be sure of being in the right place for a particular service. Taxis are also available.

WALK 16

Levada do Barreiro: Poço da Neve to Monte

Start	Poço da Neve, near Pico do Areeiro
Finish	Monte, above Funchal
Distance	9km (5½ miles)
Total ascent	50m (165ft)
Total descent	1140m (3740ft)
Time	3hr
Terrain	Paths are vague at first, becoming rugged and slippery. Wooded slopes can be overgrown. Old roads and tracks are used towards the end.
Maps	Carta Militar 6 and 9
Refreshments	Bar and café at Monte.
Transport	Taxi to Poço da Neve. Urban buses 20, 21 and 48 link Monte with Funchal. Taxis at Monte.

The Levada do Barreiro offers a fine route down from the slopes of Pico do Areeiro to Monte, above Funchal. The levada is mostly confined to the Parque Ecológico do Funchal. This area is having its original forest cover re-established and is popular with Madeiran school parties. The levada crosses bare and forested areas, with roads and tracks finally leading to Monte. This route suffered storm damage in 2010, then was devastated by a forest fire in 2015, and is slowly recovering.

Use a taxi to reach **Poço da Neve**, at 1640m (5380ft), where there is a small roadside parking space. A signpost reveals a paved path leading down to a stone ice-house covering a deep and dark pit. There is a view all the way down to the harbour at Funchal.

POÇO DA NEVE

The ice house was filled with compacted snow whenever it fell on the mountainside. This would be conserved throughout the hot summer months. Before the advent of refrigeration, runners would carry precious ice at speed down to Funchal, where it commanded a high price and was used for certain medical treatments.

The ice house at Poço da Neve, at the start of the levada walk

Poço da Neve
Altitude 1620m

A path runs downhill from the icehouse, bearing red and yellow marker posts. Continue straight down a track on a slope of grass and bracken, with boulders dotted about. Cross a road as marked and notice the very narrow **Levada do Barreiro**. Walk past heather bushes and pick a way down

The Levada do Barreiro passes areas destroyed by forest fires

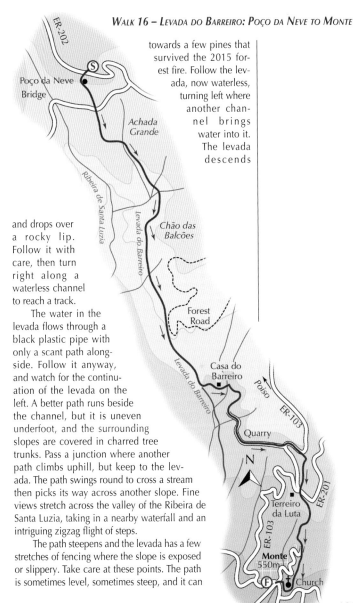

towards a few pines that survived the 2015 forest fire. Follow the levada, now waterless, turning left where another channel brings water into it. The levada descends

and drops over a rocky lip. Follow it with care, then turn right along a waterless channel to reach a track.

The water in the levada flows through a black plastic pipe with only a scant path alongside. Follow it anyway, and watch for the continuation of the levada on the left. A better path runs beside the channel, but it is uneven underfoot, and the surrounding slopes are covered in charred tree trunks. Pass a junction where another path climbs uphill, but keep to the levada. The path swings round to cross a stream then picks its way across another slope. Fine views stretch across the valley of the Ribeira de Santa Luzia, taking in a nearby waterfall and an intriguing zigzag flight of steps.

The path steepens and the levada has a few stretches of fencing where the slope is exposed or slippery. Take care at these points. The path is sometimes level, sometimes steep, and it can

101

be rugged. The open slopes offer views across the valley or down towards Funchal. The Estrada Florestal, a loop of forest road, can be reached by climbing a path on the left and offers easy walking towards Poiso.

Walk steeply down a ridge, taking care where log steps are a bit rickety. Cross a cobbled track and walk down a narrow levada path, landing on the track further downhill. ◄ Turn left to leave the levada and follow a dirt road round the valley, passing white buildings at **Casa do Barreiro**, at 960m (3150ft). The road leads through gates to leave the Parque Ecológico do Funchal and a tarmac road leads onwards. Cross a slope of tall eucalyptus and pine then pass a **quarry** on the left, and a house on the right. The road leads to a junction with the **ER-103** road on a hairpin bend. Follow the main road up to a higher bend then turn right down a very steep cobbled road to reach a road junction at **Terreiro da Luta**. ◄

Alternatively, follow a path along a crest to a hilltop viewpoint first, then drop down to the levada.

Restaurant and interurban bus stop.

Turn left down a cobbled track signposted as the Caminho do Monte. ◄ Walk down past pine, mimosa and gorse. Street lights accompany the track and there is a little levada too. After turning a couple of bends, reach some houses and keep straight ahead down the Caminho das Lajinhas, which is mostly steep, narrow and cobbled. Cross a road at the bottom and continue down a steep, narrow, cobbled road.

Stations of the Cross are passed and a notice explains how Our Lady of Monte appeared in a vision to a shepherd girl in the 15th century.

The old road runs downhill as a patchy affair, again called the Caminho do Monte, passing more houses. When it reaches a junction with another road, either head for a prominent church, or go down a flight of steps to reach a fine cobbled square at **Monte**, shaded by tall plane trees, at 550m (1805ft). Here you'll find Snack Bar Alto Monte, Café do Parque, souvenir stalls, toilets, taxis and the urban bus to Funchal.

CAMINHO DE FERRO DO MONTE

Madeira never developed a railway network, but an idea for a short funicular railway was promoted in 1893. The line was fully operational between Funchal, Monte and Terreiro da Luta by 1912. It closed in 1943, though recently there have been plans to restore at least the top part of it. There is a small museum about the railway at Terreiro da Luta, while down at Monte the old station is being restored to its former glory and there are plans for a café to open on site.

WALK 17

Levada da Negra: Poço da Neve to Barreira

Start	Poço da Neve, near Pico do Areeiro
Finish	Barreira, above Funchal
Distance	8km (5 miles)
Total ascent	50m (165ft)
Total descent	1040m (3410ft)
Time	2hr 30min
Terrain	The path is narrow and stony in places, occasionally exposed, crossing steep and rocky mountain slopes. Woodland near the end gives way to a steep road.
Maps	Carta Militar 5, 6 and 8
Refreshments	None on the route, but plenty around Funchal.
Transport	Taxi to Poço da Neve. Urban bus 10A links Barreira with bus 11 for Funchal.

The narrow channel of the Levada da Negra carries water at speed from the flanks of Picos do Areeiro and Cedro to thirsty Funchal. This walk starts at the Poço da Neve ice house, and the levada is picked up on the other side of a rugged valley. In reverse, and despite its steepness, this route offers the easiest ascent from the suburbs of Funchal to the highest peaks on Madeira.

Use a taxi to reach **Poço da Neve**, at 1640m (5380ft), where there is a small roadside parking space. A signpost reveals a paved path leading down to a stone ice house covering a deep and dark pit, with a glimpse of the harbour down at Funchal. ▶

For more information about the ice house, see Walk 16.

A path runs downhill from the ice house, bearing red and yellow marker posts. Follow it down to a track on a slope of grass and bracken with boulders dotted about. Turn right to follow the track across the slope, reaching a junction where there are waymark posts. Then left, then the rugged old track turns left alongside a valley. Watch carefully for a path down to the Ribeira de Santa Luzia. Normally, the riverbed is dry and boulder-strewn, but note the concrete dams built at intervals along its course to control flash floods.

There is a view of Pico do Areeiro, which will not be visible from this walk again, the next big mountain in view being Pico do Cedro.

Cross the riverbed and turn left as if walking downstream, but be sure to pick up the course of the **Levada da Negra**, which is a mere trickle in a very narrow channel. It slices across the mountainside and crosses a scree slope. ◄ Simply follow the water downstream. Route-finding couldn't be easier, and the channel runs through a small, but prominent rock cutting.

Cross a road and don't be tempted to follow a stony track. The

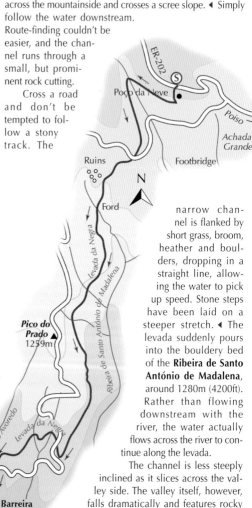

narrow channel is flanked by short grass, broom, heather and boulders, dropping in a straight line, allowing the water to pick up speed. Stone steps have been laid on a steeper stretch. ◄ The levada suddenly pours into the bouldery bed of the **Ribeira de Santo António de Madalena**, around 1280m (4200ft). Rather than flowing downstream with the river, the water actually flows across the river to continue along the levada.

The channel is less steeply inclined as it slices across the valley side. The valley itself, however, falls dramatically and features rocky

Look to the right to see several round, dry-stone structures which were formerly sheepfolds.

The narrow Levada da Negra traverses steep and rugged slopes, but always has a good path alongside

gorges and deep pools. ▶ Turn round a corner to look down to Funchal and the sea. Look for traces of an older levada cut into the rock just above the current channel.

When there is a good flow of water there are fine waterfalls.

The path hugs the levada, except when it crosses two small gullies. Floods in February 2010 broke two small sections of the channel, which have been replaced with plastic pipes. Step above the first pipe, and later step below the second pipe. Lush clumps of heather grow on the rocky slopes and a descent features steps. While some parts of the path are narrow and rocky, other parts are easier and a fairly level stretch passes a few pines on a steep slope. These are all that survived a fire, along with a few chestnuts beside the

105

Looking back along the levada towards the head of the valley

Note the flood barriers in the riverbed far below.

river. ◄ The water picks up speed for another downhill run, levelling out after turning a corner. The slope is steep and rocky, but the path is often wide and supported by a stout drystone buttress, and some parts are level and grassy. Enjoy a last view back up the valley, then continue into dense eucalyptus forest.

A narrow path runs beside the levada, reaching a small concrete hut at an intersection with another narrow levada. Keep level, in effect curving to the right to continue following the Levada da Negra downstream. The path crosses a road as it runs in and out of a little valley, then turns sharply to enter another little valley, making a tight turn to leave it. The path curves more gently, passing eucalyptus and tall chestnut. Head down a broad, cobbled track and continue straight along a tarmac road, passing a house. The road has a narrow levada on either side.

Regular urban bus 10A, requiring a change to urban bus 11 to reach Funchal.

Walk downhill to pass a water intake building and continue down a steep concrete road with steps alongside. When tarmac is reached again at **Barreira**, at around 750m (2460ft), there are bus stops. ◄

WALK 18

Levada do Curral: Curral das Freiras to Funchal

Start	Curral das Freiras
Finish	São Martinho, Funchal
Distance	15km (9¼ miles)
Total ascent	15m (50ft)
Total descent	400m (1310ft)
Time	5hr
Terrain	The levada path is uneven in places as it crosses steep, wooded slopes and sheer, exposed cliffs. Beware of rock-falls at first, then steep and slippery rock at Fajã. A good head for heights and steady feet are required. The final stretch into Funchal is much easier.
Maps	Carta Militar 5 and 8
Refreshments	Plenty at Curral das Freiras. Restaurants at Santa Quitéria. A couple of bars are passed on the way to São Martinho.
Transport	Interurban bus 81 serves Curral das Freiras from Funchal. Urban bus routes proliferate between Santa Quitéria and São Martinho.

The Levada do Curral e Castalejo, to use its full name, is one of the more frightening levadas on Madeira, slicing south from Curral das Freiras through an impressively steep-sided gorge. The route suffers regular rock-falls and landslides, but debris is generally cleared soon afterwards to keep the water flowing. The levada clings to sheer cliffs and there is a notoriously awkward stretch at Fajã where cliffs continually weep with water, making it treacherously slippery. The continuation into Funchal is much easier.

CURRAL DAS FREIRAS

Translated as the 'Nuns' Valley', the name recalls how the nuns from the convent at Santa Clara fled from pirates in 1566 and re-settled far inland, deep in the valley. A badly thought-out geological theory states that the valley is a volcanic crater, but this is nonsense. It is simply a deeply eroded valley cut into thick volcanic rock. The village has a few shops, bars and restaurants, as well as an annual autumn chestnut festival. Interurban bus 81 runs to and from Funchal, passing through a tunnel almost 2.5km (1½ miles) long.

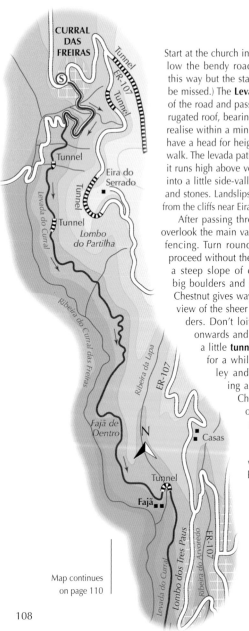

CURRAL DAS FREIRAS

Tunnel
ER-107
Tunnel

Tunnel

Eira do Serrado

Tunnel

Levada do Curral

Tunnel

Lombo do Partilha

Ribeira do Curral das Freiras

Ribeira da Lapa

ER-107

Fajã de Dentro

Casas

Tunnel

Fajã

N

Map continues
on page 110

Levada do Curral

Lombo dos Tres Paus

Ribeira do Arvoredo

ER-107

Start at the church in **Curral das Freiras** and follow the bendy road downhill. (The bus runs this way but the start of the walk could easily be missed.) The **Levada do Curral** is on the left of the road and passes above a hut with a corrugated roof, bearing a number 91. You should realise within a minute of starting whether you have a head for heights and steady feet for this walk. The levada path is narrow and concrete as it runs high above vegetable plots, then it turns into a little side-valley and is covered by earth and stones. Landslips and rock-falls are common from the cliffs near Eira do Serrado!

After passing through mixed woods, views overlook the main valley from a short stretch of fencing. Turn round another side-valley and proceed without the security of a fence across a steep slope of chestnut. There are some big boulders and still a danger of rock-fall! Chestnut gives way to a stand of pines and a view of the sheer cliff that spawns the boulders. Don't loiter, but follow the levada onwards and step round the outside of a little **tunnel**. The channel is covered for a while. There are splendid valley and peak views before turning a corner into woods again. Chestnut and eucalyptus grow on old cultivation terraces, along with malfurada and prickly pears. Turn round a bare hollow of steep rock, where the levada rushes beside an uneven path with brambles alongside. After passing a few chestnuts and more thorny scrub, turn a steep-sided rocky gully by negotiating a short, **bent tunnel**.

Turn a corner where there is a sheer drop into the valley then head into

A view of the Curral valley from the Levada do Curral

a more vegetated ravine, side-stepping a covered stretch of the levada. Continue past eucalyptus, with some mimosa and chestnut, where wet and dripping rock overhangs. Laurel flourishes in a tight little side-valley below **Lombo da Partilha**; the path can be wet and slippery, and subject to rock-falls. Leave and turn round into the next little side-valley, where the path narrows alarmingly and it is not possible to walk beside the levada. Use a wet, crumbling and vegetated path below the levada then climb to continue. Turn a rocky corner with wonderful views then follow a path below the levada again. There is more laurel and another splendid view up through the valley.

Watch out for thorny scrub and overhanging vegetation on the cliffs above the bouldery Ribeira do Curral das Freiras.

The levada makes a series of descents on a crumbling path and crude stone steps, with an awesome view of the main valley and a waterfall. After being covered for a while the water chases along the foot of a cliff. Beware of rock-falls and be careful as the path is wet, slippery and uneven. The levada loops across a steep, well-vegetated slope, so there is little sense of exposure. ◄

Look across the valley to see the village of Fajã da Galinhas and its steep terraces; then there is a significant turn round a rock outcrop. Pass a ruined cottage and old cultivation terraces at **Fajã de Dentro**. A few chestnuts grow here, then it is mostly laurels again. After some exposed moments and scrubby vegetation the levada makes a sudden downhill rush. Use a stony, crumbling path to stay below the levada then continue along an exposed path. Turn round a corner and walk down exposed steps to reach a stand of eucalyptus. There is a view back up the valley to Fajã da Galinhas.

Turn another corner, where the levada is covered with rock-fall detritus, then the water rushes downhill. If the concrete path is wet and slippery, take care, though the steeper stretches have steps built into them. Rampant

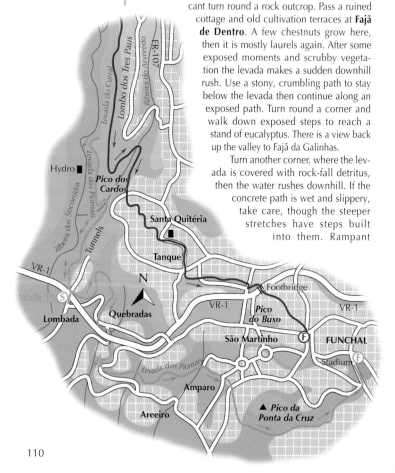

growths of cane and brambles fill old cultivation terraces at **Fajã**. ▶

Reach a gateway and pause to study an awesome side-valley, which is the most dangerous part of the walk, so take great care. Walk down the path and pass a wedged boulder. Enter a high and wide **tunnel**, with the water rushing noisily through it. The tunnel is bent and the exit can't be seen, but there are a series of 'windows' allowing light to enter. A waterfall pours down outside the first 'window' and there are 10 'windows' to pass. Leave the tunnel and walk carefully down 35 steep and exposed steps with a cable alongside. The levada is hidden and an overhang continually streams with water. Use waterproofs or an umbrella, or get soaked,

One of the old houses is seen and there is a view down the Socorridos valley to the sea.

A reasonably safe stretch of the levada downstream from Fajã

then continue along a fenced parapet to reach dry ground. The path beyond has a fence and passes a small rock arch. Pass another gateway to reach safer ground. Take a break, get a few things dried and look back into the deeply-cut valley.

The deserted houses at Fajã are seen from this stance. Later, a vine trellis straddles the levada at Casa Perreira. A good path leads through woods and along a cliff, with views from Fajã da Galinhas down to the sea. The levada goes through a tiny rock arch, but the path stays outside.

Turn round a corner where it doesn't feel so exposed with trees growing alongside. Go through a rock cutting where slabs lie over the channel for a short stretch, then look down along the Ribeira dos Socorridos, which is quite industrial.

Bananas dominate the scene, but all sorts of fruit and vegetables grow. The paved stretch of the levada is called the Vereda da Viana, and some slabs are wobbly and broken.

Pass a few houses near **Pico dos Cardos** and the levada is covered in slabs as it swings left into another valley. ◄ Cross a concrete and iron footbridge over the bouldery **Ribeira do Arvoredo**, where eucalyptus grows. The paved levada path is now the Vereda de Santa Quitéria, and is cut into a cliff as it passes more houses.

After crossing a steep concrete road the path is the Travessa do Tanque. Water is seen in the levada until the next steep concrete road, where it is covered again. Pass

The levada crosses a motorway and finishes in an urban area

WALK 18 – LEVADA DO CURRAL: CURRAL DAS FREIRAS TO FUNCHAL

vine trellises and bananas, then join and follow a bit of road round into the next valley. The channel is covered in slabs, but the water is seen again on leaving a little valley. Join a road and head straight through a roundabout, passing below the large 'Maxmat' store at **Santa Quitéria**. ▶ The levada is buried beneath the road, but watch for steps on the right and see the water again beside the Entrada do Tanque on the way to a main road at **Tanque**. Turn right at the Baleia Verde car wash, following the road for Câmara de Lobos.

Turn left to follow the Caminho do Pico do Funcho, then turn left again along the Vereda da Levada do Poço Barral. The levada runs beneath slabs, but is open later. Cross a road and continue slightly downhill, still signposted for the vereda. Beware of holes in the slabs, passing bananas and crossing a concrete path, the Rampa do Poço Barral. Continue along the path, passing bananas and the Recheio Cash and Carry.

Emerge on the busy Caminho do Esmereldo, use a pedestrian crossing and turn right. ▶ Turn left along the Travessa do Moinho, where the levada is covered at first, but turn right down steps later to find it in a concrete aqueduct. Cross the **VR-1** motorway using a blue aqueduct footbridge and continue between a tall wall and more bananas. Descend a flight of steps to the left to reach a road called the Rua do Ninho. Turn right to follow the levada downhill and the road running parallel becomes quite narrow at the end.

Turn right along the Rua do Doctor Barreto to reach the busy Caminho de São Martinho and catch any bus into **Funchal**.

Madeira Shopping, banks, ATMs, post office, restaurants, bus and taxi.

Restaurante O Moinho.

WALK 19
Levada dos Piornais: Lombada to Funchal

Start	Lombada
Finish	Estádio do Marítimo, Funchal
Distance	6.5km or 11km (4 or 6¾ miles)
Total ascent	35m (115ft)
Total descent	25m (80ft)
Time	2hr 15min or 4hr
Terrain	The first stage crosses exposed cliffs and passes through tiny tunnels where great care is needed. The second stage is easier, crossing cultivated and urban slopes.
Maps	Carta Militar 8 and 9
Refreshments	Small shops and bars at Lombada, Quebradas and Amparo.
Transport	Urban buses 1 and 3 serve Lombada. Urban buses 2 and 3 serve Quebradas. Urban bus 2 serves Caminho do Areeiro. Urban buses 4 and 48 serve Caminho do Amparo. Urban bus 45 serves the Estádio dos Barreiros.

This is one of the oldest levadas on Madeira, dating from the 15th century. It has been overhauled many times and carries water from the Socorridos valley to the sunny slopes around São Martinho. Sugar was once grown extensively, but bananas now cover the slopes. This walk can be rocky, difficult and exposed, or short, simple and easy, depending on a choice made at the start.

Start at **Lombada**, on the Caminho da Lombada, near a shop/bar/bakery. There is a view into the industrial Socorridos valley, spanned by the **VR-1 motorway bridge**. Climb steeply up the Rua do Pico da Lombada and cross a bridge over the motorway. The **Levada dos Piornais** is immediately beyond and can be followed left (difficult) or right (easy). The endemic Madeiran plant 'piorno' gave the levada its name.

Turn left to head upstream only if you are agile, sure-footed and have a head for heights, because the exposure gets worse with distance. The levada is covered and protected by railings at first, but soon afterwards a narrow parapet path passes bananas and mimosa, a few eucalyptus and pine. Another stretch is covered by metal sheeting. Note a flight of steps leading downhill, allowing a difficult and spectacular stretch to be avoided. The levada is partly cut into an overhanging cliff and partly supported on stone arches.

To stay beside the levada crouch low, or even crawl through a complex gash of a **tunnel**. ▶ Slabs lie across the levada where the parapet is too narrow to walk. Continue through another small tunnel, then cross a stone aqueduct arch. Walk on slabs through short rock cuttings, then cross another arch. A low, fractured tunnel comes next, then walk on slabs across another arch.

There are railings, but some walkers still find the exposure unnerving.

The upper half of the Levada dos Piornais is very exposed and crosses a number of cliff faces

115

The levada crosses a stepped concrete path with street lights, then the parapet path leads into a side-valley, passing eucalyptus. There are railings, but it is exposed in places. Railings also stand either side of a narrow, arched stone bridge over the bouldery **Ribeira do Arvoredo**. ◀ Swing round into the main Socorridos valley again, taking care where the smooth concrete parapet turns into an uneven stone parapet. There is a tunnel with good headroom and three 'windows', then the levada crosses a sheer cliff. A pipeline is passed and a cliff has to be negotiated opposite a hydro-electric station. After passing a house and cultivation terraces, a sign warns 'perigo/danger' though the path isn't difficult. However, after turning a corner, there is a locked gate surrounded by spikes and further access is denied. Turn round and retrace steps to where the walk started, above the motorway bridge.

There are no railings on leaving the valley, no matter how narrow or exposed the path becomes.

Leaving the bridge, the Levada dos Piornais is covered in concrete and runs between walls, houses and extensive banana terraces. Views can be described as bananoramic! Cross over a road at the head of a valley (urban bus 16A). Walk round another little valley drained

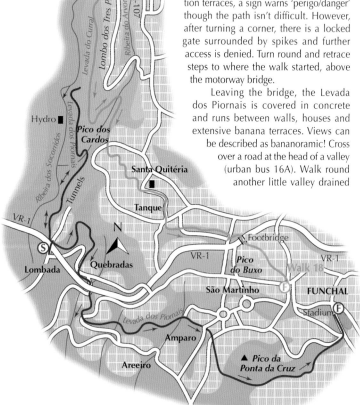

The levada passes built-up areas near Funchal

by a small stream. Mountain views include the summit of Pico do Cedro. The levada crosses a road bend at **Quebradas** then a short road walk leads along the Caminho das Quebradas to a shop bar, the Super das Quebradas. ▶

Turn right as signposted for Funchal and follow the road under a motorway bridge. Turn right down the Caminho das Quebradas de Baixo, then almost immediately turn left down steps to regain the levada. The channel is covered and there is a tall wall alongside.

A house sits on the levada, so go down steps and continue along a cobbled road. When the road rises a little, go down a couple of steps to the right to continue along the slab-covered channel. Climb a few steps and cross a road bend on the Caminho do Areeiro. ▶ Walk between a wall and a slope of prickly pears, then the slabs finish and water is seen again. A wall stands left of the levada. ▶ A steep concrete road crosses the levada on a bend, then the water is covered. A flight of steps, Escadinhas do Papagaio Verde, forms an arch on another bend, when the levada becomes open.

Pass a cave and go under a small stone arch while turning a slab-covered corner. The church tower at **São Martinho**

Urban buses 2, 3, 16A and 50.

Urban bus 2.

Vegetables and bananas grow down towards the sea at Areeiro, where big hotels and apartments are seen.

is seen on a hill, while terraces fill the valley below. The levada parapet is stone for a while, then concrete again. A concrete tunnel takes the levada beneath a busy road. Cross a busy bend on the Caminho do Amparo, where there are buses and a bar called A Casa da Levada.

The levada leaves **Amparo** and continues between houses, partly covered by slabs and partly open. Cross a minor road and walk along a slab-covered section, then follow the open levada using a stone parapet. Looking back, there is a view of the summit tor on Pico Grande. The parapet features slabs that ring musically when anyone walks on them! ◄ While following another slab-covered stretch, there are views of the Ilhas Desertas, as well as the built-up southernmost point of Madeira at Ponta da Cruz.

Look down to large buildings, while Pico da Ponta da Cruz rises above, thick with prickly pears and crowned with masts.

The levada drops a little while passing under a concrete road, then goes through a cutting. The parapet path leads round a slope offering views over Funchal and its harbour. The levada is covered in slabs for a short way until it crosses a road. Continue along a short slab-covered stretch and an open stretch then walk parallel to a busy road. Steps lead up onto this road close to a stadium, the **Estádio do Marítimo**. Keep left of stadium to finish. A restaurant and a stop for urban bus 45 lie nearby.

ESTÁDIO DO MARÍTIMO

Observe the view near the stadium if considering further levada walks near Funchal. Looking left of the stadium, the highest suburb of Funchal is Barreira, terminus of Walk 17 on the Levada da Negra. Look for the twin spires of the church at Monte, terminus of Walk 16 on the Levada do Barreiro and start of Walk 1 on the Levada dos Tornos. Spot the floodlights of the Estádio da Madeira, high above Funchal, which is near the start of Walk 3 along the Levada da Serra.

3 THE HIGH MOUNTAINS

A popular paved path gives way to a less-used path to Ilha (Walk 24)

Many walkers want to climb the highest mountains in Madeira, and the two highest peaks are remarkably easy to visit. Pico Ruivo can be climbed in an hour or so by following a stone-paved path from a high car park to the summit. Pico do Areeiro can be climbed in mere seconds using a flight of steps from a car park.

Walkers venturing far into the mountains must be aware that they are phenomenally steep, rather unstable, prone to rock-falls, with a limited number of paths available. However, given good weather, good stamina, a head for heights and a sure foot, walks through the mountains are astoundingly scenic and incredibly interesting. Paths are often carved from the rock, with thousands of stone steps piled one on top of

another. While some areas are bare and rocky, other parts are covered in dense *laurisilva* that almost blocks out the sunlight. Sadly, fires have destroyed some forests and invasive broom and brambles have colonised the mountainsides, crowding out other species.

Walkers can head for the heights and attempt to follow rugged ridges, but this isn't always possible as the paths tend to meander round the shoulders of the peaks. On the northern slopes of Pico Ruivo a couple of fine old paths are best used for long descents. Both of them cross the Levada do Caldeirão Verde, which penetrates into deep, remote, forested gullies, where it is fed by waterfalls. A handful of routes traverse the Boca das Torrinhas – a gap in the middle of Madeira's mountains.

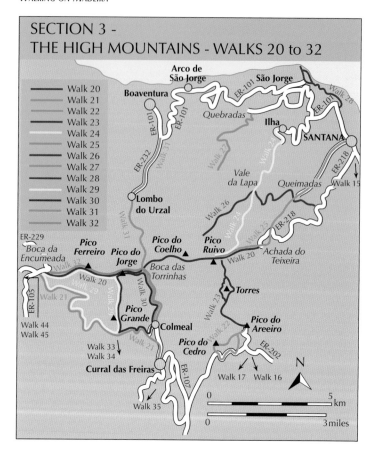

SECTION 3 - THE HIGH MOUNTAINS - WALKS 20 to 32

Walk 20
Walk 21
Walk 22
Walk 23
Walk 24
Walk 25
Walk 26
Walk 27
Walk 28
Walk 29
Walk 30
Walk 31
Walk 32

Arco de São Jorge
São Jorge
Boaventura
Quebradas
Ilha
SANTANA
Vale da Lapa
Queimadas
Walk 15
Lombo do Urzal
Pico Ferreiro
Pico do Jorge
Pico do Coelho
Pico Ruivo
Achada do Teixeira
Boca da Encumeada
Boca das Torrinhas
Torres
ER-229
Pico Grande
Colmeal
Pico do Areeiro
Pico do Cedro
Walk 44
Walk 45
Walk 33
Walk 34
Curral das Freiras
Walk 17 Walk 16
N
Walk 35

0   5 km
0   3 miles

Approaching the high mountains requires careful planning. Driving a car to Pico do Areeiro or Achada do Teixeira means returning to it, which is frustrating. Careful use of taxis and juggling with interurban and Rodoeste bus timetables will allow the use of some remarkable mountain paths. Keen walkers can link routes together to create tough long-distance routes, especially around Boca da Encumeada and Curral das Freiras. Links with low-level routes are available around Santana.

WALK 20

Boca da Encumeada to Achada do Teixeira

Start	Boca da Encumeada
Finish	Achada do Teixeira
Distance	13.5km (8½ miles)
Total ascent	1480m (4855ft)
Total descent	900m (2950ft)
Time	7hr
Terrain	Mountainous, with paved paths and steps, as well as some steep and stony stretches. Paths are generally clear throughout, but take care at junctions in mist.
Maps	Carta Militar 5 and 6
Refreshments	Snack Bar Restaurante Encumeada at the start of the walk. Small bar occasionally open below Pico Ruivo.
Transport	Rodoeste buses 6 and 139 serve Boca da Encumeada from Funchal, Ribeira Brava and São Vicente. Taxi from Achada do Teixeira to Santana.

It is possible to walk from the Boca da Encumeada, along the main mountain crest of Madeira, to Achada do Teixeira. If tempted to do this, then be sure to make an arrangement to be collected either by a taxi or by someone else at the end of the day. The route will take a little longer from west to east, than from east to west, since there is considerably more climbing involved.

Start at the **Snack Bar Restaurante Encumeada** and follow the road through a rock cutting on the Boca da Encumeada at 1007m (3304ft). Turn right to follow a stony track uphill, signposted as the PR1.3 trail. The track curves right towards some masts, so keep left to follow a narrow path further up stone steps. ▶ Climb steep flights of stone steps, often fenced and buttressed, to reach the crest of the mountain range around 1250m (4100ft) near **Pico do Meio**. Continue along the ridge and enjoy good views from a bare shoulder, looking directly down to Ribeira Brava. Cross the gentle dome of **Pico da Encumeada** to reach a narrow and well-vegetated gap, where São Vicente and Ribeira Brava can be seen.

The dense vegetation is remarkably mixed and includes everything from laurisilva species to brambles.

Cloud rises on the slopes above Boca da Encumeada

At an open corner there are views of the surrounding mountains, particularly Pico Grande.

Climb stone steps, some of them buttressed and fenced, heading left then swinging right to pass a cave with a stone seat. Climb more steps, turning left and right while climbing. ◄ Tall tree heather and ancient til trees were destroyed by a fire where the path passes along the base of a cliff on the southern flank of **Pico Ferreiro**. The path exploits a thin, crumbling layer in the rock. Zigzag up a wooded slope to reach a gap on the ridge, around 1420m (4660ft), overlooked by rocky pinnacles.

The path on the right, hacked through dense broom, is a very rugged route to Pico Grande.

Climb again, reaching fenced stone steps at a higher level, then enjoy the view. When a junction is reached, take care to keep left. ◄ The main path climbs more steps on the northern flanks of Pico do Jorge, among tree heather and bilberry, reaching a shoulder where views take in Pico

Signpost for Pico Ruivo at the Boca das Torrinhas

do Cedro, Pico Grande, Paúl da Serra and the north-west coast. ▶ Head downhill to reach a shoulder with fine views. Continue up and along the crest, then cross a gritty gap around 1650m (5415ft) near **Pico Casado**.

Pass a blade-like outcrop of rock and zigzag downhill, noticing that some of the stones make musical chinking sounds underfoot. Pass a cave and head down steps on a slope of dense heather. The path levels out and squeezes through a rocky cleft full of ferns and exotic plants.

The way ahead is more rugged but becomes gentler as the path crosses the ridge. Walk

Enjoy a stretch along the crest with good views, looking down from a stout stone buttress to São Vicente.

Map continues
on page 124

123

Signposts give destinations along all the paths that leave this point, which are covered in turn on Walks 30, 31 and 32.

A path junction might be noticed, marked by a stone painted 'S Jorge'. This offers a route to São Jorge.

Look along the rugged ridge to Pico do Areeiro, and look deep into the valley towards Curral das Freiras. Pico Grande has a prominent summit tor, with the plateau of Paúl da Serra beyond. Densely wooded slopes fall to the north coast.

Right is for Pico do Areeiro, used on Walk 23.

down a fenced flight of stone steps to land on the **Boca das Torrinhas** at 1450m (4760ft). ◄

Unless tempted to switch routes at this point, follow the path up along the ridge and up a ramp-like buttress, enjoying views in most directions before passing through a wooded area. Steep flights of stone steps with fencing alongside lead downhill on the sunless northern flank of **Pico da Laje**, where the surroundings are like a jungle. Another long flight of stone steps climbs to a gap overlooking the Curral valley. Keep left at path junctions to avoid being drawn off-course into the valley.

Climb easily across the broom-covered slopes of **Pico das Eirinhas** with views back to Pico Grande and ahead to Pico Ruivo. The path rises and falls, switching from one side of the crest to the other, then runs past broom and skeletal, burnt heather trees on the south-facing slopes of **Pico do Coelho**. ◄ A paved path appears and runs mostly downhill, often with good views of the Curral valley, crossing slopes of broom while avoiding Pico da Lapa da Cadela, then running level. The path climbs through broom and swings right along a stony crest of red pumice. Simply follow the paving to reach a signposted junction with another path.

Turn right to follow a paved path to the top of **Pico Ruivo**. There is a tall trig point at 1862m (6109ft) beside a monument. The summit is entirely stone-paved, surrounded by a fence, with a couple of fenced paths leading off to subsidiary viewpoints. ◄ Retrace steps down from the summit and turn right to follow a paved path and steps down to a **refuge** where refreshments are occasionally available.

Walk down a flight of stone steps from the refuge, reaching another signposted junction of paths. ◄ Keep straight ahead past bare pumice then walk down stone

Pico do Coelho 1733m

Pico da Lapa da Cadela

Refuge

Pico Ruivo 1862m

Santana

■1590r

Empenas

Achada do Teixeira

N

F

steps to go through a gap in a wall. Pass tree heather, broom, big boulders and rocky outcrops, reaching a stone shelter on a gap, where there is a superb view back to the peaks of Torres. Walk down to a signposted path junction and keep straight ahead. ▶ The paved path climbs to pass another stone shelter and a water source. The path regains the ridge to pass yet another stone shelter. Views take in mountains, valleys and the sea, so enjoy them all before the path finally leads down to a car park at **Achada do Teixeira**, around 1580m (5185ft). (If you reach this point and haven't made any transport arrangements, there are sometimes taxis parked here, waiting for their clients to return from Pico Ruivo. They might be willing to run you down to Santana.)

The path down to the left is used on Walk 24.

WALK 21
Boca da Encumeada to Curral das Freiras

Start	Boca da Encumeada
Finish	Curral das Freiras
Distance	15km (9¼ miles)
Total ascent	680m (2230ft)
Total descent	1040m (3410ft)
Time	5hr
Terrain	Mountainous, with a well-wooded path at first, then a paved path. There is a danger of rock-falls at a higher level. The descent is along a steep and stony path.
Maps	Carta Militar 5
Refreshments	Snack Bar Restaurante Encumeada at the start. Small bar at Fajã Escura. Plenty of choice at Curral das Freiras.
Transport	Rodoeste bus 6 and 139 serve Boca da Encumeada from Funchal, Ribeira Brava and São Vicente. Interurban bus 81 links Curral das Freiras with Funchal.

This walk avoids the peaks, but includes good views of them from various vantage points. Leaving the Boca da Encumeada, a well-wooded valley has to be crossed before the route climbs around the steep slopes of Pico Grande. Beware of rock-falls on the way to the Boca do Cerro. A steep and winding path leads down into a deep and rugged valley to finish at Curral das Freiras.

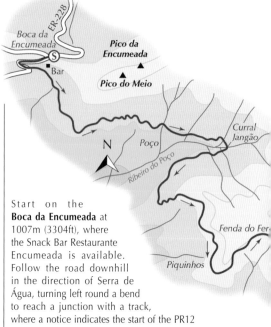

Boca da
Encumeada

ER-228

Pico da
Encumeada

S

Bar

Pico do Meio

N

Poço

Curral
Jangão

Ribeiro do Poço

Fenda do Fer

Piquinhos

*Footbridges span
streams around
the Poço valley*

Start on the
Boca da Encumeada at
1007m (3304ft), where
the Snack Bar Restaurante
Encumeada is available.
Follow the road downhill
in the direction of Serra de
Água, turning left round a bend
to reach a junction with a track,
where a notice indicates the start of the PR12

trail. ▶ Laurel, heather, broom and brambles grow on the slope. Keep right at a junction. The track narrows and at one bend there is a fine view of Pico Grande. Drop down a flight of stone steps and pass a pipeline feeding the generating station at Serra de Água.

Buses might stop here if given due notice, but it is an awkward bend.

Follow the path across and down a slope dominated by eucalyptus. Cross rocky and bouldery stream-beds at **Poço**, unless broken footbridges have been repaired. The path later passes cultivation terraces and climbs gently through pines, also passing eucalyptus, candleberry and bilberry. A shaded, stone-paved path leads to the head of the valley at **Curral Jangão**, where there are cultivated slopes

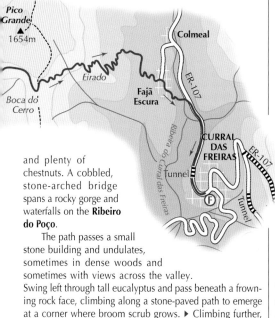

and plenty of chestnuts. A cobbled, stone-arched bridge spans a rocky gorge and waterfalls on the **Ribeiro do Poço**.

The path passes a small stone building and undulates, sometimes in dense woods and sometimes with views across the valley. Swing left through tall eucalyptus and pass beneath a frowning rock face, climbing along a stone-paved path to emerge at a corner where broom scrub grows. ▶ Climbing further, the path is flanked by bracken, broom and brambles, passing only a few trees. The route picks out a line of weakness between two cliff faces, working its way round a steep-sided hollow, then turning a prominent corner into another

There are good views of the valley and mountains. Another path descends to a dirt road that offers a convoluted descent to Serra de Água.

awesome hollow at **Fenda do Ferreiro** on the slopes of Pico Grande.

Pass round the base of a monstrous tower of rock, climbing through tree heather and passing some old til trees. There is rock-fall debris on the slopes and some stretches are wet, muddy, slippery and well-vegetated. Follow a drier path across the next cliff face, then after another wet patch the path levels out on a slope of gorse. There is a fine view ahead to Pico do Serradinho (see Walk 33). For today, turn left at a signposted junction, up a few stone steps to cross the gorse-covered crest of **Boca do Cerro**, around 1300m (4265ft). ◄

To climb Pico Grande, turn left again and see Walk 29 or Walk 30.

A narrow path descends gently from the gap with good views into the Curral valley. ◄ A few chestnuts offer shade on the slope, then the path goes through broom scrub and crosses a bouldery stream-bed. Brush past broom, turn round a corner and zigzag down between fences on a steep spur at **Eirado**. A well-engineered path, carved from rock or stoutly buttressed, is often stony underfoot. Chestnut and other trees clothe the slope as the zigzag path leads downhill. There are flights of log steps, but beware of following these too far downhill. Watch carefully to spot a track on the right, and follow it further downhill. It descends past cultivated plots

A pinnacle of rock lies to the right, while views across the valley include Pico Ruivo and Pico do Areeiro.

A band of cloud stretches across the Curral valley

to a road-end at **Fajã Escura**, where the Snack Bar O Lagar is available and occasional buses turn around.

Catch a bus if one is due or walk to Curral das Freiras. Walk straight down the Caminho da Fajã Escura, following a concrete road, a steeper stone track, then steps down a wooded slope with street lights alongside. Cross a metal footbridge over the bouldery **Ribeira do Curral das Freiras**, where a path and steps lead up to the ER-107 road. There is a bus stop here, otherwise turn right to keep walking. Cross a bridge over the Ribeira do Cidrão then follow the road up through a tunnel to **Curral das Freiras**. ▶

For facilities see Walk 18.

WALK 22
Pico do Cedro and Pico do Areeiro

Start/finish	Pico do Areeiro
Distance	7.5km (4¾ miles)
Total ascent/descent	400m (1310ft)
Time	3hr
Terrain	Mostly good mountain paths, linking with a mountain road.
Maps	Carta Militar 5 and 6
Refreshments	Bar/restaurant on Pico do Areeiro.
Transport	Taxi to Pico do Areeiro.

From certain vantage points, Pico do Areeiro and Pico do Cedro look smooth, seeming to offer easy walking. This is partly true, if following the skyline crest, but there are cliffs falling into the Curral valley, and awkward slopes dropping to the nearest road. A circular walk has only become practicable in recent years, following the construction of a mountain road and forest tracks.

Start at the car park beside the visitor centre, restaurant and souvenir shop on **Pico do Areeiro**. Arrive as early as possible for the clearest views. Climb steps behind the building to reach the 1818m (5965ft) summit. The adjacent air force radome was constructed in 2011 and contrasts starkly with the impressive mountain vista.

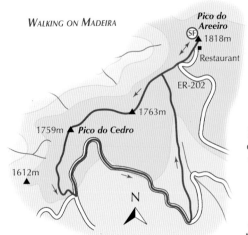

Look carefully to find a path running downhill from the **restaurant**, avoiding the car park to reach a sharp bend down the access road. There are a couple of red and yellow marker posts. Don't step onto the road, but simply walk straight down the path to reach a gap. Step across a fence and follow a path up the crest of the mountain. The path is mostly clear, but there are rocks and bushy broom to tackle on the ascent.

A boundary marker stands on a broad summit, around 1763m (5784ft). The path joins a grassy track to descend to another gap. There is a track junction and a plantation of young pine trees. Follow a track gently uphill, but watch carefully on the right to spot a path passing between the pines. The path climbs straight to a trig point at 1759m (5771ft) on **Pico do Cedro**. ◄

Look back to Pico do Areeiro, take in the peaks round the Curral valley to Pico Grande, and note Paúl da Serra and Terreiros beyond.

A marker post between Pico do Areeiro and Pico do Cedro

130

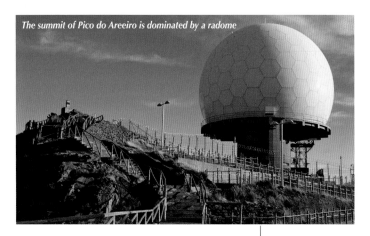

The summit of Pico do Areeiro is dominated by a radome

Follow the path downhill, spotting occasional wooden posts to stay on course. The slope to the left has been planted with pines, while the slope to the right eventually gives way to fearsome cliffs dropping to the Curral valley. Watch carefully to the left to spot a track, and when it is fairly close, walk across to it. Turn right and follow its bendy course down to a road junction. ▶

It is possible to continue down the mountain crest, eventually reaching viewpoints on Montado do Paredão, but only do this if a pick-up is arranged.

Turn left to follow the road, which is quite bendy as it works its way round a mountain valley at around 1600m (5250ft). The road passes a viewpoint and descends gradually to reach a prominent bend. Look carefully to spot a very narrow water channel on either side of the road. This is the Levada Negra, which is followed in its entirety on Walk 17.

Turn left and follow the levada as it runs parallel to the road, but further uphill. Pass through a small, but prominent rock cutting and cross a scree slope. ▶ The levada leads to the boulder-strewn bed of the Ribeira de Santa Luzia, which is normally dry. Cross over it and walk upstream a little, then climb to find an old track. Turn left and follow it to a junction, where there are marker posts.

There is a view of Pico do Areeiro ahead.

Turn left and follow a path up through the head of the valley to reach a gap. This point was reached earlier in the day. Turn right and climb to a road bend, then either follow the road up to the car park on **Pico do Areeiro**, or use the path avoiding the road to finish.

131

WALK 23
Pico do Areeiro to Pico Ruivo

Start/finish	Pico do Areeiro
Distance	12km (7½ miles) there and back
Total ascent/descent	1300m (4265ft)
Time	6hr
Terrain	Mountainous, with a narrow path, several flights of steps and five tunnels. Steep, rocky and exposed slopes are often protected by fencing, but a head for heights and steady feet are required.
Maps	Carta Militar 5 and 6
Refreshments	Bar/restaurant on Pico do Areeiro. Small bar occasionally open below Pico Ruivo.
Transport	Taxi to Pico do Areeiro.

The most popular mountain walk on Madeira is from Pico do Areeiro to Pico Ruivo. It is not suitable in bad weather, being prone to rock-falls, and the route would upset vertigo sufferers. Apart from that, the engineering of the path is superb. It is almost entirely carved from rock and offers close-up views of mountains while linking the highest peaks. The walk is there-and-back, possibly using a more rugged alternative (currently closed), but it could be finished at Achada do Teixeira instead, with reference to Walk 25.

Start at the car park beside the visitor centre, restaurant and souvenir shop on **Pico do Areeiro**, studying a notice about the Vereda do Areeiro, or PR1 trail. Arrive as early as possible for the clearest views. Climb steps behind the building to reach the 1818m (5965ft) summit. The adjacent air force radome was constructed in 2011 and contrasts starkly with the impressive mountain vista.

The path is paved and runs gently down to a gap, then crosses a small hump. Stone steps lead down to another gap, then the path slices across a rocky slope, exploiting a weak and crumbling layer in the basalt bedrock. Detour to the right to reach a viewpoint at **Ninho da Manta**, overlooking the Metade valley. Take the opportunity to look ahead and spot other sections of the mountain trail.

Continue along the main path, which turns a sharp corner and crosses a ridge. Fenced steps lead down a steep, sharp, rocky edge to a gap at Pedra Rija, where there is another viewpoint and an information board. Climb a little and cut across a cliff face on **Pico do Cidrão**, then descend with a vengeance using zigzag flights of stone steps. Duck beneath a huge, leaning boulder, pass rocky pinnacles and go down through a hole punched through an

upstanding wall-like basalt dyke. An easier terrace path leads to a tunnel beneath the sheer-sided **Pico do Gato**. There is good

Leaving Pico do Areeiro early in the morning

133

The right hand option over Torres has been closed for some years. Should it re-open, it offers steep ascents and descents on stone steps, with some very exposed paths.

headroom and if you have a torch, use it. When you emerge, there are two alternatives at a path junction, around 1600m (5250ft). ◄

Keep left to follow a path that has been carved deeply into a cliff face, running more or less horizontally, with a fence alongside. It is horribly exposed, but technically easy to follow, offering dramatic views. However, beware of low headroom at times and ensure that your pack or clothing doesn't snag on protruding rocks.

Go through another **tunnel**, which is bent, so the exit can't immediately be seen. This is followed by another long tunnel. There are two more short tunnels to be negotiated, then a closed-off junction with the alternative route is reached. Keep left to descend steeply to around 1500m (4920ft). Some walkers might feel that they are descending too far, with the mountains rising steeply above, but there is only one path and this is it.

If it re-opens, bear it in mind for the return journey.

A steep zigzag climb is made using a series of 'fire-escape' metal stairways. Hold on carefully and hope that these remain securely attached to the mountainside. After crossing a gap and descending a little, another junction is reached with the closed-off alternative route. ◄

Look back along the exposed cliff path before climbing to a refuge and the summit of Pico Ruivo

The path has been carved deeply into a cliff face, running more or less horizontal with a fence for protection. It is horribly exposed, but technically easy to follow. Follow it gingerly onwards, enjoying dramatic views but watching for low headroom. Climb a winding path and steps through heather and broom to reach a signposted junction of paths. ▸ Turn left to climb a flight of stone steps to reach a **refuge** where refreshments are occasionally available.

Climb stone steps and follow a stone-paved path up a heather-clad slope. At another signposted junction of paths, turn left to follow a paved path to the top of **Pico Ruivo**. There is a tall trig point at 1862m (6109ft) beside a monument. The summit is entirely stone-paved and surrounded by a fence, with a couple of fenced paths leading off to subsidiary viewpoints. ▸ Retrace the steps down from the summit and turn right to return to the refuge.

To finish this walk, there are four options. The easiest exit is via Achada do Teixeira, only 2.5km (1½ miles) from the refuge along an easy path, but if heading that way, a taxi is needed from a road-end car park high above Santana. The statistics for this walk assume that you will retrace your steps back to **Pico do Areeiro**, again bearing in mind that a taxi is needed unless you parked a car there. Only the fittest walkers could hope to continue to the Boca da Encumeada, or down to Ilha or Santana. ▸

Turning right offers the easiest exit via Achada do Teixeira, see Walk 25.

Look along the rugged ridge to Pico do Areeiro, and look deep into the valley towards Curral das Freiras. Pico Grande has a prominent summit tor, with the plateau of Paúl da Serra beyond. Densely wooded slopes fall to the north coast.

See Walks 20, 24 and 25.

WALK 24
Pico Ruivo, Vale da Lapa and Ilha

Start	Pico Ruivo
Finish	Ilha
Distance	8.5km (5¼ miles)
Total ascent	30m (100ft)
Total descent	1530m (5020ft)
Time	3hr 30min
Terrain	The path down from Pico Ruivo is paved, but the spur to Ilha is less obvious at first, becoming clearer as it descends a forested ridge. An old levada, steep paths, steps, tracks and roads finally reach Ilha.
Maps	Carta Militar 3, 5 and 6
Refreshments	Bar below Pico Ruivo. Small shops and bars at Ilha.
Transport	Taxi from Santana to Achada do Teixeira. Interurban bus 103 occasionally serves Ilha from Funchal, Santana and São Jorge.

Signposts between Ilha and Pico Ruivo point uphill, but this route seems better suited for descending, especially on a hot and humid day. The path is waymarked as the PR1.1 trail, heading down a steep ridge covered in tree heather, becoming easier further downhill. It levels out for a while after crossing the Levada do Caldeirão Verde in dense forest, but there are further steep drops to Ilha.

The statistics for this walk assume that the summit of Pico Ruivo has been reached by other means, such as via Walks 20 or 23, leaving this route purely for the descent. However, the route can be restructured by starting from Achada do Teixeira, either walking 2km (1¼ miles) to the start of the path to Ilha, or 3km (2 miles) to climb to the summit of Pico Ruivo first.

Enjoy wide-ranging views of the mountains of Madeira from the stone-paved summit of **Pico Ruivo**, at 1862m (6109ft). Walk down through the heather along a paved path and steps, passing red pumice to reach a signposted junction. Turn right to follow the path and steps down a heather-clad slope to reach a **refuge** where refreshments are occasionally available.

Looking down on the refuge perched below Pico Ruivo

Walk down a flight of stone steps from the refuge, reaching another signposted junction of paths. ▶ Keep straight ahead past bare pumice then walk down stone steps to go through a gap in a wall. Pass tree heather, broom, big boulders and rocky outcrops, reaching a stone shelter on a gap. Walk down to a signposted path junction and turn left as signposted for Ilha via the PR1.1 trail. ▶ The path has stone steps and is marked with red and yellow paint flashes.

Cross a water pipe where the path is a grassy ribbon with steps and the slope is liberally scattered with stones. The path crosses a steep and rugged slope, generally descending with good views. Other mountain ridges drop very steeply, but this route heads for the **Lombo dos Bodes**, which is gentler. There are some rocky outcrops, but the path slips off to the left down steps, passing a rock-face, then switches to the right down into tree heather on a lower part of the ridge. Here the path is good, with earth and log steps. Reach a junction in denser tree heather, where a signpost points back to Pico Ruivo and left for Semagral, but keep right to continue downhill.

There are good views across Caldeirão Verde and Caldeirão do Inferno. The path swings right and drops down log steps through a deep rut where the ground is mossy.

Turn right for Pico do Areeiro, used on Walk 23.

The path straight ahead is used on Walk 25.

137

Pass a few little caves where views are limited. There is a pronounced bend steeply down to the left and tree heather gives way to til trees. Watch for a gap on the left, where there is a fine view. Continue down the path, which levels out at a junction. Straight ahead is signposted for the **Posto Florestal Vale da Lapa,**

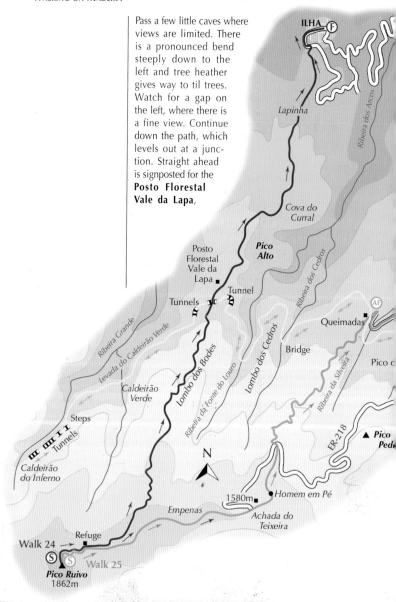

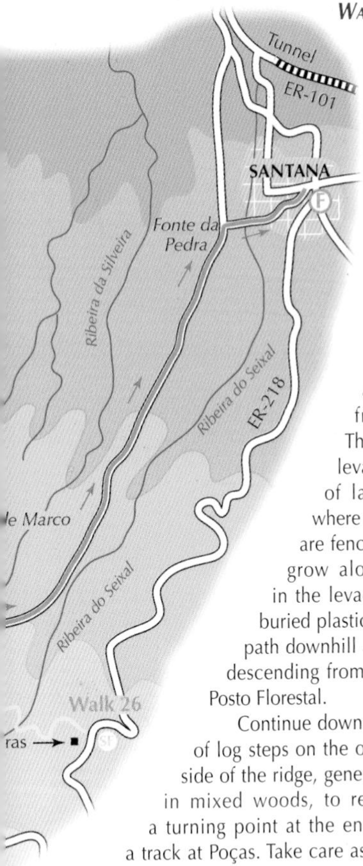

but turn sharply right and left to walk down log steps to another junction, close to a point where the **Levada do Caldeirão Verde** goes into a **tunnel**. ▸

The levada could be followed for 4.5km (2¾ miles) to Queimadas, see Walk 26.

To continue to Ilha keep left, in effect straight ahead as signposted from the junction. The course of an old levada crosses a slope of laurel and heather, where some rock outcrops are fenced, and hydrangeas grow alongside. The water in the levada is confined to a buried plastic pipe. ▸ Follow the path downhill and re-join the path descending from the Posto Florestal.

Note a path leading up to a spring and small shrine.

Continue down lots of log steps on the other side of the ridge, generally in mixed woods, to reach a turning point at the end of a track at Poças. Take care as the surface can be slippery, but follow the track until a right-hand bend is reached. Head left along a grassy path on a crest of gorse, heather and brambles. Drop down steps in a deep, dark cutting to reach the track again at a lower level. Cross over it and continue down more steps through another deep and dark cutting to land on the track yet again at **Lapinha**. Turn right along it then turn left along another track to reach a cultivated brow. A sign points to Garnal,

Walking down a flight of earth steps on the way to Ilha

but keep right to follow a path beside a narrow levada. This drops past a few sheds, with earth steps giving way to concrete steps, the Vereda do Lombo Grande, landing on a road.

Turn left to walk down the road, reaching a small shop and the Snack Bar Parada opposite the church in **Ilha**. Only occasional bus services call here, so be absolutely sure of timetables.

WALK 25
Pico Ruivo, Queimadas and Santana

Start	Pico Ruivo
Finish	Santana
Distance	10.5km (6½ miles)
Total ascent	50m (165ft)
Total descent	1490m (4890ft)
Time	3hr 30min
Terrain	The path down from Pico Ruivo is paved, but the forested descent to Queimadas can be steep and slippery. The last stretch is along a road.
Maps	Carta Militar 3, 5 and 6
Refreshments	Bar below Pico Ruivo. Café at Queimadas. Plenty of choice at Santana.
Transport	Taxi from Santana to Achada do Teixeira or from Queimadas. Interurban buses 56, 103 and 138 serve Santana from Funchal and São Jorge.

This descent may seem long, but it is quite direct and comes in three distinct stages. A paved path runs downhill from Pico Ruivo to Achada do Teixeira. A steep and rugged path zigzags down past heather trees and through laurisilva forest to Queimadas, where the walk could finish early if a pick-up is arranged. The final stretch to Santana is along an easy minor road.

The statistics for this walk assume that the summit of Pico Ruivo has been reached by other means, such as on Walks 20 or 23, leaving this route purely for the descent. However, the route can be restructured by starting from Achada do Teixeira, saving 3km (2 miles) by heading straight downhill.

▸ Enjoy wide-ranging views of the mountains of Madeira from the stone-paved summit of **Pico Ruivo**, at 1862m (6109ft). Walk down through the heather along a paved path and steps, passing red pumice to reach a signposted junction. Turn right to follow the path and steps down a heather-clad slope to reach a **refuge** where refreshments are occasionally available.

Walk down a flight of stone steps from the refuge, reaching another signposted junction of paths. ▸ Keep straight ahead past bare pumice then walk down stone steps to go through a gap in a wall. Pass tree heather, broom, big boulders and rocky outcrops, reaching a stone shelter on a gap, where there is a superb view back to the peaks of Torres. Walk down to a signposted path junction and keep straight ahead. ▸ The paved path climbs to pass another stone shelter and a water source. The path regains the ridge to pass yet another stone shelter. Views take in mountains, valleys and the sea, so enjoy them all before the path finally leads down to a car park at **Achada do Teixeira**, around 1580m (5185ft). ▸

Pass in front of and below the house, picking up a path and turning left downhill to go through a gap in a wall and fence, entering a shallow valley. Keep to the right of a peculiar, tall, blocky outcrop called **Homem em Pé**. Walk down a grassy path to a hut, then just below it turn left and roughly

For map, see Walk 24.

Right is for Pico do Areeiro, see Walk 23.

The path down to the left is used on Walk 24.

The nearby house was once available for hire as a refuge.

Homem em Pé, or Standing Man, on the way downhill

Other tree species appear in due course, along with gorse and brambles.

Arrange to be collected here to avoid the last 5km (3 miles) of road-walking.

contour across a slope of tall heather. The path narrows and zigzags, needing care where it drops suddenly down onto a bend on the ER-218 road. Cross over the road to continue.

Walk down 70 concrete steps and continue down eroded, steep, crudely-cut steps that can be slippery in wet weather. The path is often in a deep rut flanked by tree heather, and seems to zigzag forever. ◄ A steep cobbled track is reached, which leads down through dense laurisilva to a couple of houses. Continue down to a car park at **Queimadas** and look left to see lovely thatched houses, where there is a café available. The Levada do Caldeirão Verde is crossed at this point, at 883m (2897ft) (see Walk 26). ◄

The cobbled road leaves the car park and turns right, becoming a tarmac road descending steeply. It runs more gently around and across a bouldery stream and is flanked by laurels and hydrangeas. The road rises a little among eucalyptus then descends again in mixed woodlands. After a fairly level stretch above **Vale Marco** it descends more steeply, passing eucalyptus, pine and mimosa. Pass a junction at **Fonte da Pedra** and keep straight ahead, but turn right at another junction. Drop steeply into a valley and climb up the other side, then head for the middle of Santana (for facilities, see Walk 15).

WALK 26
Levada do Caldeirão Verde from Pico das Pedras

Start/finish	Pico das Pedras or Queimadas
Distance	16km or 20km (10 or 12½ miles) there-and-back
Total ascent/descent	100m (330ft)
Time	6hr or 7hr
Terrain	The levada path is easy and well-wooded at the start. There are nine tunnels and some require a torch. Several narrow, rugged paths are followed, especially towards the end, with some being exposed and slippery
Maps	Carta Militar 5 and 6
Refreshments	Café at Queimadas.
Transport	Taxi from Santana, to and from Pico das Pedras or Queimadas.

Walking the Levada do Caldeirão Verde can be easy or difficult. Two starting points offer easy paths in well-wooded surroundings. Tunnels and narrow paths feature further along. Either turn round after visiting a slender waterfall at Caldeirão Verde, or continue into a steep-sided, densely-wooded valley, climbing to Caldeirão do Inferno where waterfalls spill into a deep gorge.

The starting point for this walk can be Pico das Pedras or Queimadas. Neither place has a bus service, but both can be reached by car or taxi from Santana. Either place can serve as a finishing point, and the route also intersects with Walks 24 and 25. The Levada do Caldeirão Verde is waymarked as the PR9 trail.

▶ Leave the ER-218 road at **Pico das Pedras**, at 875m (2870ft), as if visiting a bungalow complex. Walk past the bungalows along a narrow road flanked by stone gateposts. A winding track runs through mixed woodlands dominated by eucalyptus, with the **Levada do Caldeirão Verde** alongside. Head upstream following the track through a rock cutting while the levada runs round the outside. Stone slabs cover the channel in places, then after turning round a couple of little valleys, cross the **Ribeira da Silveira** and follow the levada to **Queimadas**. ▶ The Parque das Queimadas is an alternative starting point with a car park. A cobbled path leads past a couple of attractive thatched houses and is signposted for Caldeirão Verde and Caldeirão do Inferno. Pass through a picnic area among tall trees then cross a small duckpond. The levada has a broad and clear path with tall trees alongside. Cross over a track, the Caminho dos Folhadeiros. ▶ The broad path gives way to a narrow path, with views of wooded ridges and valleys.

For map, see Walk 24.

Walk 25 crosses here, and a café is available.

Note the hydrangeas and oaks beside the levada, though the slopes are covered in laurisilva forest.

The path has some fencing, but isn't particularly exposed. There are some drippy and slippery stretches then steps lead below a drippy hollow. There is more fencing alongside the path on the way round to the next valley. Cross a stone-arch **bridge** over the **Ribeira dos Cedros** at the head of the valley, but note how the levada once went further round the deep, green gorge. The path continues with more fencing, making a pronounced turn into the next valley. Pass through a small rock cutting on a densely-wooded slope of *laurisilva*. There are views from time to time, taking in a slender waterfall and peaks high above. Cross a concrete bridge to face a waterfall on the **Ribeira da Fonte do Louro**, which cascades across the levada.

Walkers emerge from a tall and narrow tunnel on the levada

Walk 24 crosses over the top of this tunnel and runs close to the tunnel mouth.

Leave the valley and continue along the fenced path. There are views for a while but also plenty of vegetation, with tree heather leaning low across the path. Watch out for rock cuttings with low headroom. The path winds across a slope and some parts are covered in landslip debris. Go through a low, bendy **tunnel** with an uneven path then continue across a slope of tree heather and laurel. A signpost for Caldeirão Verde points straight through another **tunnel**. ◀

The tunnel is high and the path is broad, while a fence separates the path from the water. Later the path becomes uneven and the roof lowers. Exit with a fine view of a deep valley then enter the next **tunnel**. There is a high wall between the path and the water inside the tunnel, with low headroom and some constricted spaces. The path is narrow, uneven and wet, with a 'window' offering a view out to the valley of the Ribeira Grande. The tunnel is quite bendy and the exit is higher and drier.

The path is fenced, though not too exposed, but the parapet needs care. Part of the parapet is avoided by switching to a lower path. The way is partly fenced while winding across a steep slope to the next tunnel. Slabs cover part of the levada and the tunnel is short and curved. Continue across long, steep slopes and cliffs, well-vegetated in places, but quite exposed in other places. A pronounced turn leads into a huge green gully. This is **Caldeirão Verde**, where a path leads up to a fine slender waterfall spilling into a large pool. ▶

Note that the path gets rougher further along and the fencing isn't always in good order. Leave Caldeirão Verde to pick a way across a fenced slope to leave the green gully. Turn round beside a big stump of rock to re-enter the main valley. Continue across an unfenced slope, then pass some tattered fencing. When the levada channel narrows, go down a path and cross a stony slope, then head up on the other side. After passing tall til trees, watch for a badly-eroded flight of steps up to the left.

Climb around **200 steps**, though there may have been twice that number at one time. Take care as the slope is steep and rugged, reaching a flat area beside a higher levada at a junction of **three tunnels**. Don't go through the tunnel on the left, except maybe for the view. The tunnel straight ahead has railway lines and leads deep beneath Pico Ruivo to reach the generating station at Fajã da Nogueira (see Walk 14). Enter this **tunnel**, but immediately turn right through a very short **tunnel** and pass a wide, deep water tank to continue.

Walk along an uneven and exposed path to find a waterfall pouring down in front of another short **tunnel**. Go through this and immediately turn round into the next **tunnel**. This is long and bendy with a good path and good headroom. Later, there is plenty of headroom but the path is wet. Towards the end, the roof is rather lower and the path is stony. Walk along an even, but unfenced parapet and take care if it is wet and slippery. The final **tunnel** is bendy and rumbles ominously, featuring a stony path and low headroom. Although the exit can't be seen at first, there are a few 'windows' looking out into a deep, dark, narrow, green gorge. The rumbling noise becomes louder as you climb out of the tunnel to find two waterfalls thundering down into the gorge at **Caldeirão do Inferno**. Admire them, but obviously there is no way out of this place except by retracing your steps, negotiating all those tunnels a second time. Return to **Queimadas** or **Pico das Pedras** to finish, or end elsewhere by linking with Walk 24 or Walk 25.

The waymarked trail ends at this point, but adventurous explorers with a head for heights can delve further into the valley to reach the Caldeirão do Inferno.

WALK 27
Levada do Rei from Quebradas

Start/finish	Quebradas, above São Jorge
Distance	10km (6¾ miles) there-and-back
Total ascent/descent	150m (490ft)
Time	3hr 30min
Terrain	After an initial steep ascent, the levada path climbs gradually round increasingly forested slopes into a deep, steep-sided valley.
Maps	Carta Militar 2 and 3
Refreshments	Quinta Levada do Rei café at Quebradas.
Transport	Taxi from São Jorge to Quebradas. Interurban buses 103 and 138 serve São Jorge from Funchal and Santana.

The Levada do Rei is waymarked as the PR18 trail, following the watercourse upstream to its source, penetrating deep into the valley of the Ribeira Bonito. Lush *laurisilva* forest features tall til trees in an exceptionally steep-sided valley. When returning to São Jorge afterwards, it is worth visiting the nearby working watermill and sawmill, which are both powered by the Levada do Rei.

Either drive up through a maze of minor roads above São Jorge, or arrange for a taxi to take you and collect you later. To navigate the roads, watch for signs pointing the way to Moinho de Água (watermill) and Serragem a Água (sawmill). The starting point is further up the road at **Quebradas**, where there is a the Quinta Levada do Rei café and a car park.

A dirt road called Caminho do Curralinho leads off a minor road. A notice explains about the PR18 trail and the track leads quickly to a waterworks. The **Levada do Rei** runs beside the track in a concrete channel and is fringed with agapanthus and eucalyptus. Pass the **waterworks** and a concrete dam, then turn right as signposted for Ribeiro Bonito, up concrete and earth steps parallel to the levada, where the water rushes furiously.

Turn left at a little water intake to follow the level levada path further upstream. It meanders, but swings noticeably to the right into a well-wooded little valley with limited views at

Achada do Milheiro. Leaving the valley, cross an earth track. ▸ The path is good and isn't really exposed, but has short stretches of fencing as it slices across the side of a wooded valley. Longer fences feature where the levada is cut into rock, and

Enjoy views of Pico Ruivo, its forested northern ridges and valleys, with Ilha and Santana beyond.

The start of the Levada do Rei at Quebradas

in a couple of places the channel is covered. Turn round the head of a jungle-like valley and cross a river.

Dense woodlands obscure views on the way round into the next little side-valley, where triangular stepping stones cross a stream. Leaving the valley, turn a wooded corner and go through a short, bent **tunnel** where slabs lie on the channel. Views before the tunnel look to the head of valley, while afterwards they look down it.

Turn right round a rocky corner, where there is fencing

147

and overhanging rock. Don't be tempted to drop below the levada parapet when a path is seen, but keep to the parapet even if it seems narrow.

More fencing appears across a rock face, with views from top to bottom through the valley. There is a likelihood of getting wet while passing a dripping overhang. After passing another fenced overhang, the steep and wooded valley sides draw in noticeably. The Levada do Rei drinks greedily from the mossy, boul-dery, fern-hung **Ribeiro Bonito** in a deep gorge full of tall til trees.

To finish this walk, retrace steps back to the road at **Quebradas**. If a taxi was used for access and a pick-up wasn't arranged, it is possible to walk back to São Jorge by road in an hour or so. Before leaving, find the time to visit the working sawmill, Serragem a Água, and watermill, Moinho de Água, which are both powered by the Levada do Rei.

WALK 28
Santana, Calhau and São Jorge

Start	Pico de Tanoeiro, near Santana
Finish	São Jorge
Distance	5.5km or 6km (3½ or 3¾ miles)
Total ascent	300m (985ft)
Total descent	330m (1082ft)
Time	2hr or 2hr 30min
Terrain	Mostly along winding cobbled tracks on steep slopes.
Maps	Carta Militar 3
Refreshments	Restaurant at Quinta do Furão. Café Cabo Aéreo. Bars and restaurants at São Jorge.
Transport	Interurban buses 103 and 138 link Santana and São Jorge with Funchal.

The main road from Santana to São Jorge is anything but direct. In the past people followed a more direct cobbled road, which still exists and offers a fine short walking route. Leaving Santana, the old road zigzags down to the sea at Calhau, then zigzags up to São Jorge. Other coastal and cliff paths can also be explored, taking the walk towards the rugged Ponta de São Jorge.

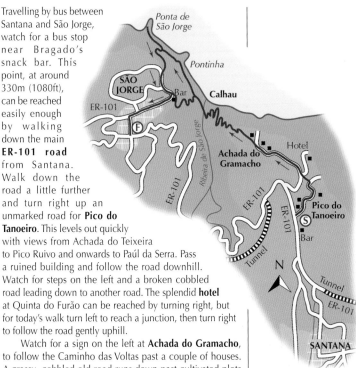

Travelling by bus between Santana and São Jorge, watch for a bus stop near Bragado's snack bar. This point, at around 330m (1080ft), can be reached easily enough by walking down the main **ER-101 road** from Santana. Walk down the road a little further and turn right up an unmarked road for **Pico do Tanoeiro**. This levels out quickly with views from Achada do Teixeira to Pico Ruivo and onwards to Paúl da Serra. Pass a ruined building and follow the road downhill. Watch for steps on the left and a broken cobbled road leading down to another road. The splendid **hotel** at Quinta do Furão can be reached by turning right, but for today's walk turn left to reach a junction, then turn right to follow the road gently uphill.

Watch for a sign on the left at **Achada do Gramacho**, to follow the Caminho das Voltas past a couple of houses. A grassy, cobbled old road runs down past cultivated plots

Traditional red-and-white thatched houses at Santana, part of a group containing the Tourist Information Office

149

Look inland to see the village of Ilha perched halfway up towards Pico Ruivo.

and terraces. It is broad and zigzags downhill on a well-engineered course, making light of what is almost a cliff face, with prickly pears growing on the lower slopes. ◄ Cross an arched bridge over the **Ribeira de São Jorge** and pass a swimming pool. Keep right to walk through the little seaside settlement of **Calhau**, reaching a junction of cobbled tracks and a choice of routes.

For a short walk, turn left to follow a zigzag path up past a few plots and terraces. There are wild tangles of vegetation, as well as an undercut cliff where the track has been hacked from rock. Tall pines and eucalyptus grow at the top. Reach a cobbled car park and the Café Cabo Aéreo, named after an old winch that used to serve Calhau.

Beware of rock-falls as the cliff sheds huge boulders.

For a longer walk, continue straight ahead at Calhau, following a cobbled track and path across a cliff face. ◄ One stretch of path is well-buttressed and then stone steps cross an old landslip. Continue along the path and turn a corner to see the rocky **Ponta de São Jorge**, with a fisherman's path perched precariously over deep water. Walkers will probably not wish to go there so turn round and walk back along the cliff path, with a view along the coast to the distant Ponta de São Lourenço. Don't walk all the way back to Calhau, but turn right up another cobbled track, zigzagging up a slope covered in cane and malfurado. Turn left to follow a road to a cobbled car park and the Café Cabo Aéreo.

The short and long walk join at the car park and all that remains is a road-walk up to **São Jorge**. Two roads leave the car park, so take the higher one and climb up a slope covered in pines to reach a walled cemetery. Follow the road called the Rua São Pedro to reach a junction with another road beside a chapel. Walk straight along the Rua Dr Leonel Mendonça to reach the church in **São Jorge**.

SÃO JORGE

Note the typical style of the little old houses in the area, which are wooden with thatched roofs. The church contains some extravagant gilded carvings and is worth visiting. There is a post office, a few shops, bars and restaurants. Interurban buses 103 and 138 link São Jorge with Santana and Funchal, and there are taxis.

WALK 29

Boca da Encumeada and Pico Grande

Start/finish	Boca da Encumeada
Distance	17.5km (10¾ miles)
Total ascent/descent	1100m (3610ft)
Time	6hr
Terrain	Mountainous, with a well-wooded path, a paved path and the danger of rock-falls. Hands-on scrambling is required on Pico Grande. A very rough and rocky path leads onwards, with an easier path to finish.
Maps	Carta Militar 5
Refreshments	Snack Bar Restaurante Encumeada at the start/finish.
Transport	Rodoeste buses 6 and 139 serve Boca da Encumeada from Funchal, Ribeira Brava and São Vicente.

A rugged, circular mountain walk can be attempted from the Boca da Encumeada, reaching the summit of Pico Grande by a rocky scramble, then passing close to other summits on the main mountain crest of Madeira. The outward and return paths are quite popular, but the path in the middle of the route was for many years in a very poor condition. It now has its vegetation hacked back occasionally by local mountain runners, who regard it as **one of the toughest mountain trails in Madeira. Bear this in mind before considering this route, because it does require plenty of time and effort.**

Start on the **Boca da Encumeada** at 1007m (3304ft), where the Snack Bar Restaurante Encumeada is available. Follow the road downhill in the direction of Serra de Água, turning left round a bend to reach a junction with a track, where a notice indicates the start of the PR12 trail. ▶ Laurel, heather, broom and brambles grow on the slope, then keep right at a junction. The track narrows and at one bend there is a fine view of Pico Grande. Drop down a flight of stone steps and pass a pipeline feeding the generating station at Serra de Água.

Follow the path across and down a slope dominated by eucalyptus. Cross rocky and bouldery stream-beds at **Poço**, unless broken footbridges have been repaired. The path

Buses might stop here if given due notice, but it is an awkward bend.

151

later passes cultivation terraces and climbs gently through pines, also passing eucalyptus, candleberry and bilberry. A shaded, stone-paved path leads to the head of the valley at **Curral Jangão**, where there are cultivated slopes and plenty of chestnuts. A cobbled, stone-arched bridge spans a rocky gorge and waterfalls on the **Ribeiro do Poço**.

The path passes a small stone building and undulates, sometimes in dense woods and sometimes with views across the valley. Swing left through tall eucalyptus and pass beneath a frowning rock face, climbing along a stone-paved path to emerge at a corner where broom scrub grows. ◄ Climbing further, the path is flanked by bracken, broom and brambles, passing only a few trees. The route picks out a line of weakness between two cliff faces, working its way round a steep-sided hollow, then turning a prominent corner into another awesome hollow at **Fenda do Ferreiro** on the slopes of Pico Grande.

There are good views of the valley and mountains. Another path descends to a dirt road that offers a convoluted descent to Serra de Água.

Pass round the base of a monstrous tower of rock, climbing through tree heather and passing some old til trees. There is rock-fall debris on the slopes and some stretches are wet, muddy, slippery and well-vegetated. Follow a drier path across the next cliff face, then after another wet patch the path levels out on a slope of gorse. There is a fine view ahead to Pico do Serradinho (see Walk 33). For today, turn left at a signposted junction, up a few stone steps to cross the gorse-covered crest of **Boca do Cerro**, around 1300m (4265ft). ◄

Walk 21 runs straight ahead to descend to Curral das Freiras.

Turn left again at a signposted junction and follow a path past a sheepfold in the shade of chestnuts, then climb to a cave hewn into a cliff. A cable is fixed to the rock where fenced steps climb a steep and rocky slope. A zigzag path climbs further, passing occasional chestnuts on a steep slope of rock and broom. There are stone steps and rock steps. Keep climbing and swing well to the left to reach a rocky ridge, then scramble with great care

Map continues on page 162

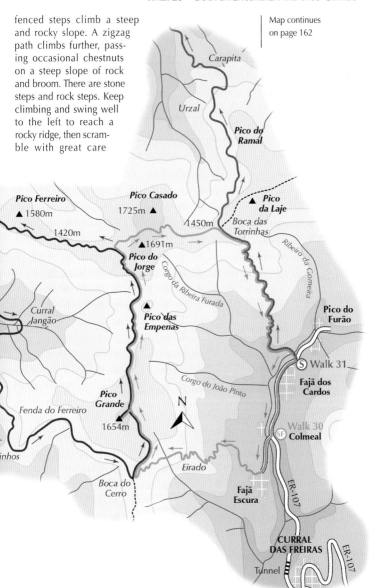

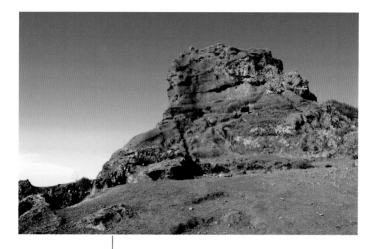

*A cable offers
protection on a
rocky scramble
to Pico Grande*

along a route marked with a fraying cable to reach the highest rocky peak of **Pico Grande**, at 1654m (5426ft).

Scramble down from the summit and retrace steps downhill, but watch for another path heading off to the left, cutting through dense broom. This crosses a gap where there is a dry-stone wall. Cross the wall and look carefully to the left to spot the path among rocks and boulders. A short flight of stone steps climbs uphill to confirm the route. On the other side, stone steps and broken steps drop steeply downhill and need care as there is so much loose rock. Watch very carefully for the line of the path, which passes beneath towering, overhanging cliffs. Broom scrub flanks the path, but is usually trimmed back, then there is a climb past some dead, blasted trees. Turn round a rocky corner for views of a rugged gap with Pico do Jorge beyond. Walk down past more blasted trees and short broom scrub to pass below a gap near **Pico das Empenas**.

There are views as the path undulates across the slope. A towering peak of rock rises ahead as the path levels out. Climb steps and steep, stony slopes, leaving the bushes and trees behind to climb a well-buttressed flight of steps. The zigzag path climbing higher is loose and worn, while the steps are crumbling, so there is a danger of rock-fall. Stone steps and a zigzag path lead up to a slope of broom as the path gains a high crest around 1550m (5085ft) near **Pico do Jorge**. Turn left at a junction, along a clearer path, which goes down fenced stone steps and eventually lands on a gap at 1420m (4660ft).

The path slips off to the left to avoid rocky pinnacles, zigzagging down a wooded slope to pass through a gateway. Pass along the base of a cliff on the southern flank of **Pico Ferreiro**, exploiting a thin, crumbling layer in the rock. ▶ Continue through tall tree heather, crossing a slope and going down steps. The path turns right then swings left to go down more steps. Pass a cave with a stone seat, then the path heads off to the left down buttressed, fenced steps, going through a gate to reach a narrow and well-vegetated gap, where São Vicente and Ribeira Brava can be seen.

Climb gently while walking across the dome of **Pico da Encumeada**, crossing a bare shoulder offering good views. The path leads along the ridge past **Pico do Meio**, around 1250m (4100ft), then steep flights of stone steps follow, often fenced and buttressed. Views are lost among the dense vegetation, which is remarkably mixed and includes everything from laurisilva species to brambles. The final steps are rough and ready, with the narrow path reaching a stony track at a mapboard. Continue straight down to a road junction and turn left through a rock cutting on the **Boca da Encumeada**, at 1007m (3304ft). Hopefully you reach the Snack Bar Restaurante Encumeada in good time for the last bus!

At an open corner, there are views of the surrounding mountains, particularly Pico Grande.

Flights of stone steps on the way to Boca da Encumeada

155

WALK 30
Colmeal and Pico Grande

Start/finish	Colmeal, in the Curral valley
Distance	14km (8¾ miles)
Total ascent/descent	1450m (4760ft)
Time	6hr
Terrain	Mountainous, with a steep and stony climb. Hands-on scrambling is required on Pico Grande. A very rough and rocky path leads onwards, then a steep and well-wooded zigzag path leads downhill.
Maps	Carta Militar 5
Refreshments	Small bars at Fajã Escura, Fajã dos Cardos and Colmeal.
Transport	Interurban bus 81 serves Curral das Freiras from Funchal and some services run to Colmeal, Fajã Escura and Fajã dos Cardos.

This arduous mountain circuit starts deep in the Curral valley, climbing steep and rocky slopes, with hands-on scrambling required to reach the summit of Pico Grande. The path in the middle of the route was for many years in a very poor condition. It now has its vegetation hacked back occasionally by local mountain runners, **who regard it as one of the toughest mountain trails in Madeira**. The walk continues to Pico do Jorge and the Boca das Torrinhas. A steep and stony zigzag descent leads back into the Curral valley.

For map, see Walk 29.

◄ Start at **Colmeal**, where the Snack Bar Costa Verde is located, or if the bus is heading to nearby **Fajã Escura**, then stay on board to avoid a short road-walk. Climb from the last bus stop to pass the Snack Bar O Lagar. The road ends and a track climbs past cultivated plots, drifting right to enter a forest. Watch out for a path climbing to the right at a bend, with flights of log steps. Climb past pines, eucalyptus and tall chestnuts, later climbing more open slopes. Follow the zigzag path faithfully uphill, passing occasional chestnut and other trees. The ground is often stony underfoot, but the path is well-engineered, carved from rock or stoutly buttressed. Climb past a steep spur at **Eirado** and zigzag up between fences. Pass broom scrub and cross a bouldery stream-bed. A few chestnuts offer shade on the slope and a pinnacle of rock lies to the left. The narrow path finally climbs to the gorse-covered crest of **Boca do Cerro** around 1300m (4265ft).

Turn right at a signposted junction and follow a path past a sheepfold in the shade of chestnuts, then climb to a cave hewn into a cliff. A cable is fixed to the rock where fenced steps climb a steep and rocky slope. A zigzag path climbs further, passing occasional chestnuts on a steep slope of rock and broom. There are stone steps and rock steps. Keep climbing and swing well to the left to reach a rocky ridge, then scramble with great care along a route marked with a fraying cable to reach the highest rocky peak of **Pico Grande**, at 1654m (5426ft). ▶

Views stretch from the plateau of Paúl da Serra, around the Curral valley to Pico Ruivo and Pico do Areeiro, with Funchal down by the sea.

Scramble down from the summit and retrace steps downhill, but watch for another path heading off to the left, cutting through dense broom. This crosses a gap where there is a dry-stone wall. Cross the wall and look carefully to the left to spot the path among rocks and boulders. A short flight of stone steps climbs uphill to confirm the route. On the other side, stone steps and broken steps drop steeply down-hill and need care as there is so much loose rock. Watch very carefully for the line of the path, which passes beneath towering, overhanging cliffs. Broom scrub flanks the path,

Very rugged and complex terrain beyond Pico Grande needs careful attention to route-finding

but is usually trimmed back, then there is a climb past some dead, blasted trees. Turn round a rocky corner for views of a rugged gap with Pico do Jorge beyond. Walk down past more blasted trees and short broom scrub to pass below a gap near **Pico das Empenas**.

A towering peak of rock rises ahead as the path levels out. Climb steps and steep, stony slopes, leaving the bushes and trees behind to climb a well-buttressed flight of steps. The zigzag path climbing higher is loose and worn, while the steps are crumbling, so there is a danger of rock-fall. Stone steps and a zigzag path lead up to a slope of broom as the path gains a high crest around 1550m (5085ft).

Turn right and the path climbs steps on the northern flanks of **Pico do Jorge**, among tree heather and bilberry, reaching a shoulder where views take in Pico do Cedro, Pico Grande, Paúl da Serra and the north-west coast. ◀ Head downhill to reach a shoulder with fine views. Continue up and along the crest, then cross a gritty gap around 1650m (5415ft) near **Pico Casado**.

Pass a blade-like outcrop of rock and zigzag downhill, noticing that some of the stones make musical chinking sounds underfoot. Pass a cave and head down steps on a slope of dense heather. The path levels out and squeezes through a rocky cleft full of ferns and exotic plants.

The way ahead is more rugged but becomes gentler as the path crosses the ridge. Walk down a fenced flight of stone steps to land on the **Boca das Torrinhas** at 1450m (4760ft). ◀

Unless tempted elsewhere, turn right to continue descending, as signposted for Curral das Freiras, or the PR2 trail. The path is narrow as it slices across a rocky slope, and it can be grassy, stony or rocky underfoot, with a few stone steps, while some parts are buttressed and paved. Descend through broom and go down a flight of log steps. Dense eucalyptus follows, and the path zigzags down several flights of stone steps. ◀ A few chestnuts stand among the eucalyptus, along with charred and fallen pine trees. Zigzag further downhill on flights of log steps to pass pine trees. Houses can be seen at the head of the valley with Pico Ruivo and other peaks high above. Follow the path from the woods to pass cultivation terraces, and the path links with flights of steps. Walk down to a concrete bridge and cross a river. The Vereda de Fajã Capitão runs up a few steps to reach a road near **Pico do Furão**.

Enjoy a stretch along the crest with good views, looking down from a stout stone buttress to São Vicente.

Signposts give destinations along all the paths that leave this point, which are covered in turn on Walks 20, 31 and 32.

There are occasional views back down to houses at the head of the valley with Pico Ruivo and other peaks high above.

Rock towers rise high above Fajã dos Cardos

Turn right to walk down the road, passing a couple of small bars near a bridge and a few houses at **Fajã dos Cardos**. There are bus stops, if a bus is due, otherwise follow the road to a junction beside a bridge at **Colmeal**. ▶ If there is a long time to wait, follow the main ER-107 road onwards and up through a tunnel to Curral das Freiras.

The Snack Bar Costa Verde is immediately available if waiting for a bus.

WALK 31
Fajã dos Cardos to Fajã do Penedo

Start	Fajã dos Cardos, in the Curral valley
Finish	Bar A Frontera, Fajã do Penedo
Distance	13km (8 miles)
Total ascent	950m (3115ft)
Total descent	1400m (4595ft)
Time	5hr
Terrain	Forested zigzag mountain paths, which are quite steep at times, with roads at the end.
Maps	Carta Militar 2 and 5
Refreshments	Small bars at Fajã dos Cardos. Bar A Frontera at Fajã do Penedo.
Transport	Interurban bus 81 serves Curral das Freiras from Funchal and some services run to Fajã dos Cardos. Rodoeste bus 6 passes the Bar A Frontera at Fajã do Penedo, linking with São Vicente, Ribeira Brava and Funchal. The bus occasionally serves Falca de Cima.

Roads are gradually advancing through the mountains of Madeira. For the most part they terminate at remote settlements, where old mountain paths and tracks can be followed further. This walk, which is designated as the PR2 trail, crosses from the Curral valley, over the mountain gap of Boca das Torrinhas, to descend through *laurisilva* forest to reach Lombo do Urzal, for Fajã de Penedo.

For map, see Walk 29.

◄ Start at **Fajã dos Cardos**, where a couple of small bars are located near a mapboard and signpost for the PR2. A path called the Vereda de Fajã Capitão leads down concrete steps to a concrete bridge crossing a river. Rocky mountains rise on all sides, including Pico Grande, Pico do Jorge and the rugged flanks of Torres.

There are occasional views back down to houses at the head of the valley with Pico Ruivo and other peaks high above.

Climb concrete steps and follow a narrow, winding path up from houses, passing cultivation terraces. Zigzag up through tall eucalyptus where there are a couple of long flights of log steps. These are followed by shorter flights of log steps and some rugged stretches of path. ◄ Log steps later give way to several flights of stone steps as the path zigzags

higher. Dense eucalyptus gives way to steep slopes of broom at a path junction. Keep left, or straight ahead, but note that turning right leads towards Pico Ruivo.

View of Pico Ruivo while climbing from Fajã dos Cardos

The path can be grassy, stony or rocky underfoot, with a few stone steps, while some parts are buttressed and paved. Enjoy views to Pico Grande and its summit tor, as well as down through the Curral valley, before slicing across a rocky slope to reach the **Boca das Torrinhas** at 1450m (4760ft). Signposts give destinations along all the paths that leave this point (see Walks 20, 30 and 32).

Cross the gap at its lowest point as signposted for Lombo do Urzal, and note the immediate change in character of the route as it enters *laurisilva* forest. The path is narrow and a little overgrown as it is rarely used. The path is well-engineered in places but look ahead carefully as it is not always possible to see far through dense tree heather, laurel, bilberry and flowery undergrowth. Watch for brambles and take care where the path edge has soft and crumbling earth.

Climb a little from time to time as the path negotiates a steep and densely wooded valley head below **Pico da Laje**. Contour across the steep slope, pass along the base of a cliff and turn a rocky corner where there may be a small waterfall. Later, the path runs along the base of another cliff, where there is a breach in the rock and steps zigzag uphill. Later,

161

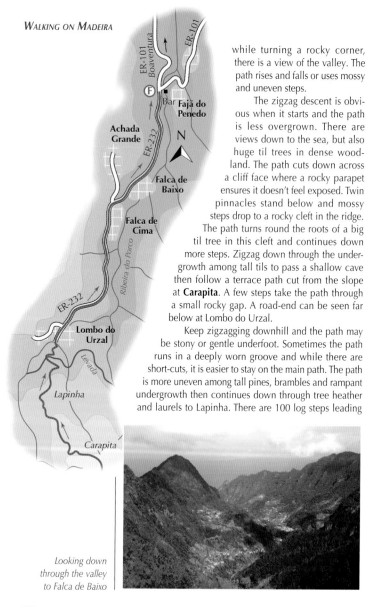

while turning a rocky corner, there is a view of the valley. The path rises and falls or uses mossy and uneven steps.

The zigzag descent is obvious when it starts and the path is less overgrown. There are views down to the sea, but also huge til trees in dense woodland. The path cuts down across a cliff face where a rocky parapet ensures it doesn't feel exposed. Twin pinnacles stand below and mossy steps drop to a rocky cleft in the ridge. The path turns round the roots of a big til tree in this cleft and continues down more steps. Zigzag down through the undergrowth among tall tils to pass a shallow cave then follow a terrace path cut from the slope at **Carapita**. A few steps take the path through a small rocky gap. A road-end can be seen far below at Lombo do Urzal.

Keep zigzagging downhill and the path may be stony or gentle underfoot. Sometimes the path runs in a deeply worn groove and while there are short-cuts, it is easier to stay on the main path. The path is more uneven among tall pines, brambles and rampant undergrowth then continues down through tree heather and laurels to Lapinha. There are 100 log steps leading

Looking down through the valley to Falca de Baixo

down to a levada. ▸ Continue down almost 300 stone steps to reach another levada. Pass the first house at **Lombo do Urzal** and walk down a concrete road to cross a concrete bridge over the bouldery **Ribeira do Porco**. Walk up the road to reach a mapboard and signpost. Look round the densely-wooded mountains enclosing the valley. ▸ Walk up a tarmac road to reach a bus shelter and a junction. Keep right to pass **Falca de Baixo** and its church. The road descends between a cliff and a river. Cross a bridge at the bottom and note the huge boulders in the riverbed. The road reaches a junction at a bend on the **ER-101** road near **Fajã do Penedo**, and the Bar A Frontera is to the right, with a bus shelter opposite.

The water flows through one of the longest tunnels in Madeira.

Steep terraces and red-roofed storage sheds are features of the valley, with plenty of vine trellises, while levadas can be seen on the slopes.

WALK 32
Boca da Encumeada to Colmeal

Start	Boca da Encumeada
Finish	Colmeal, in the Curral valley
Distance	9.5km (6 miles)
Total ascent	740m (2425ft)
Total descent	1110m (3640ft)
Time	5hr
Terrain	Mountainous, with paved paths and steps, as well as steep and stony stretches. A steep, forested zigzag path leads downhill at the end.
Maps	Carta Militar 5
Refreshments	Snack Bar Restaurante Encumeada at the start. Small bars at Fajã dos Cardos and Colmeal.
Transport	Rodoeste buses 6 and 139 serve Boca da Encumeada from Funchal, Ribeira Brava and São Vicente. Interurban bus 81 serves Curral das Freiras from Funchal and some services run to Colmeal.

One of the problems of walking through the mountains of Madeira is timing your arrival at a bus stop before the last bus leaves. On this walk, the main mountain crest is followed from the Boca da Encumeada to the Boca das Torrinhas. A descent is made into the Curral valley, where buses run quite late back to Funchal. This should allow plenty of time for slow walkers to finish.

Start at the Snack Bar Restaurante Encumeada and follow the road through a rock cutting on the **Boca da Encumeada** at 1007m (3304ft). Turn right to follow a stony track uphill, signposted as the PR1.3 trail. The track curves right towards some masts, so keep left to follow a narrow path further up stone steps. ◄ Climb steep flights of stone steps, often fenced and buttressed, to reach the crest of the mountain range around 1250m (4100ft) near **Pico do Meio**. Continue along the ridge and enjoy good views from a bare shoulder, looking directly down to Ribeira Brava. Cross the gentle dome of **Pico da Encumeada** to reach a narrow and well-vegetated gap, where São Vicente and Ribeira Brava can be seen.

The dense vegetation is remarkably mixed and includes everything from laurisilva species to brambles.

Climb stone steps, some of them buttressed and fenced, heading left then swinging right to pass a cave with a stone seat. Climb more steps, turning left and right while climbing. ◄ Tall tree heather and ancient til trees were destroyed by a fire where the path passes along the base of a cliff on the southern flank of **Pico Ferreiro**. The path exploits a thin, crumbling layer in the rock. Zigzag up a wooded slope to reach a gap on the ridge, around 1420m (4660ft), overlooked by rocky pinnacles.

At an open corner there are views of the surrounding mountains, particularly Pico Grande.

Climb again, reaching fenced stone steps at a higher level, then enjoy the view. When a junction is reached, take care to keep left. The path on the right, hacked through dense broom, is a very rugged route to Pico Grande. The main path climbs more steps on the northern flanks of **Pico do Jorge**, among tree heather and bilberry, reaching a shoulder where views take in Pico do Cedro, Pico Grande, Paúl da Serra and the north-west coast. ◄ Head downhill to reach a shoulder with fine views. Continue up and along the crest, then cross a gritty gap around 1650m (5415ft) near **Pico Casado**.

Enjoy a stretch along the crest with good views, looking down from a stout stone buttress to São Vicente.

Pass a blade-like outcrop of rock and zigzag downhill, noticing that some of the stones make musical chinking

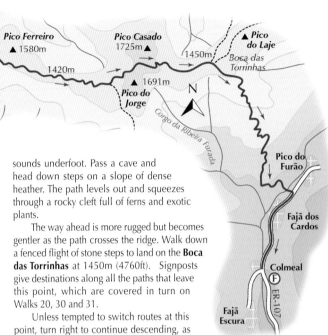

Pico Ferreiro
▲ 1580m

Pico Casado
1725m ▲

1450m

▲ Pico
do Laje

*Boca das
Torrinhas*

1420m

▲ 1691m
**Pico do
Jorge**

N

Corgo da Ribeira Furada

**Pico do
Furão**

**Fajã dos
Cardos**

Colmeal
Ⓕ

ER-107

**Fajã
Escura**

sounds underfoot. Pass a cave and head down steps on a slope of dense heather. The path levels out and squeezes through a rocky cleft full of ferns and exotic plants.

The way ahead is more rugged but becomes gentler as the path crosses the ridge. Walk down a fenced flight of stone steps to land on the **Boca das Torrinhas** at 1450m (4760ft). Signposts give destinations along all the paths that leave this point, which are covered in turn on Walks 20, 30 and 31.

Unless tempted to switch routes at this point, turn right to continue descending, as

Boca das Torrinhas is a prominent gap in the mountains

signposted for Curral das Freiras, or the PR2 trail. The path is narrow as it slices across a rocky slope, and it can be grassy, stony or rocky underfoot, with a few stone steps, while some parts are buttressed and paved. Descend through broom and go down a flight of log steps. Dense eucalyptus follows, and the path zigzags down several flights of stone steps. ◀ A few chestnuts stand among the eucalyptus, along with charred and fallen pine trees. Zigzag further downhill on flights of log steps to pass pine trees. Houses can be seen at the head of the valley with Pico Ruivo and other peaks high above. Follow the path from the woods to pass cultivation terraces, and the path links with flights of steps. Walk down to a concrete bridge and cross a river. The Vereda de Fajã Capitão runs up a few steps to reach a road near **Pico do Furão**.

There are occasional views back down to houses at the head of the valley with Pico Ruivo and other peaks high above.

Turn right to walk down the road, passing a couple of small bars near a bridge and a few houses at **Fajã dos Cardos**. There are bus stops, if a bus is due, otherwise follow the road to a junction beside a bridge at **Colmeal**. ◀ If there is a long time to wait, follow the main ER-107 road onwards and up through a tunnel to Curral das Freiras.

The Snack Bar Costa Verde is immediately available if waiting for a bus.

Looking up to the mountains from Fajã dos Cardos

4 JARDIM DA SERRA

Rocky peaks rise steeply above the Curral valley (Walk 35)

Jardim da Serra is literally the 'Garden of the Mountains'. The name refers to a loose conglomeration of little villages tucked into the mountains between Funchal and Ribeira Brava, and the name is also used for the Posto Florestal on the Boca da Corrida. Terreiros is the highest mountain in this region, and is also one of the easiest to climb on Madeira. Its southern flanks are criss-crossed with paths and tracks. In fact, there are enough paths, tracks and acceptable gradients to allow for a couple of circular walks, which are rare in the mountains of Madeira.

The Levada do Norte wraps itself round most of this area and is something of a 'Jekyll and Hyde' route. The stretch between Serra de Água and Boa Morte is one of the most frightening levadas on the island, with a crumbling path cutting across sheer cliffs. A notice was erected in recent years stating that the levada was closed to walkers. The continuation from Boa Morte to Estreito de Câmara de Lobos, on the other hand, is relatively easy and quite popular.

This region is easily reached using Rodoeste buses from Funchal, but walkers who want to stay in quieter places will find good access by bus from Ribeira Brava. Take careful note of all the walking routes that use the road to and from Boca da Corrida. This steep road becomes a bit wearing if you walk it too many times, and walkers who wish to arrive by taxi should hire one from Estreito de Câmara de Lobos.

Several walks in this region link with each other, and there are even more

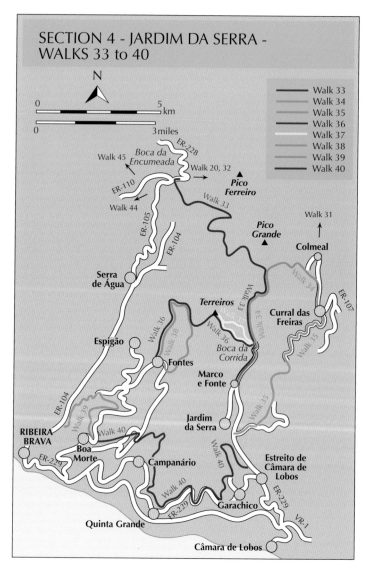

SECTION 4 - JARDIM DA SERRA -
WALKS 33 to 40

N

0 ————— 5 km

0 ————— 3 miles

Walk 33
Walk 34
Walk 35
Walk 36
Walk 37
Walk 38
Walk 39
Walk 40

ER-228

Boca da Encumeada

Walk 45

Walk 20, 32

ER-110

Pico Ferreiro

Walk 44

ER-105

Walk 33

Pico Grande

Walk 31

Colmeal

ER-104

Serra de Água

Terreiros

Walk 34

Curral das Freiras

ER-107

Walk 36

Espigão

Walk 38

Fontes

Boca da Corrida

Walk 35

Marco e Fonte

ER-104

Walk 39

Jardim da Serra

RIBEIRA BRAVA

Walk 40

Boa Morte

ER-229

Campanário

Walk 40

Estreito de Câmara de Lobos

ER-229

ER-229

Garachico

VR-1

Quinta Grande

Câmara de Lobos

The village of Fontes (Walk 36)

opportunities to link with other rugged paths leading to the higher mountains. In fact, the longer the maps are studied, the greater the number of choices that present themselves, especially around the Boca da Encumeada and Curral das Freiras. However, few walkers would relish dropping deep into the Curral valley only to have to climb up the other side. Interurban buses link Curral das Freiras with Funchal.

WALK 33
Boca da Encumeada to Marco e Fonte

Start	Boca da Encumeada
Finish	Marco e Fonte
Distance	15km (9¼ miles)
Total ascent	600m (1970ft)
Total descent	700m (2300ft)
Time	6hr
Terrain	Mountainous, with a well-wooded path at first, then a paved path, with the danger of rock-falls at a higher level. A good path leads from gap to gap, descending to link with a road leading further down a wooded slope.
Maps	Carta Militar 5
Refreshments	Snack Bar Restaurante Encumeada at the start. Bar O Mário at Marco e Fonte.
Transport	Rodoeste buses 6 and 139 serve Boca da Encumeada from Funchal, Ribeira Brava and São Vicente. Rodoeste bus 96 links Marco e Fonte with Funchal.

This route is waymarked as the Caminho Real da Encumeada, or PR12 trail. It links the Boca da Encumeada with the Boca da Corrida. Explore a wooded valley then follow a stone-paved path across the cliffs flanking Pico Grande. After passing the Boca da Cerro the path winds along a rugged crest to reach the Boca da Corrida, where a cobbled road leads down to Marco e Fonte.

Start on the **Boca da Encumeada** at 1007m (3304ft), where the Snack Bar Restaurante Encumeada is available. Follow the road downhill in the direction of Serra de Água, turning left round a bend to reach a junction with a track, where a notice indicates the start of the PR12 trail. ◄ Laurel, heather, broom and brambles grow on the slope, while the track narrows and at one bend there is a fine view of Pico Grande. Cross a flight of stone steps and pass a pipeline feeding the generating station at Serra de Água.

Follow the path across and down a slope dominated by eucalyptus. Cross rocky and bouldery stream-beds at **Poço**, unless broken footbridges have been repaired. The path later

Buses might stop here if given due notice, but it is on an awkward bend.

passes cultivation terraces and climbs gently through pines, also passing eucalyptus, candleberry and bilberry. A shaded, stone-paved path leads to the head of the valley at **Curral Jangão**, where there are cultivated slopes and plenty of chestnuts. A cobbled, stone-arched bridge spans a rocky gorge and waterfalls on the **Ribeiro do Poço**.

The path passes a small stone building and undulates, sometimes in dense woods and sometimes with views across the valley. Swing left through tall eucalyptus and pass beneath a frowning rock face, climbing along a stone-paved path to emerge at a

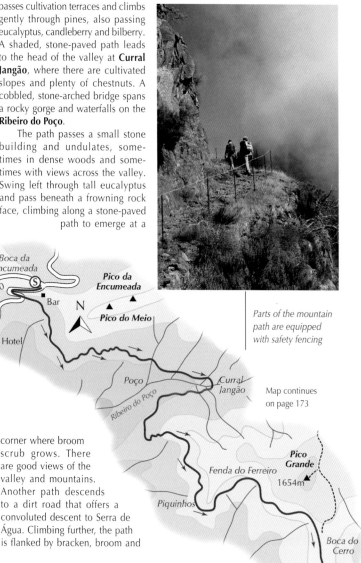

Parts of the mountain path are equipped with safety fencing

corner where broom scrub grows. There are good views of the valley and mountains. Another path descends to a dirt road that offers a convoluted descent to Serra de Água. Climbing further, the path is flanked by bracken, broom and

Map continues on page 173

brambles, passing only a few trees. The route picks out a line of weakness between two cliff faces, working its way round a steep-sided hollow, then turning a prominent corner into another awesome hollow at **Fenda do Ferreiro** on the slopes of Pico Grande.

Pass round the base of a monstrous tower of rock, climbing through tree heather and passing some old til trees. There is rock-fall debris on the slopes and some stretches are wet, muddy, slippery and well-vegetated. Follow a drier path across the next cliff face, then after another wet patch the path levels out on a slope of gorse. Reach a signposted junction near the gorse-covered gap of **Boca do Cerro**, around 1300m (4265ft). ◄

To climb Pico Grande, turn left and left again and see Walk 29 or Walk 30.

Keep straight ahead along the path towards **Pico do Serradinho**. The path doesn't climb over it, but passes broom and chestnut, turning interesting corners with good views. The path later drops and levels out then crosses the gap of **Passo de Ares**, around 1250m (4100ft). Climb and follow the path around and down the flank of Pico do Cavalo, where it is variously buttressed or cut from rock, with stone steps and fencing in places. There are fine views of the mountains across the Curral valley. Reach yet another gap, the **Boca dos Corgos**, where there are chestnuts around 1230m (4035ft).

The path to Boca da Corrida is plain and obvious throughout

Climb steep zigzags and steps to follow a broad path across a slope, levelling out among broom and chestnuts before descending. More than 160 stone steps drop to a track on the **Boca da Corrida**, around 1220m (4000ft). There is a small car park and picnic area beside the **Posto Florestal Jardim da Serra**, as well as a shrine to São Cristovão in the shade of a tree. The walk can be ended here if a pick-up or a taxi can be arranged.

To reach the nearest bus, walk down an attractively cobbled road, which bends sharply to the right and left, giving way to a steep tarmac road at a cattle grid. Nearby slopes are dominated by chestnut, with some pine and eucalyptus, giving way to cultivated plots further downhill. Rodoeste bus 96 turns round at a bus stop, but only those specifically timetabled for 'Corrida'. If a bus isn't due for a while, keep walking downhill and wait at the **Bar O Mário** at a road junction at **Marco e Fonte**.

WALK 34
Boca da Corrida and Curral das Freiras

Start	Marco e Fonte
Finish	Curral das Freiras
Distance	10.5km (6½ miles)
Total ascent	660m (2165ft)
Total descent	920m (3020ft)
Time	4hr
Terrain	A steep road gives way to a good path leading from gap to gap. The descent is along a steep, stony, wooded path.
Maps	Carta Militar 5
Refreshments	Bar O Mário at Marco e Fonte. Plenty of choice at Curral das Freiras.
Transport	Rodoeste bus 96 serves Marco e Fonte from Funchal, or take a taxi from Estreito de Câmara de Lobos to Boca da Corrida. Interurban bus 81 links Fajã Escura and Curral das Freiras with Funchal.

Walkers who find themselves on the Boca da Corrida enjoy splendid views of the Curral valley. Some may wonder if there is a way down there. There is, but first it involves following a path from gap to gap along a rugged ridge, then taking a very steep zigzag path into the Curral valley. There are options to shorten the walk at the start and finish, but plan in advance if you wish to do this. Buses marked 'Corrida' pass Marco e Fonte and run part-way up the steep Estrada da Corrida. If you wish to avoid the steep climb to Boca da Corrida, you should get off the bus at Estreito de Câmara de Lobos and hire a taxi. To finish early at Fajã Escura, arrive in time for one of the infrequent buses.

The bus marked 'Corrida' reaches a turning space above **Marco e Fonte**. The road continues to climb steeply past cultivated plots onto slopes dominated by chestnut, with some pine and eucalyptus. After crossing a cattle grid, a cobbled stretch bends right and left, leading to **Boca da Corrida** at around 1220m (4000ft). There is a small car park and picnic area beside the **Posto Florestal Jardim da Serra**, as well as a shrine to São Cristovão in the shade of a tree.

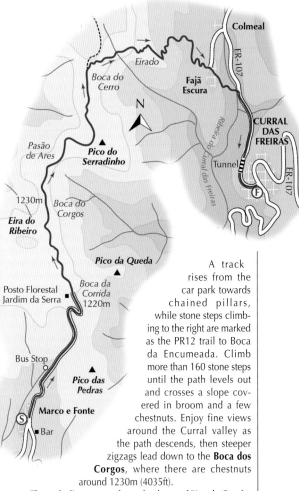

A track rises from the car park towards chained pillars, while stone steps climbing to the right are marked as the PR12 trail to Boca da Encumeada. Climb more than 160 stone steps until the path levels out and crosses a slope covered in broom and a few chestnuts. Enjoy fine views around the Curral valley as the path descends, then steeper zigzags lead down to the **Boca dos Corgos**, where there are chestnuts around 1230m (4035ft).

The path slices across the rocky slopes of Pico do Cavalo, where the path is cut from rock or buttressed as it climbs, with some stretches protected by fences. Cross the ridge and descend to a gap at **Passo de Ares**, around 1250m (4100ft). A level stretch goes through a gateway, then climb round the slopes of **Pico do Serradinho**, where there are interesting corners with good views. Pass broom-covered slopes that give way to gorse scrub on the **Boca do Cerro**, around 1300m (4265ft). The path appears to run level towards cliffs on the flank of Pico Grande, but look out for a signposted right turn up a few stone steps and cross the gorse-covered crest, passing another junction. ◄

To climb Pico Grande, see Walk 29 or Walk 30.

A narrow path descends gently from the gap with good views into the Curral valley. A pinnacle of rock lies to the right, while views across the valley include Pico Ruivo and Pico do Areeiro. A few chestnuts offer shade on the slope, then the path goes through broom scrub and crosses a bouldery stream-bed. Brush past broom, turn round a corner and zigzag down a steep spur at **Eirado**. A well-engineered path, fenced at first, then carved from rock or stoutly buttressed, it is often stony underfoot.

Snack Bar O Lagar and a bus shelter.

Chestnut and other trees clothe the slope as the zigzag path leads downhill. There are short flights of stone or log steps on a slope bearing tall chestnut, eucalyptus and pine. Literally hundreds of log steps lead further downhill. These eventually link with concrete steps past houses, leading to a road. However, watch carefully on the right to spot a concrete forest track, which soon leads down past cultivated plots to a road-end at **Fajã Escura**. ◄

Curral das Freiras is signposted downhill from Boca do Cerro

Catch a bus if one is due, otherwise continue to Curral das Freiras. Walk down the Caminho da Fajã Escura, following a concrete road, a steeper cobbled track and steps down a wooded slope, with street lights alongside. Cross a metal footbridge over the bouldery **Ribeira do Curral das Freiras**, then take a path and steps that lead up to the ER-107 road. There is a bus stop, otherwise turn right to keep walking. Cross a bridge over the Ribeira do Cidrão then follow the road up through a **tunnel** to reach **Curral das Freiras**. ▸

For facilities see Walk 18.

WALK 35
Boca dos Namorados and Curral das Freiras

Start	Cabo Podão
Finish	Lombo Chão or Curral das Freiras
Distance	4.5km or 9km (2¾ or 5½ miles)
Total ascent	260m or 590m (855ft or 1935ft)
Total descent	600m or 730m (1970ft or 2395ft)
Time	1hr 45min or 3hr 15min
Terrain	Wooded slopes. A clear track is used for the ascent and a steep and stony zigzag path is used on the descent, ending with a road walk.
Maps	Carta Militar 5 and 8
Refreshments	Bars at Cabo Podão. Snack Bar Hostia in the Curral valley. Plenty of choice at Curral das Freiras.
Transport	Rodoeste bus 96 serves Cabo Podão from Funchal. Interurban bus 81 links Lombo Chão and Curral das Freiras with Funchal.

No buses run to the Boca dos Namorados, overlooking the Curral valley, but cars can be driven there. An old cobbled track can be followed up there, climbing through forest from Cabo Podão then dropping down a steep and rugged zigzag path to Lombo Chão. There are buses you could take at that point, or you could follow the road across the valley and up to Curral das Freiras. Not all buses heading for Jardim da Serra serve Cabo Podão. Taking the wrong bus means additional walking up steep roads from Corticeiras.

The bus goes a short way up the road.

Curral das Freiras can be reached on foot or by bus

Start at a road junction at **Cabo Podão**, where the Bar Bilhares Pestana and a few spots are located. A school, the Escola Básica Foro, is situated above, with a modern church dominating the area. Walk up the bendy road signposted for the Boca dos Namorados. ◄ Eventually, turn left up a very steep cobbled road called the Caminho Velha da Boca dos Namorados. This climbs to a horse-riding centre, or Centro Hípico, then continues as a rough and broken cobbled road, fringed with gorse bushes, into eucalyptus forest.

A cobbled path leads onwards and upwards, crossing a track and finally climbing a few steps to reach a road-end car park on the **Boca dos Namorados**, around 1050m (3445ft). Enjoy the view down into the Curral valley and up to the high peaks.

Follow a paved path from the car park to start descending gently at first. When the path starts to drop down a very steep slope, it zigzags and features flights of log steps but the tall eucalyptus, pine and chestnut trees prevent any sense of exposure. The zigzags end for a while and there is a slight climb along a well-vegetated path to reach a little gap where an electricity pylon stands beside **Pico do Cedro**. Despite the intrusion of the pylon, there is a good view to the head of the Curral valley, taking in the rugged peaks that surround it.

Descend more steeply on rocky and stony zigzags, with more log steps, passing clumps of laurel, broom, gorse and brambles on an otherwise open slope with good views. The path levels out a little as it passes a little knoll where chestnuts grow. Zigzag further downhill among tall eucalyptus and pine, continuing down a densely-wooded slope of laurel and chestnut. The lower parts of the path have cobbled steps with mimosa alongside. Swing into a damp little valley to cross a stream, then follow a narrow concrete path and steps uphill. Prickly pears grow on a rocky slope and a few houses are reached at a road-end at **Lombo Chão**. Finish here for the short walk.

Either wait for a bus, or if one isn't due for a while, walk along the road to enjoy good views across to Curral das Freiras. There are sweeping loops along the road, but there are odd short-cuts down flights of steps with street lights alongside. The Snack Bar Hostia is reached near a bridge over the bouldery **Ribeira do Curral das Freiras**. Climb up the other side of the valley and the road rises in loops, crossing the **Levada do Curral**. The road levels out near the church in **Curral das Freiras**. ▸

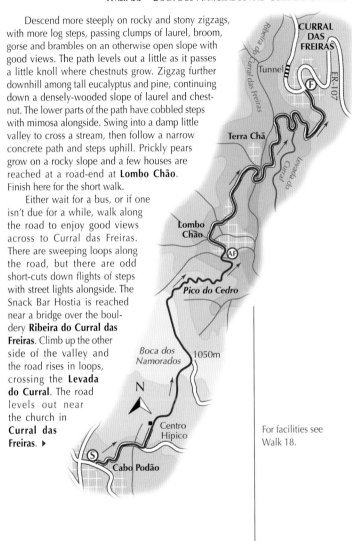

For facilities see Walk 18.

WALK 36

Marco e Fonte to Fontes

Start	Marco e Fonte
Finish	Fontes
Distance	8km (5 miles)
Total ascent	520m (1705ft)
Total descent	480m (1575ft)
Time	3hr 30min
Terrain	A steep road gives way to good tracks on open slopes, but the ascent of Terreiros crosses rugged slopes where care is needed in mist.
Maps	Carta Militar 5
Refreshments	Bar O Mário at Marco e Fonte. Bar Fontes at Fontes.
Transport	Rodoeste bus 96 serves Marco e Fonte from Funchal, or taxi to Boca da Corrida. Rodoeste bus 127 links Fontes with Ribeira Brava.

With careful reference to bus services, a fairly straightforward walk can be followed from Marco e Fonte to Boca da Corrida, over the summit of Terreiros to head down into Fontes. Good tracks are used most of the way and there are fine views of Madeira's highest mountains from Terreiros. Fontes is a very quiet little village with limited buses to Ribeira Brava.

Plan in advance if you wish to shorten this walk. Buses marked 'Corrida' pass Marco e Fonte and run part-way up the steep Estrada da Corrida, but get off the bus early if the shop or Bar O Mário is needed. If you wish to avoid the initial steep climb to Boca da Corrida, you should get off the bus at Estreito de Câmara de Lobos and hire a taxi. Time your arrival at Fontes to pick up one of the infrequent buses to Ribeira Brava.

The bus marked 'Corrida' reaches a turning space above Marco e Fonte. The road continues to climb steeply. After crossing a cattle grid, an attractively cobbled stretch bends right and left, leading to Boca da Corrida at around 1220m (4000ft). There is a car park and picnic area beside the **Posto Florestal Jardim da Serra**, and a shrine to São Cristovão.

A track rises from the car park, passing between chained pillars, then turning left to climb up and across a slope covered in broom and brambles. The track turns right and zigzags further uphill. Pass through an area of burnt chestnuts and keep walking to reach a junction of tracks. Take the track on the right, rising to an isolated **concrete building** close to a gap in a ridge near Terreiros.

Pico Grande and Pico Ruivo from the summit of Terreiros

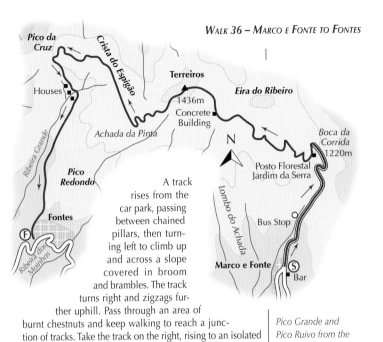

181

Views stretch from the sea near Ribeira Brava to the sloping plateau of Paúl da Serra, then along the rugged mountain crest of Madeira and down towards Funchal.

Walk above the building to follow a narrow path leading through broom to the ridge. Bear left to follow the rugged ridge, crossing a gap and following a fence uphill through broom. There are a few arrows painted on rocks for assistance. There is a short, steep, rocky stretch, then more broom on the higher parts. Cross a fence at a junction, using a crude ladder stile, then follow a path beside the fence to reach the summit of **Terreiros** at 1436m (4711ft), where a fence and wall meet. ◄

Cross the wall on the summit and walk down a narrow path. Swing right across a gentle slope to follow a grassy track gently downhill. The track winds and goes through a gateway, then there is a broad zigzag on grass or stones before another gateway. Reach a junction with a broader dirt road. Turn right here to follow it, running gently down and around the head of a valley. There is a gap in the ridge of **Crista do Espigão**, offering a view across a deep, steep-sided valley to lofty Pico Grande and other high mountains. Much the same view is gained from the next gap. When the track zigzags downhill, there is a water-hole to the right and a fine view over a very steep slope to Serra de Água.

The track wriggles away from the edge and drops down into a valley, passing three tiny houses and entering an area of chestnut and eucalyptus beside the **Ribeira Grande**. You will emerge from the trees to see old cultivation terraces and signs of former occupation. Continue down the stony track, and tangles of broom and brambles give way to cultivation terraces and small buildings. The track is rough and stony in places, but always clear to follow, with a narrow levada alongside after passing through a gate. You will pass more chestnut and eucalyptus then, all of a sudden, little houses and farms. A road, the Caminho das Fontes, leads down to a junction beside the Bar Fontes and a bus stop, back in the little village of **Fontes** at 936m (3071ft). ◄

Rodoeste bus 127 to Ribeira Brava.

WALK 37

Terreiros from Boca da Corrida

Start/finish	Boca da Corrida
Distance	5.5km (3½ miles)
Total ascent/descent	300m (985ft)
Time	2hr
Terrain	Mostly easy tracks on open slopes, but Terreiros has rough and stony slopes, while Eira do Ribeiro has vague grassy paths.
Maps	Carta Militar 5
Refreshments	None closer than the Bar O Mário at Marco e Fonte.
Transport	Taxi to Boca da Corrida.

Terreiros stands at the lofty height of 1436m (4711ft), but it can be approached using an easy track and a short, rugged path from the Boca da Corrida. This route would suit those who prefer to arrive by car, since it is possible to return to the start by another route, thereby enjoying a short, scenic mountain walk for relatively little effort. However, the route can be tricky in mist.

Cars can be driven up the Estrada da Corrida to Boca da Corrida. Walkers without cars who want to avoid the steep climb should get off the bus at Estreito de Câmara de Lobos and hire a taxi, arranging a pick-up for later.

Boca da Corrida stands around 1220m (4000ft), with a small car park and picnic area beside the **Posto Florestal Jardim da Serra**. ▶

Follow a track uphill from the car park through chained pillars, then turning left to climb up and across a

Splendid views take in mountains from Pico Grande to Pico Ruivo and Pico do Areeiro, while Curral das Freiras lies deep in the valley, with a glimpse of Funchal harbour far below.

Terreiros
▲
1436m
Concrete
Building
Eira do Ribeiro
N
SF *Boca da Corrida*
1220m
Posto Florestal
Jardim da Serra

slope covered in broom and brambles. The track turns right and zigzags further uphill. Pass through an area of burnt chestnuts and keep walking to reach a junction of tracks. Take the track on the right, rising to an isolated **concrete building** close to a gap in a ridge near Terreiros.

Walk above the building to follow a narrow path leading through broom to the ridge. Bear left to follow the rugged ridge. Cross a gap and follow a fence up through broom, where you'll see a few arrows painted on rocks for assistance. There is a short, steep, rocky stretch, then more broom on the higher parts. Cross a fence at a junction, using a crude ladder stile, then follow a path beside the fence to reach the summit of **Terreiros** at 1436m (4711ft), where a fence and wall meet.

Retrace your steps from the summit to the gap above the concrete building. Don't go down to the building, but aim to stay high instead. There is a narrow path along the crest, often flanked by broom, with occasional painted arrows. Take great care in mist, as it would be easy to lose the path and there are cliffs to the north and east. Cross the gently rounded summit of **Eira do Ribeiro** at 1410m (4626ft).

Stay faithful to the highest part of the crest, swinging right to enjoy views over the deep-cut Curral valley, with fine mountains beyond. Swing left downhill, then right again further down the crest. Walk straight down the crest to reach

Madeira's highest mountains, seen from Eira do Ribeiro

a bend on a track. This track was followed on the outward journey, so turn left to follow it quickly back down to **Boca da Corrida**.

WALK 38
Crista do Espigão from Fontes

Start/finish	Fontes
Distance	8.5km (5¼ miles)
Total ascent/descent	380m (1245ft)
Time	3hr
Terrain	Dirt roads climb through forest onto open slopes, later descending through a valley.
Maps	Carta Militar 5
Refreshments	Bar Fontes at Fontes.
Transport	Rodoeste bus 127 serves Fontes from Ribeira Brava.

A circular walk along broad and clear tracks is available above the little village of Fontes. An ascent through chestnut and eucalyptus forest passes the Posto Florestal Trompica, then climbs onto more open broom-covered slopes. The highlight of the walk is the ridge of Crista do Espigão and the views that are available from the little gaps along it, especially looking down towards Serra de Água.

Start at the Bar Fontes in the little village of **Fontes** at 936m (3071ft). Follow the road gently down and around a valley while walking through the village. The road climbs past a few more houses and turns left, then there is a slight descent and a bend to the right. Watch for a broad concrete track rising sharply left, almost immediately swinging round to the right, signposted as the Caminho da Trompica.

Apple trees quickly give way to eucalyptus as the track climbs through forest. Chestnuts are reached further uphill, where the road levels out near a **waterworks**. Continue up the concrete road, catching glimpses down through the Campanário valley and up to the shapeless form of Terreiros at its head. The road climbs past the **Posto Florestal Trompica**, then gives way to a broad a dusty dirt road at a cattle grid.

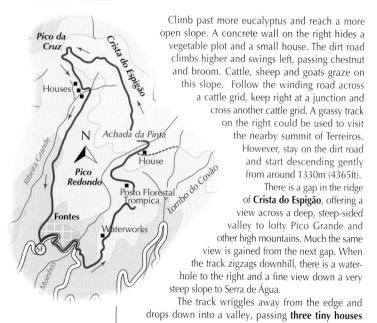

Climb past more eucalyptus and reach a more open slope. A concrete wall on the right hides a vegetable plot and a small house. The dirt road climbs higher and swings left, passing chestnut and broom. Cattle, sheep and goats graze on this slope. Follow the winding road across a cattle grid, keep right at a junction and cross another cattle grid. A grassy track on the right could be used to visit the nearby summit of Terreiros. However, stay on the dirt road and start descending gently from around 1330m (4365ft).

There is a gap in the ridge of **Crista do Espigão**, offering a view across a deep, steep-sided valley to lofty Pico Grande and other high mountains. Much the same view is gained from the next gap. When the track zigzags downhill, there is a water-hole to the right and a fine view down a very steep slope to Serra de Água.

The track wriggles away from the edge and drops down into a valley, passing **three tiny houses**

Looking down to Serra de Água from Crista do Espigão

and entering an area of chestnut and eucalyptus beside the **Ribeira Grande**. Emerge from the trees to see old cultivation terraces and signs of former occupation. Continue down the stony track, and tangles of broom and brambles give way to cultivation terraces and small buildings. The track is rough and stony in places, but always clear to follow, with a narrow levada alongside after passing through a gate. Pass more chestnut and eucalyptus then all of a sudden there are little houses and farms. A road, the Caminho das Fontes, leads down to a junction beside the Bar Fontes and a bus stop, back in the little village of **Fontes** at 936m (3071ft). ▶

Rodoeste bus 127 to Ribeira Brava.

WALK 39
Fajã da Ribeira, Levada Norte and Boa Morte

Start	Fajã da Ribeira
Finish	Boa Morte
Distance	6.5km (4 miles)
Total ascent	500m (1640ft)
Total descent	20m (65ft)
Time	2hr 30min
Terrain	Flights of many steps climb steeply and are protected by handrails. The levada path is virtually level, easy and well-wooded.
Maps	Carta Militar 8
Refreshments	Bars just off-route at Boa Morte.
Transport	Rodoeste buses 6, 100 and 139 run from Ribeira Brava, close to Fajã da Ribeira. Rodoeste bus 127 links Boa Morte with Ribeira Brava, and bus 148 links Boa Morte with Funchal.

The Levada do Norte from Serra de Água to Boa Morte was included in earlier editions of this guidebook, but there is now a notice on the northern stretch, stating that it is closed. It features a narrow path with a frightening amount of exposure, making it unsuitable for anyone who suffers from vertigo. Instead of this stretch, an impressive flight of steps can be climbed from Fajã Riberia to the Levada do Norte, then an easier stretch of the levada path is followed to Boa Morte.

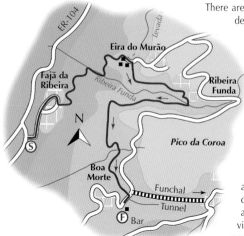

There are two ways to start this walk, depending on the availability of transport. Either walk along the road from Ribeira Brava towards **Fajã da Ribeira**, or catch a bus if one is heading that way, or take a taxi. The road serving the village is signposted for Fajã da Ribeira and it climbs steeply at one point, with 114 concrete steps alongside. These steps are merely an introduction for what comes later. The road makes a one-way circuit through the village, and at its highest point, around 150m (490ft), there is a notice about a path called the Vereda da Eira do Mourão.

Climb concrete steps between houses, looking uphill to trace the line of the path by spotting the streetlights and handrails that accompany it. After climbing 235 steps a house is passed on a steep slope. After climbing 510 steps, turn left at a junction. The gradient eases after 600 steps, offering good views before passing beneath a cliff. A prominent corner is turned after 685 steps, where there are fine views through the canyon-like valley from Serra de Água to Ribeira Brava. A couple of derelict cave houses can be inspected soon afterwards, then after 770 steps, including some that go downhill, a footbridge is crossed over the **Ribeira Funda**.

Climb rather more steeply, and after 840 steps a derelict house is passed. Then, after 1300 steps, walk between ruined buildings. There is a gentler stretch before final flights take the step count to 1553 by the time a road is reached in the tiny settlement of **Eira do Murão**. Keep walking uphill along the road to reach the **Levada do Norte** on at a bend around 550m (1805ft).

Turn right to follow the levada into a side-valley, passing a few houses and cultivation terraces. Wild and mixed woodlands are passed while crossing a footbridge where the Ribeira Funda runs through a gorge. Cross a slope of

Walkers follow the Levada do Norte near Boa Morte

eucalyptus and later turns a corner to leave the side-valley and enjoy another view into the main valley, from Ribeira Brava to Boca da Encumeada. ▶

The path loops and is attractively lined with agapanthus, crossing a track at one point. Later, you will reach a road where a prominent notice points back along the levada for Serra de Água and ahead for Quinta Grande. Walk 40 continues along the Levada do Norte, but for the time being the Snack Bar O Pinheiro and little village of **Boa Morte** lie just downhill. ▶

There are pines among the eucalyptus, but they have been burnt in the past.

Rodoeste bus 127 to Ribeira Brava and 148 to Funchal.

WALK 40

Levada do Norte: Boa Morte to
Estreito de Câmara de Lobos

Start	Boa Morte
Finish	Estreito de Câmara de Lobos
Distance	17.5km (10¾ miles)
Total ascent	30m (100ft)
Total descent	20m (65ft)
Time	5hr 30min
Terrain	The levada path is level and either crosses well-cultivated slopes or goes through wooded valleys. Some short stretches are exposed and there is a tunnel.
Maps	Carta Militar 8
Refreshments	Bars at Boa Morte, Cruz da Caldeira and Garachico. Plenty of choice at Estreito de Câmara de Lobos.
Transport	Rodoeste buses 127 and 148 serve Boa Morte from Ribeira Brava and Funchal respectively. Rodoeste bus 96 links the end of the levada and Estreito de Câmara de Lobos with Funchal.

The continuation of the Levada do Norte from Boa Morte to Estreito de Câmara de Lobos is easy and very popular. Enjoy following it across well-cultivated and well-settled slopes, passing Campanário, Quinta Grande and Garachico at a general level of 550m (1805ft). The levada also enters well-wooded valleys that are pleasant and quiet.

Stay on the bus to pass through the village of **Boa Morte**, then get off either at the Snack Bar O Pinheiro or where the road crosses the **Levada do Norte**. Turn right to follow the flow downstream, passing a water intake where the path is planted with hydrangeas. Pass tall pines and cross a slope dotted with chestnuts. A couple of houses are passed above **Corujeira**, where the path loops round a couple of tucks in the valley side. Cross a tarmac road near a former sports pitch and turn round the head of a valley drained by the Ribeiro dos Melões. Pass tall pines, a circular reservoir and chestnuts, passing the other side of the former sports pitch along a path lined with agapanthus.

Turn sharply round to the left to cross a concrete road at a water intake and pass a few houses beside terraces covered in fruit and vegetables. There are street lights beside the levada which leads to another house. ▶ The path then makes a tight turn around a side-valley. As the levada swings round into the main Campanário valley, pines give way to eucalyptus, and a narrow parapet path picks its way across the top of a stout buttress. Cross the **Ribeira do Campanário** at a road-end picnic site and continue across a well-wooded slope, passing tall pine and eucalyptus. Cultivation terraces full of fruit and vegetables are crossed before a short fenced stretch. Turn round a little side-valley where are views between tall pine and eucalyptus of the church and houses at **Campanário**.

Cultivated slopes give way to mimosa and chestnut.

Walk past pine, shady mimosa and chestnut, looking down on houses all the way across the side of the Campanário valley. The levada later crosses a couple of roads close together and follows concrete walkways. A slope above bears pine and eucalyptus, while the path passes cane and brambles, with some fencing alongside. Cross a steep cobbled steps above a church at **Quinta Grande**, then a

A ruin beside the Levada do Norte near Corujeira

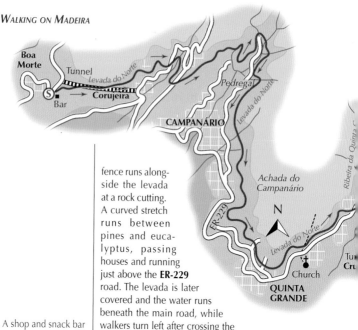

fence runs along-
side the levada
at a rock cutting.
A curved stretch
runs between
pines and euca-
lyptus, passing
houses and running
just above the **ER-229**
road. The levada is later
covered and the water runs
beneath the main road, while
walkers turn left after crossing the
road to pick up its continuation by going
down a flight of steps. Turn round the head of the valley to
cross the **Ribeira da Quinta Grande**, then pass beneath **Cruz
da Caldeira** by going through a short **tunnel** with an uneven
path. ◀

A shop and snack bar
lie above the tunnel,
with a restaurant
nearby, but it is best
to reach them via
the main road.

The levada crosses rock-faces, but has fences alongside
so it doesn't feel too exposed. Agapanthus and brambles
grow on a steep slope and prickly pears are also seen. Turn
round the head of the valley to cross the **Ribeiro da Caldeira**,
after which the levada is covered. Go up steps and cross the
main **ER-229** road above Caldeira, noting that the levada is
still covered. There is a landslip at **Nogueira**, where a building collapsed and destroyed the channel. The water flows
through a buried pipe, so go down a slope of mimosa trees,
then head uphill to continue along another covered stretch.
A house covers the levada, so walk down steps beside a
road, then turn left up steps to pick up its course again.

The levada is again covered by slabs and has plenty of
houses and street lights alongside as it swings round into a
little valley. Leave the valley and turn round a spur where

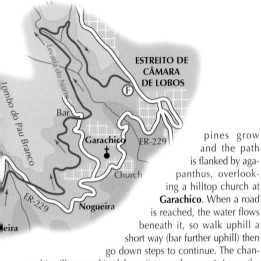

pines grow and the path is flanked by agapanthus, overlooking a hilltop church at **Garachico**. When a road is reached, the water flows beneath it, so walk uphill a short way (bar further uphill) then go down steps to continue. The channel is still covered in slabs as it passes houses. ▶ Leave the valley and turn round into the next long valley, catching a view beyond Estreito de Câmara de Lobos to distant Funchal.

Pass overhanging rock with care and walk across steep slopes and rock walls covered in mixed woodland. Cross a metal footbridge over the **Ribeira da Caixa** at the wild and wooded head of the long valley, then cross a concrete footbridge in a side-valley. Be careful of overhanging rock later, but don't worry when the parapet path narrows twice, as steps lead down to lower paths, climbing back to the levada shortly afterwards. Houses are reached on the way out of the long valley, as well as fruit and vegetable plots and vine trellises. The levada is sometimes open and sometimes covered on the way round a little valley then it is completely covered towards the end.

Follow a tarmac road and cross a concrete road, where the levada becomes a paved path leading round a little valley. Pass beneath vine trellises and reach a large sign announcing the Levada do Norte on a steep road. There are regular buses up and down this road, but it is also possible to walk down the road and finish below the prominent church in the middle of **Estreito de Câmara de Lobos**. ▶

A painted 'Bar' notice points uphill to the Snack Bar Oriental.

Market, banks with ATMs, post office, shops, bars, restaurants, taxis, Rodoeste bus 96 to and from Funchal.

5 PAÚL DA SERRA

Paúl da Serra is a high plateau with fairly gentle gradients, which would appeal to walkers who don't like steep and rugged slopes. However, not all the walking routes are gentle, especially those that run over the edge of the plateau, so be sure to read the route descriptions before launching into a route. When the mist descends, the plateau is rather featureless and good navigation is required. Note that the ER-110 road from the Boca da Encumeada to Paúl da Serra is often 'closed' due to rock-fall, but that doesn't always stop motorists from using it, but it's at your own risk.

Rodoeste buses serve the Boca da Encumeada and Porto Moniz from Ribeira Brava. There is no public transport onto Paúl da Serra, so walkers who want to explore the high plateau

SECTION 5 -
PAÚL DA SERRA -
Walks 41 to 47

— Walk 41
— Walk 42
— Walk 43
— Walk 44
— Walk 45
— Walk 46
— Walk 47

A moorland track between Estanquinhos and Bica da Cana goes on to pass several wind turbines (Walk 41)

will have to arrive by car or taxi. There is a restaurant and lodgings at Rabaçal. A restaurant is also available at Pico da Urze, which is well-placed for meals after exploring Pico Ruivo do Paúl da Serra and the gentle Levada do Paúl. The Levada das Rabaças is a there-and-back route to Cascalho. It used to be possible to continue through long tunnels to the Bocada Encumeada, but a recent landslide made it impassable. The nearby Caminho do Pináculo e Folhadal includes several tunnels. This would be unsuitable for claustrophobia sufferers.

Two long levadas have been cut on either side of the deep, well-forested and well-watered Janela valley. The Levada dos Cedros has been completely restored and is quite delightful. The Levada da Janela, which is seldom shown correctly on maps, is altogether more of a challenge, running through several long tunnels.

Both levada walks can be extended down narrow, winding old roads to the sea. Careful planning is required to follow them. The simplest approach is to use Porto Moniz as a base and arrange for taxis to the start, then simply walk back 'home' during the day. Links with several mountain walks are available at the Boca da Encumeada, but roads off the plateau also link with long levada walks high above the west coast of Madeira.

5 km

3 miles

ER-228

Walk 20, 32

Boca da Encumeada

Walk 21, 29, 33

ER-105

ouro

WALK 41

Pico Ruivo do Paúl da Serra from Estanquinhos

Start/finish	Posto Florestal Estanquinhos
Distance	13.5km (8½ miles)
Total ascent/descent	300m (985ft)
Time	4hr
Terrain	Gently sloping moorland covered in bracken, goose and broom. Paths and tracks can be vague or stony underfoot. Care is needed with route-finding in mist.
Maps	Carta Militar 5
Refreshments	Restaurant off-route at Pico da Urze.
Transport	None. The nearest taxis are at Calheta.

Paúl da Serra is a broad, gently sloping plateau around 1400 to 1600m (4600 to 5250ft), with the appearance of bleak, rolling moorland enclosed by rounded hills. Roads, tracks and paths criss-cross it in all directions. Try to start walking early on a sunny day to make the most of this area, which is often blanketed by mist in the afternoon.

The **Posto Florestal Estanquinhos**, signposted from the ER-110 road, offers a place to park around 1550m (5085ft). Walk down the access road from the forest house, but immediately turn left to rise gently along a broad, stony forest track. When this starts to descend turn right along a grassy track that runs gently downhill out of the forest. ◄ Turn left and later right to head towards prominent wind turbines.

If the original track is followed downhill far enough, it links with Walk 45.

Follow a stony access track from one turbine to another, but later fork left along a grassy track. Head downhill, then follow a rocky path and a narrow grassy path. A short walk through gorse reaches the main **ER-110** road at junction with an access road for **Bica da Cana**. ◄

It is possible to detour to a fine viewpoint on the edge of the plateau.

Cross the main road and follow a short path down to a bend on a stony track. Turn left to follow the track down into a hollow of gorse, broom and bracken, then head gently uphill. The track remains stony as it descends into a shallow valley. Cross a streambed then rise to a junction and turn right along a grassier track. ▶

Keep straight ahead along the most obvious track and note that there is a fence running parallel far away to the left. By all means approach the fence, which guards a precipitous steep slope above **Cascalho**. The track later bends to the right and left and is anything but direct as it heads for the **ER-209** road at a large 'Paúl da Serra' sign.

Wind turbines whirl on the brow to the right.

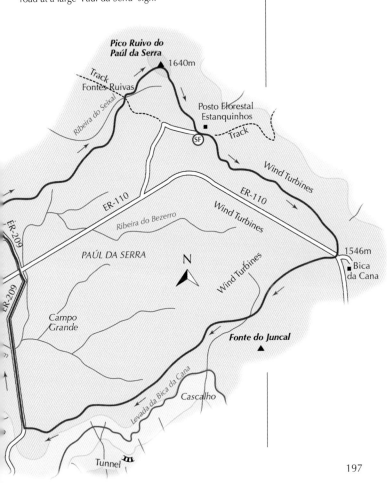

Rugged terrain on the higher slopes of Pico Ruivo do Paúl da Serra, with a view towards Fanal

Turn right to follow the ER-209 road, across the expansive **Campo Grande**, eventually passing through a well-signposted crossroads at the heart of Paúl da Serra. Continue straight ahead as signposted for Fanal, and walk straight ahead at another junction. The road bends right, then left to cross the bouldery bed of the **Ribeira do Lajeado**. Turn right after crossing and follow a vague grassy track, slightly sunken on the moorland and liberally scattered with stones. Turn right at a vague junction with another track.

The track becomes a narrow path through scratchy gorse, and it is important to follow this path faithfully, whether it is narrow or broad, passing grass or squeezing through gorse. Eventually, turn left twice in quick succession to follow a broader track. When this joins an even clearer track, turn right to follow it into a forest, reaching a picnic site and a signpost at **Fontes Ruivas**.

Turn left to follow a path alongside a narrow levada, then climb out of the forest and follow a narrow path through gorse, brambles and bracken to reach the summit of **Pico Ruivo do Paúl da Serra**. A tall trig point stands at 1640m (5380ft) and viewpoints offer fine views round the plateau. ◀ Follow a clear, well-trodden path downhill, heading south-east to reach a junction on a gap. Keep straight ahead along a path flanked by gorse then take a rugged forest path to finish back at the **Posto Florestal Estanquinhos**.

Madeira's highest peaks can be seen, and it is possible to look down to São Vicente, though sometimes an ocean of cloud laps against the edge of the plateau.

WALK 42

Rabaçal, Levada do Risco and 25 Fontes

Start/finish	ER-110 above Rabaçal
Distance	13km (8 miles)
Total ascent/descent	300m (985ft)
Time	4hr
Terrain	The levadas are level, while the paths vary from broad and easy to narrow and rugged. There are also flights of steps on steep and well-wooded slopes.
Maps	Carta Militar 4
Refreshments	Rabaçal Nature Spot Café.
Transport	A minibus shuttle serves Rabaçal from the main road. The nearest taxis run from Calheta.

Most walkers who reach Rabaçal have their own cars, as there are no bus services to this part of Madeira. However, some walking tour operators bring walkers in by bus. A steep-sided, well-forested valley bites into the flanks of Paúl da Serra, where copious quantities of water are collected to generate electricity at Calheta. This route enjoys short walks along a couple of levadas, admiring waterfalls that look spectacular after heavy rain.

Cars must be parked around 1290m (4230ft) beside the **ER-110** road above Rabaçal, where a narrow road is closed by a barrier. Either walk down the road, or use the minibus shuttle. The road winds down round both sides of a steep-sided valley to reach isolated buildings, including the Rabaçal Nature Spot Café, around 1065m (3495ft) at **Rabaçal**. Using the minibus saves walking a total of 3.5km (2¼ miles). If walking late in the day, check the time of the last run.

Leave the buildings to follow a clear and cobbled path downhill, signposted as the PR6 trail. When the path

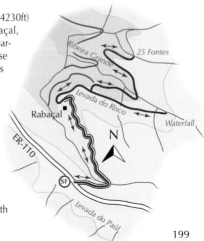

Looking down the steep and densely forested Janela valley from Rabaçal

The steep slopes are covered in contorted ancient tree heather, laurel, bilberry and broom.

levels out, keep right to pass a junction, staying on the level as signposted for Risco. The path is broad, clear and easy to follow alongside the **Levada do Risco**. ◄ There are brief glimpses down into the valley, then a bouldery patch is crossed. The path appears to narrow, but actually remains broad as far as a viewpoint with stone seating at Risco. After heavy rain the last part of the path has a waterfall spilling onto it, so use waterproofs or an umbrella. From the viewpoint a slender waterfall is seen pouring in a rock-walled amphitheatre. Further access is forbidden as the rocks are dangerously wet and slippery, so retrace your steps to the signposted path junction.

Turn right downhill as signposted for 25 Fontes. Winding steps lead down a steep and wooded slope. Turn right to follow the Levada das Vinte Cinco Fontes using a concrete path. Cross a bouldery gully and pass some pipework, then the path narrows. Walk down steps and cross a wide bridge over the bouldery **Ribeira Grande**, then climb up steps to pick up the levada again. The path loops round the valley side and is sometimes fenced. Where it runs along a buttressed wall, use the narrow levada parapet as a handrail. There are stony and uneven surfaces, so take care. ◄ Turn round a tight bend on a spur to enter a side valley. When a bouldery stream-bed is reached, leave the levada and divert upstream for a few

The tree heather is often quite dense but there are some views of the Janela valley.

paces. A rock-walled amphitheatre at **25 Fontes** drips and dribbles water, with a tall and slender waterfall pouring into a pool full of big boulders after heavy rain. There may not be as many as 25 springs here, but there are a lot!

All that remains is to retrace your steps back along the levada and climb back to the buildings at **Rabaçal**. If the narrow path is very busy, use a marked short-cut to avoid walkers still trying to reach 25 Fontes. Either walk back up the main road or use the minibus shuttle.

WALK 43
Levada do Paúl: Rabaçal to Cristo Rei

Start	ER-110 above Rabaçal
Finish	Cristo Rei statue on the ER-209 road
Distance	5.5km (3½ miles)
Total ascent	50m (165ft)
Total descent	10m (30ft)
Time	2hr
Terrain	The levada path is mostly level and easy, but narrow and stony in places.
Maps	Carta Militar 4 and 5
Refreshments	Restaurants off-route at Rabaçal and Pico da Urze.
Transport	The nearest taxis run from Calheta.

The Levada do Paúl offers a short and easy walk on the south-western fringe of the Paúl da Serra plateau. The levada can be followed easily from Rabaçal to the ER-209 road below the prominent Cristo Rei statue. This short walk can be covered in addition to Walk 42 around Rabaçal, and it is also possible to link with Walk 41 and Walk 44.

Cars must be parked at around 1290m (4230ft) beside the ER-110 road above Rabaçal. The **Levada do Paúl** lies across the main road and a little way downhill, just to the left of a small shrine. Follow the levada upstream from a reservoir. The water runs in a small concrete channel across a steep slope of grass, heather and bracken. Cross a road that climbs

Walkers enjoy a high-level stroll along the level and easy Levada do Paúl above Rabaçal

all the way from the coast at Arco da Calheta, then as the ground becomes rockier there are masses of gorse bushes. The path is uneven as it passes some small caves then there is a tight loop across a small stream at the head of the **Ribeira do Pico da Urze**.

The slope is covered in bracken while turning round a corner, then turn round another corner and cross another little stream at the head of the **Ribeira do Caldeirão**. The slope is still covered in bracken, though as it becomes more rugged it has more broom and brambles. Later, while passing a cave, there is tree heather and tall bilberry. The path swings into another little valley to cross the head of the **Ribeira do Covo**

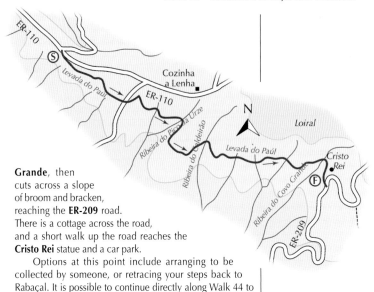

Grande, then cuts across a slope of broom and bracken, reaching the **ER-209** road. There is a cottage across the road, and a short walk up the road reaches the **Cristo Rei** statue and a car park.

Options at this point include arranging to be collected by someone, or retracing your steps back to Rabaçal. It is possible to continue directly along Walk 44 to Cascalho. Walking up the road links easily with Walk 41.

WALK 44

Levada das Rabaças and Cascalho

Start/finish	Cristo Rei statue on the ER-209 road
Distance	9km (5½ miles)
Total ascent/descent	315m (1035ft)
Time	3hr
Terrain	An easy levada path links with a track that passes through a tunnel, then is subject to rock-falls. Steps must be retraced afterwards.
Maps	Carta Militar 5
Refreshments	None closer than a restaurant at Pico da Urze.
Transport	The nearest taxis run from Calheta.

The Levada do Paúl runs fairly easily across a rugged slope. It eventually links with a track that descends steeply and passes through a tunnel. Leaving the tunnel, there are cliffs that continually shed boulders onto the track, so you must take great care. The end of the Levada das Rabaças comes very suddenly, with the water flowing through pipes suspended above an inaccessible ravine. Before 2010, it was possible to continue to Boca da Encumeada, but a landslide at Cascalho completely destroyed the levada.

Start at the **Cristo Rei** statue high on the **ER-209** road, walking down the road to find the Levada do Paúl crossing at 1310m (4300ft). Turn left and pass in front of a building to walk through a small cutting. Follow the levada upstream past heather and broom, swinging left into a little valley. The levada crosses a bracken slope and passes a solitary pine tree. Cross a cobbled road then climb alongside an inclined channel. Cross a stile over a fence on a gentle gap, then turn left into a bigger valley.

The levada leads in easy loops across a steep and rugged slope, looking down on the **Levada Seca**. There is an exposed concrete parapet, and be careful of rock leaning over the channel. The path continues as a grassy, stony or earthen line, with a few short exposed parts, crossing a steep slope. Turn right down a broad track, passing a cave carved in the pumice bedrock. Descend in loops across the steep mountainside, passing a building where there are fine views ahead. Go through a **tunnel** with an impressive amount of headroom, though it is curved and the exit isn't immediately seen. A levada channel crosses the floor, so don't step in it!

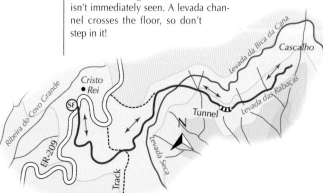

Walk down from the tunnel to pass a couple of tunnel mouths carved into the cliffs. Take great care near these cliffs, as they suffer from frequent rock-falls. The track was constructed for vehicles, but vehicles can't use it in its current state. The **Levada das Rabaças** runs downstream through an inclined channel, becoming a little exposed. The end comes suddenly, as the water is collected into four plastic pipes suspended on cables, high above a deep and rugged ravine. Look towards the head of the valley at **Cascalho** to see a raw-looking landslip and waterfalls.

The end of the line at Cascalho, where pipes carry water

It used to be possible to walk round the valley sides, following the levada path, and continue through two very long tunnels to reach Boca da Encumeada. Since the landslide, there is no way to continue around the valley, so there is no option but to retrace your steps back uphill to return to the road at **Cristo Rei**.

WALK 45
Caminho do Pináculo e Folhadal

Start/finish	Boca da Encumeada
Distance	18km (11¼ miles)
Total ascent/descent	500m (1640ft)
Time	8hr
Terrain	Two level levadas prove to be quite difficult. The lower one has a series of six tunnels (you will need a torch). A track and a rugged, densely-wooded mountain path climb to a higher levada then the descent is steep and rocky, giving way to a long road-walk.
Maps	Carta Militar 5
Refreshments	Snack Bar Restaurante Encumeada is at the start/finish.
Transport	Rodoeste buses 6 and 139 serve Boca da Encumeada from Funchal, Ribeira Brava and São Vicente.

Two remarkably different levadas can be linked on the steep north-eastern escarpment of Paúl da Serra. This route is waymarked as the PR17 trail and starts on the Boca da Encumeada. It follows the Levada do Norte through six tunnels, then climbs to the Levada da Serra, which slices across a cliff face. Even the final road-walk runs through three tunnels to return to Encumeada.

Agapanthus flanks the path and there is a fine mixture of trees and shrubs along the way, including pine, oak, laurel, heather and malfurada.

Start at the **Boca da Encumeada** beside the Snack Bar Restaurante Encumeada. Just across the road, steps lead up to the **Levada do Norte** and a sign points upstream for Folhadal. The route is waymarked as the PR17 trail and the way is easy at first. Although well-wooded, there are breaks offering views down the valley. ◀ Pass a cottage and enjoy easy loops, with a view back to Encumeada from an over-hanging rock cutting. Pico Grande and other mountains can be seen across the deep valley.

When a **tunnel** is seen to the right, reach for a torch. There is low headroom at the start, but the path is good. Later, there is more space to manoeuvre and plenty of headroom, but the path is uneven. There are drippy bits in the middle. Exit onto a good path flanked by agapanthus and hydrangea.

The steep slopes are covered in ancient, dense *laurisilva* forest supporting mosses and ferns. The path is fenced in places, looping gently round a slope with little sense of exposure and few views between the trees.

Go through a short, tall **tunnel** cut through unstable boulders; there is a slender waterfall off to the left and the surroundings are very green, moist and jungle-like. Ahead is a long **tunnel**, the entrance of which is rich with mosses. There is low headroom on entering and it is rather narrow, with an uneven path. There is more room later, with a better path, though it remains narrow. The levada is deep and wide, so don't fall into it! It is usually wet at the exit, and the levada is covered in stone slabs. Tree heather, laurel and malfurada grow along the next few easy loops and the levada is covered in places.

The next **tunnel** has low entrance, with a narrow path, though the path is mostly even and there is more room in the middle. It narrows again towards the exit, then crosses a well-wooded gully with a little waterfall to the left. Almost immediately, you will walk into another **tunnel**. There is mostly good headroom and the path is even, but some parts are a bit narrow. You will emerge on a wooded slope, then walk a short way to enter yet another **tunnel**, which is quite

The Levada das Rabaças near Boca da Encumeada

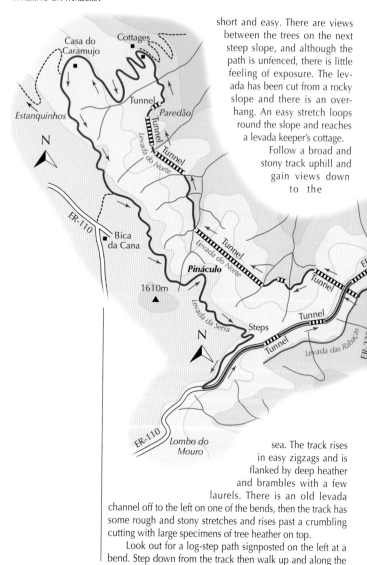

short and easy. There are views between the trees on the next steep slope, and although the path is unfenced, there is little feeling of exposure. The levada has been cut from a rocky slope and there is an overhang. An easy stretch loops round the slope and reaches a levada keeper's cottage.

Follow a broad and stony track uphill and gain views down to the

sea. The track rises in easy zigzags and is flanked by deep heather and brambles with a few laurels. There is an old levada channel off to the left on one of the bends, then the track has some rough and stony stretches and rises past a crumbling cutting with large specimens of tree heather on top.

Look out for a log-step path signposted on the left at a bend. Step down from the track then walk up and along the narrow path through dense *laurisilva* forest. There is tall tree heather, laurel, tall bilberry and bracken. The path climbs gradually and is mossy and stony, but fairly clear despite being narrow. There are some level stretches and a couple of fallen trees, as well as a short bouldery stretch. Continue climbing along the foot of some cliffs. The path is usually good, but may be very narrow where it runs through bracken, heather and bilberry, and take care if there is a crumbling earth edge. ▶ If an exit is needed, watch for a path marked for **Bica da Cana** and the main **ER-110** road. The path passes tall bilberry, crosses muddy patches, runs through heather and traverses beneath dripping cliffs.

Enjoy a view of Madeira's highest peaks from time to time.

Look ahead to see the line of the **Levada da Serra**. Turn round a steep-sided hollow to find the

narrow levada channel. Little streams and drips from the cliff are gathered and flow downstream. The path is often narrow and flanked by dense heather. There are some steep, but fenced drops, though little sense of exposure because of the vegetation. Take care where the levada path is broken, usually because of rock-falls from the cliff above.

The Levada da Serra passes the prominent domed rock tower of Pináculo before dropping to a road

The path becomes easier and there is a wide stance where a break can be taken beside the big stump of rock called **Pináculo**. Again, you can enjoy a view of the highest peaks on Madeira.

The levada suddenly runs down a steep chute. Don't follow it, but look for stone steps to descend. The flow remains vigorous and an easy path passes tall tree heather. There are a couple more steep chutes while turning a corner, then a splendid view of the peaks and valleys beyond Encumeada. ◄ Follow a narrow, well-trodden path well to the left of the levada chute. Start zigzagging down a steep and rocky slope covered in broom and heather, crossing the levada chute twice. A terrace path and a flight of steps leads along and down a cliff into tree heather. There is wonderfully mixed vegetation while crossing the levada again, now seen as a lovely little waterfall. Walk beside the channel again using a good path through dense vegetation. Cross a drippy, slippery rock lip and continue past weeping walls, then the water runs through a pipe. Take care when stepping onto a blind bend on the **ER-110** road.

Turn left to follow the road downhill from Lombo do Mouro. There is no way of avoiding the final road-walk, but maybe a motorist will offer a lift. ◄ The road runs down through **three tunnels** to return to the **Boca da Encumeada**. A café and souvenir shop offers access to a viewpoint. Turn right at a road junction to return to the Snack Bar Restaurante Encumeada and bus stops.

The road seems far below and you may wonder how to reach it.

The road is often 'closed' due to rock-falls, but motorists tend to use it regardless.

WALK 46

Levada dos Cedros: Fanal to Ribeira da Janela

Start	Vâo da Fanal
Finish	Central da Ribeira da Janela
Distance	12km (7½ miles)
Total ascent	Negligible
Total descent	1200m (3940ft)
Time	4hr 30min
Terrain	A steep, forested descent and an easy levada walk, then another steep, forested descent followed by an old road down to the coast.
Maps	Carta Militar 1
Refreshments	Bars at Ribeira da Janela.
Transport	Taxi to Fanal. Rodoeste bus 150 links Ribeira da Janela with Porto Moniz and Sâo Vicente. Rodoeste bus 139 offers an evening link to Porto Moniz, but other services pass through a tunnel.

Two waymarked paths can be joined together to provide a splendid route from high in the *laurisilva* forest at Fanal all the way down to the sea at Ribeira da Janela. Hundreds of steps lead down a steep, forested slope to the restored 17th century Levada dos Cedros. This offers easy walking to Curral Falso, where a continuation runs down to Ribeira da Janela and the coast.

This route starts very suddenly at 1200m (3940ft) beside the **ER-209** road above the **Posto Florestal Fanal**. There are no bus services and only small parking spaces beside the road, so it is best to arrive by taxi, then walk down to the coast to intercept a bus. The starting point is at **Vâo da Fanal**, where a prominent notice beside a bay tree explains about the way-marked PR14 trail, which forms the first half of the route.

Walk gently down a narrow path through forest dominated by heather trees, then drop more and more steeply down impressive flights of log steps. Cross a footbridge and walk down more steps close to a stream, crossing the course of an old levada. The path pulls away from the stream to continue its long descent, with tight zigzags appearing before

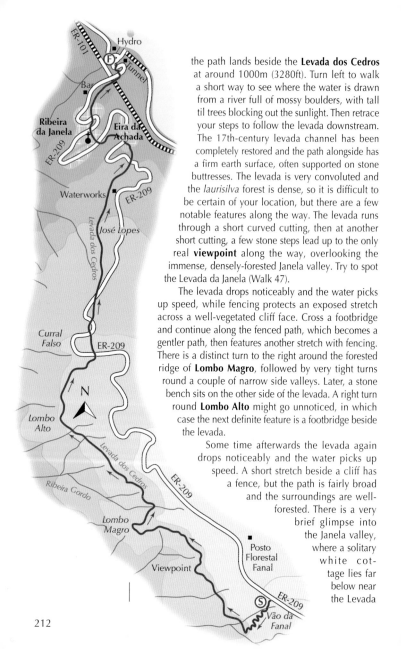

the path lands beside the **Levada dos Cedros** at around 1000m (3280ft). Turn left to walk a short way to see where the water is drawn from a river full of mossy boulders, with tall til trees blocking out the sunlight. Then retrace your steps to follow the levada downstream. The 17th-century levada channel has been completely restored and the path alongside has a firm earth surface, often supported on stone buttresses. The levada is very convoluted and the *laurisilva* forest is dense, so it is difficult to be certain of your location, but there are a few notable features along the way. The levada runs through a short curved cutting, then at another short cutting, a few stone steps lead up to the only real **viewpoint** along the way, overlooking the immense, densely-forested Janela valley. Try to spot the Levada da Janela (Walk 47).

The levada drops noticeably and the water picks up speed, while fencing protects an exposed stretch across a well-vegetated cliff face. Cross a footbridge and continue along the fenced path, which becomes a gentler path, then features another stretch with fencing. There is a distinct turn to the right around the forested ridge of **Lombo Magro**, followed by very tight turns round a couple of narrow side valleys. Later, a stone bench sits on the other side of the levada. A right turn round **Lombo Alto** might go unnoticed, in which case the next definite feature is a footbridge beside the levada.

Some time afterwards the levada again drops noticeably and the water picks up speed. A short stretch beside a cliff has a fence, but the path is fairly broad and the surroundings are well-forested. There is a very brief glimpse into the Janela valley, where a solitary white cottage lies far below near the Levada

da Janela. The path ends with stone steps dropping to the main **ER-209** road near **Curral Falso**, around 840m (2755ft). Cross the road to find a notice about the Vereda da Ribeira da Janela, designated as the PR15, to continue the walk. A good path leaves the road, with the Levada dos Cedros now on the left. The path steepens and has long flights of log steps. The water rushes downhill, but drifts away into dense *laurisilva*, and although it cannot be seen it can be heard. Beware of trailing brambles, cross the main road and use a short and direct path to cut a road bend. Cross the road again and follow a gentle track onwards. This becomes a steep path with more steps. When the road is reached yet again, turn right to walk down it, but watch for more log steps down to the left.

Follow a grassy path with rock poking through, while the levada crosses from left to right. When a track is reached at **José Lopes**, turn right, then immediately left to continue down a path. There are some log steps, but the path is mostly rugged and runs down through mixed forest dominated by tall pine and eucalyptus. When you reach a gateway in a wall, don't go through it. Turn right to follow a path downhill, which may be a bit muddy and brambly, but it gets better. Go

The Levada dos Cedros follows a very convoluted course round several ravines deep in the laurisilva

213

through a small gateway and walk down a broadening path, then turn right at a track junction among tall eucalyptus.

Follow the track almost to the levada, where there is a picnic site and **waterworks**, but turn left beforehand to continue downhill. The path uses all kinds of steps, including log steps and rough-hewn steps. ◀ Cross a track and walk down log steps in a deep cutting through crumbling ancient beds of volcanic ash. Steps finally lead down to the main **ER-209** road where there is a notice about the PR15 trail.

Cross the road and walk down a concrete road with steps down the middle, the Caminho da Terra da Fonte, leading into the hilltop village of **Eira da Achada**. Walk down round a bend on the main road to reach a bus stop, turning left down the Caminho Fundo. This road is concrete, cobbled and tarmac, leading down to the main road and another bus stop. Cross over to go down the Caminho da Voltinha, which is a steep, bendy tarmac road with steps down the middle. Cross a road halfway down it to pass a little shop/bar and reach the church in the village of **Ribeira da Janela**.

Walk down steps from the church, the Travessa da Igreja, then cross the main road to go down the Caminho do Ribeirinho, a steep concrete road with steps. Cross the main road again to walk down the Caminho dos Casais de Baixo, another steep concrete road with steps. The road becomes

There is a glimpse of a village huddled on a hill, which will be reached in due course.

The striking forms of the Ilhéus da Ribeira da Janela, seen from a bouldery beach at the mouth of the river

stone-paved and gentler, but misses the shop and Bar O Negrinho just down on the main road. ▶ The stone-paved track ends where steps lead down to the main road.

Turn right down the road for a few paces then follow the Caminho do Piquinho, which has rough steps followed by cobbles. It bends left to reach steps dropping back down onto the main road again. Pick up the continuation of the path to avoid one last bend, reaching the main road near a bridge over the Ribeira da Janela. ▶

If time can be spared, follow the road to the cobbly beach to admire the towering rock pillars of the Ilhéus da Ribeira da Janela. Another point of interest is the **Central da Ribeira da Janela hydro-electric station**, fed by water collected from the deep and densely-forested Janela valley.

Notice the heather windbreaks around tiny fruit and vegetable plots.

Bar, campsite, Rodoeste bus 150 to Porto Moniz and São Vicente.

WALK 47
Levada da Janela:
Fonte do Bispo to Porto Moniz

Start	Fonte do Bispo
Finish	Lamaceiros or Porto Moniz
Distance	14km, 17km (to the source of the levada) or 18.5km (to Porto Moniz) (8¾, 10½ or 11½ miles)
Total ascent	15m (50ft)
Total descent	850m (2790ft) or 1250m (4100ft)
Time	7hr, 8hr or 9hr 30min
Terrain	The descent is on a stony or grassy track and a steep and crumbling path. The levada goes through eight tunnels, including a very long and wet one, and a torch is required. Some parts of the path are exposed, but the slopes are mostly well-forested.
Maps	Carta Militar 1
Refreshments	Small bar at Lamaceiros. Plenty of choice at Porto Moniz.
Transport	Taxi to Fonte do Bispo. Rodoeste bus 80 from Porto Moniz to Ponta do Pargo, Ribeira Brava and Funchal. Rodoeste bus 139 from Porto Moniz to São Vicente, Ribeira Brava and Funchal. Rodoeste bus 150 from Porto Moniz to São Vicente.

This interesting and exciting levada is absent from many maps. It draws water from a deep, forested valley to feed a hydro-electric station. A taxi is required to Fonte do Bispo, where a steep track and path drop to the levada. There is an option to walk to the source, otherwise head downstream through eight tunnels to Lamaceiros. Another extension allows for a descent to Porto Moniz.

Start high on the ER-110 road at **Fonte do Bispo**, where there is a signpost at 1230m (4035ft) pointing along a grassy track for Galhano. The track rises slightly from a barrier gate then descends through chained gateposts and is stony as it winds downhill, with rough concrete strips. Cross a cattle grid and pass plenty of tree heather, laurel and tall bilberry, with some broom and candleberry.

There is good shade and occasional views across to Fanal on the far side of the valley (Walk 46).

◀ Pass **Colmeias** and walk down past tall, dense til trees where it is quite dark at times. Emerge at a small rock cutting and a little wooden **hut**. A narrow path runs behind the hut, dropping steeply and stonily, with an open stretch subject to landslips. Cross a small concrete footbridge over a rocky gorge then pick a way across the base of a cliff, rising gently. Walk downhill again on battered wooden steps. There are a few more substantial concrete and stone steps later, then a final series of steps lead down to the **Levada da Janela**, around 420m (1380ft). ◀

An optional detour is possible here, but consider the time.

Detour to the source of the levada

A sign reading 'Origem Levada 3km' is a bit misleading. It is actually 3km (2 miles) to the source of the levada and back to this point. To make the detour, head upstream round a corner to pass a **levada keeper's cottage**. The winding levada is occasionally fenced, then covered in slabs, reaching a **tunnel**. It is a bit drippy inside, but the path and headroom are mostly good. Emerge from the tunnel and later cross an exposed wall to reach the source of the levada in the broad and bouldery bed of the **Ribeira da Janela**. Retrace your steps back through the tunnel and past the levada keeper's cottage to continue with the main route.

Enter a long **tunnel** that has good headroom and a good path, though the path slopes awkwardly towards the water. Exit into a deep, rocky, wooded gorge then enter the next

tunnel. This is a longer one, measuring 1.2km (¾ mile). There is good headroom for the most part but the path is narrow at the start. The path widens but is uneven and bouldery in places. ▶ A much better path leads out in a wooded side-valley, where the levada goes through a rock arch and continues with an overhanging lip where it has been cut from a rock-face. Note the lovely ferns alongside on leaving the valley, and swing round into another side-valley. Cross the **Ribeira do Bonito** and notice the coverings over the levada to catch landslip debris. There is a tremendous view through the main, densely-forested Janela valley, taking in the riverbed, steep slopes and thick beds of volcanic boulders.

Go through a short **tunnel**. There are a couple of squeezes, but otherwise no problems.

There are constant showers from cracks in the roof, and a vicious 'power shower' from a crack in the rock wall to the right. Wear waterproofs or get very wet!

Map continues on page 218

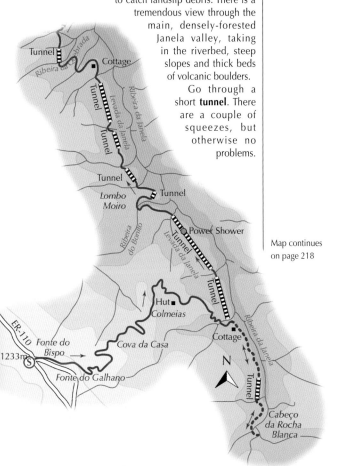

217

Curve round a rock wall and enter a longer **tunnel**, with low headroom in places and a narrow path. Exit and continue along a broad path, which narrows and leads into another little side-valley. A narrow levada path leads out of the valley and it is partly fenced as it crosses a wooded, rocky slope high above the **Ribeira da Janela**. There are splendid valley views and an easy stretch of path, then another short **tunnel**. This one has a low entry and exit, but good headroom in between. The path inside is good, but narrow. Walk a short way across a slope to reach the next **tunnel**, which is longer. It has good headroom most of the time, but beware of projecting rock. The path can be narrow but is mostly good. Emerge in a tight little side-valley with plenty of ferns, and leave by following a narrow, fenced path. The woodlands are laurisilva but the levada has a border of hydrangeas. Swing round into the main Janela valley again and pass a **levada keeper's cottage**.

Walk round into another side-valley, passing a dripping cliff covered in ferns, mosses and liverworts. Leave this valley and turn round into the next little valley, where the levada is covered with concrete slabs. There are awesome rock walls on both sides and no room for a path beside the levada. Enter the **penultimate tunnel**, where there is good headroom and a good path, but puddles in the middle. Swing to the right to eave, ready for low headroom and lots of drips. There is a **waterfall** outside, so use stepping stones on the levada and go through a shelter to avoid the water. The path is fenced round a sheer-sided valley head then goes through the final **tunnel**, which is a bit wet and muddy, has a good path, but is narrow and has low headroom in places. The levada swings left at

Ilhéu Mole

PORTO MONIZ

ATLANTIC OCEAN

ER-101

Ladeira

Miradouro do Redondo

Lamaceiros
Bar

Reservoir

N

Viewpoint

Achada da Fonte Vermelha

Winch huts

Ribeira da Janela

Ribeira da Janela

Ribeira da Lova Negra

Tunnel
Waterfall

Tunnel

Cottage

Ribeira da Cobrada

Emerge from a tunnel to pass beneath a tin shelter where a waterfall pours down before the final tunnel

the end while walkers exit separately. Enter a tight, ferny, wooded side-valley and follow the levada onwards.

The path is mostly fenced leaving the side-valley, then it swings round to overlook the main Janela valley. Enter a much more densely-wooded side-valley and, leaving this, walk round into a wet and dripping side-valley, crossing its bouldery head before leaving. There is a rock cutting to walk through while returning to the main valley, where a couple of small **concrete winch huts** are passed. The levada has no fencing, but isn't particularly exposed either. The levada

219

An easy stretch of the Levada da Janela is followed before a road is joined near Lamaceiros

An easy stretch of the Levada da Janela is followed before a road is joined near Lamaceiros

widens into a deep trough and there is a sudden mixture of trees and shrubs, including hydrangeas and apples. Pass a concrete overspill and walk back among dense laurel, then pass another viewpoint with a picnic bench. Tall pine and eucalyptus stand above the levada, then there is a water intake before reaching a road.

Either follow the road straight away, or follow the levada as it turns a loop to pass a circular reservoir in an attractively-planted area before joining the road. The road runs up to a junction where a right turn leads down into **Lamaceiros**. ◀

Shop/bar, bus, with taxis only a phone-call away in Porto Moniz.

Extension to Porto Moniz

To extend the walk a little further, it is possible to walk down to Porto Moniz. Simply head straight through a crossroads along the Caminho do Lombinho, then turn right along the Caminho da Assomada. Walk straight ahead and go steeply down the Caminho da Ladeira. This road is bendy as it passes the **Miradouro do Redondo**, where there are splendid aerial views of Porto Moniz. Continue the very steep descent to **Ladeira** ending on tarmac. Turn right down the main ER-101 road through the upper part of **Porto Moniz**, and continue down to the rocky coast.

PORTO MONIZ

This isolated resort is best explored by staying for a couple of nights. It is relatively modern, with the older parts of town clinging to a steep slope above. Signs for 'piscinas naturais' lead to rock-walled swimming pools kept topped-up with water when waves break over them. An aquarium allows the sea-life to be studied while the interesting Centro Ciência Viva (tel 291–854274, www.porto-moniz.pt) is themed around the *laurisilva* for which Madeira is famous. There are banks with ATMs, hotels, bars, restaurants, a post office, buses, taxis and a Tourist Information Centre (tel 291–853075).

Looking down on Porto Moniz from Miradouro do Redondo

Walk 47 → Tornadouro

Walk 48
Walk 49
Walk 50
Walk 51
Walk 52
Walk 53
Walk 54
Walk 55
Walk 56
Walk 57

Achadas da Cruz

Cabo

Ponta do Pargo

Walk 50

Lombo

Walk 48

Walk 51

Fajã da Ovelha

Raposeira

ER-223

Paúl do Mar

Prazéres

Walk 52

Jardim do Mar

Estreito da Calheta

Calheta

Madalena do Mar

PONTA DO SOL

Fonte do Bispo →

Walk 47

ER-110

N

0   5 km

0   3 miles

SECTION 6 -
WESTERN MADEIRA -
Walks 48 to 57

ER-210

Walk 53

ER-211

Walk 42, 43 →

Walk 41, 42, 43 →

Lombo dos Faias

Walk 41, 43, 4 →

ER-222

Carvalhal

ER-101

Walk 49

6 WESTERN MADEIRA

Following the levada through gentle country to Raposeira (Walk 51)

The western coast of Madeira is steep and rugged, though from time to time there is access to the shore, where a handful of little villages are located. At a higher level there are well-cultivated slopes and forested valleys, with small farmsteads dotted everywhere. Few tourists explored the area until recently, as the convoluted roads and sparse bus services meant that a lot of time was spent travelling. New roads and tunnels have been built and the Rodoeste bus company has increased its services.

This well-cultivated area needs plenty of water, so there are lengthy levada walks available. Villages along the way have accommodation so there is an opportunity to enjoy long-distance levada walks, simply breaking the journey with minimal fuss and continuing walking the following day. The Levada do Moinho above Porto Moniz is easily linked with the lengthy, looping Levada da Calheta – Ponta do Pargo, and once this has been followed all the way to Ponta do Sol, walkers can climb to pick up the course of the Levada Nova, with a view to reaching Ribeira Brava.

Both Ribeira Brava and Ponta do Sol have a good range of services and provide a choice of accommodation options, while Rodoeste buses head westwards to other villages that lie on or near the walking routes. While there are no direct links with walking routes high above on Paúl da Serra, there are steep and winding roads that allow cars and taxis to reach the high plateau.

Adventurous long-distance walkers could proceed beyond Ribeira Brava and simply keep linking routes end-to-end to continue through the middle of Madeira, passing Funchal to reach the eastern parts of the island. Creating long-distance walks from simple day walks is just a

Long flights of steep, 'rolled', cobbled steps drop down to the coast at Paúl do Mar (Walk 52)

matter of studying the maps and looking for links, then checking whether there is accommodation, or buses off-route, along the way.

WALK 48

Ponta do Pargo to Fonte do Bispo

Start	Farol de Ponta do Pargo
Finish	Fonte do Bispo
Distance	10.5km (6½ miles)
Total ascent	1210m (3970ft)
Total descent	10m (30ft)
Time	3hr 30min
Terrain	Quiet roads and clear tracks climb from cultivated slopes to forested slopes, ending on a high moorland road.
Maps	Carta Militar 1
Refreshments	Bars at Ponta do Pargo.
Transport	Rodoeste bus 142 serves Ponta da Pargo from Funchal and Ribeira Brava. Rodoeste bus 80 also serves Ponta do Pargo from Porto Moniz. No transport from Fonte do Bispo.

The red and white lighthouse, or 'farol', at Ponta do Pargo stands on 300m (1000ft) high cliffs at the extreme western end of Madeira. There is accommodation nearby at the Residencial O Farol. A fairly easy walk follows roads up through the village of Ponta do Pargo, where tracks continue up through forest to reach heathery heights around Fonte do Bispo. Of course, the walk finishes in the middle of nowhere and a pick-up needs to be arranged, but it is no hardship to walk back down.

The road serving the lighthouse emerges from a tunnel and ends abruptly at a clifftop viewpoint. Follow a dirt road uphill to reach another clifftop viewpoint at **O Fío**. Enjoy coastal views then follow the road uphill and inland, climbing to the church in the village of **Ponta do Pargo**. ▸

Here you'll find banks with ATMs, a post office, bars, shops and buses.

Either follow the road uphill from the church, or use the narrower Travessa da Eira Velha running parallel. Pass the Bar Girasol. Go straight through a crossroads on the main ER-101 road, around 500m (1640ft). ▸ Follow a road uphill, swinging right and left to climb past houses on the way out of the village. Pass the tall wall surrounding **Quinta da Serra**

The crossroads offers an alternative starting point.

and continue uphill from a junction, on slope of burnt pines, to reach a **waterworks**.

The road swings right and a concrete road on the left crosses the Levada da Calheta – Ponta do Pargo. ◀ Turn right to follow it, crossing little cattle grids to enter and leave a field. Turn left up a concrete road, the Caminho da Corujeira, and continue up a clear, sunken track on a slope of pine and eucalyptus, where bracken and gorse form the undergrowth.

Another track rises from the left, but keep climbing and avoid lesser tracks, sometimes passing through deep clay cuttings. One of the cuttings has hollowed-out caves to the left. There is a small levada to the left and a cattle grid is crossed at a fork. Keep right, climbing among tall pines with plenty of clearance between them. Other tracks converge on the main track, then cross a hump and descend a little. Keep left to climb again, always following the broadest and clearest track uphill. Tree cover is sparse and eventually peters out on extensive slopes of bracken. The summit to the left is the **Alto da Ponta do Pargo**, rising to 998m (3274ft).

Cattle and goats may be noticed grazing grass among the bracken. The track levels out and swings to the right onto the other side of a valley, even descending slightly. Tall heather, bilberry and gorse grow in places. The

The entire levada is followed on Walks 50, 51, 53 and 54.

track makes a wide loop to the left as it climbs, and at least part of this can be short-cut if the opportunity to do so is spotted. Cross broken rock at a higher level where bracken gives way to clumps of heather. The track undulates gently, with tall heather alongside, then there is a final pull, keeping left at a fork, up a grassy track to the ER-110 road near **Fonte do Bispo**.

There is a road junction at 1233m (4045ft) signed for Fonte do Bispo, Prazéres, Paúl da Serra, Canhas and Porto Moniz. Arrange to be collected here or, if this is not possible, it is quick and easy to walk back down to Ponta do Pargo; just take care to reverse the route exactly and avoid being drawn down the wrong tracks. Very strong walkers could continue from this high road and walk down to Porto Moniz via the Levada da Janela (Walk 47).

Steep forested slopes give way to gentler high moorland slopes as the track passes Alto da Ponta do Pargo

WALK 49
Levada do Moinho: Tornadouro to Ribeira da Cruz

Start	Tornadouro
Finish	ER-101 at Ribeira da Cruz
Distance	10.5km (6½ miles)
Total ascent	400m (1310ft)
Total descent	130m (425ft)
Time	3hr 30min or 4hr
Terrain	The levada path is narrow at first, though broader paths and tracks are used later. Cultivated slopes give way to forested slopes and areas of laurisilva.
Maps	Carta Militar 1
Refreshments	Shop/bar off-route at Pinheiro.
Transport	Rodoeste bus 150 serves Levada Grande from Porto Moniz and São Vicente. Rodoeste bus 80 serves Achadas da Cruz and Porto Moniz from Ribeira Brava and Ponta do Pargo.

The Levada do Moinho is a rough and ready watercourse. It wasn't a state-sponsored enterprise but was cut by people in the far north-west of Madeira. The name 'moinho' refers to watermills and some ruined examples can be seen as the water is followed upstream from Tornadouro to its source in the Ribeira da Cruz. Study bus timetables carefully to catch a bus at the end.

Tournadouro lies above the main **ER-101** road at **Levada Grande**, reached by firstly following signposts for the Levada da Ribeira da Janela, then watching for a notice about the **Levada do Moinho** beside the road. The levada is waymarked as the PR7 trail and starts by climbing 25 fenced steps. The channel is followed upstream and it is quite narrow as it crosses a road. The path leads onwards to a water store. Turn left to continue upstream, passing cultivated plots and crossing a concrete road. After a very short stretch of path, turn left along a road, with the levada running alongside.

Turn left to leave the road and continue along levada path. There is a steep climb beside the channel, or nearby steps could be used instead. Continue upstream and turn right at a junction of levadas, heading gradually up among eucalyptus. Cross a concrete road below a few houses while crossing small fields. Later, go up log and stone steps on a steeply inclined stretch of the levada, continuing a little less steeply upstream.

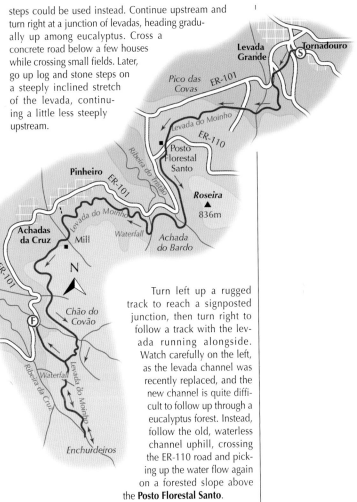

Turn left up a rugged track to reach a signposted junction, then turn right to follow a track with the levada running alongside. Watch carefully on the left, as the levada channel was recently replaced, and the new channel is quite difficult to follow up through a eucalyptus forest. Instead, follow the old, waterless channel uphill, crossing the ER-110 road and picking up the water flow again on a forested slope above the **Posto Florestal Santo**.

Follow the levada further upstream. The path enters woodland and is fenced where it crosses a steep wooded slope above the main ER-101 road. Climb a flight of 38 stone steps beside an inclined channel on a slope of *laurisilva*

Stone steps beside the levada above Posto Florestal Santo

Note the Ribeira do Tristão feeding into the levada.

There is a brief glimpse down to Pinheiro, where there is a shop/bar and bus stops.

forest. Squeeze past a dark, dripping cliff and turn round the head of a fern-hung valley. ◄ The water channel is cut through rock in dark *laurisilva* forest, then is fenced where it makes a very tight turn round a gully to pass a **waterfall** and a pool. Walk gently up through the *laurisilva* and emerge on a slope where pine and eucalyptus have been felled. Climb log steps and continue through the remaining forest. Concrete steps are reached where bamboo grows beside the path. ◄

Pass dense bamboo and head back into mixed woodland, turning round a side-valley. There is a small gate and a ruined levada-powered **mill**. Climb log steps and turn left, then go up more log steps on the left to follow the levada up a steep incline where the water flows fast and furious. A gentler path runs onwards from a concrete tank. Cross a slope of gorse then cross a dirt road and continue past burnt pine trees. The levada crosses a slope of gorse and bracken, then continues through *laurisilva*. Pass in and out of small valleys, later reaching a valley where the levada draws water directly from a river at **Chão do Covão**.

Cross the dry riverbed and follow a path up several flights of log steps on a steep, wooded slope. Pass a signposted junction and follow the levada upstream to another signposted path junction. If time is pressing, turn right downhill to finish early. Otherwise, turn left to follow the levada to its source, bearing in mind that you'll need to retrace your steps later. ▶ A pleasant **waterfall** can be seen in one little side-valley, with a smaller one in the next. Continue onwards to pass a dripping cliff, reaching a gorge deep in the *laurisilva* to find the source of the levada, where care needs to be taken on a narrow, mossy parapet. A little waterfall splashes into a pool in the **Ribeira da Cruz**.

Retrace your steps to the path junction and turn left downhill. Pass heather trees and other trees then go down flights of log steps. A final flight of log steps leads down to a road bend near a little river on the **ER-101** road.

There is a view across a forested valley, then eucalyptus, then dense laurisilva.

An open stretch of the levada passes gorse bushes

If catching a the Rodoeste 80 bus at this point, be on the road in good time and find a place where the driver can see you. Alternatively, turn right to follow the road another 2km (1¼ miles) to Achadas da Cruz. For a longer walk, turn left to follow the road for another 3km (2 miles) to reach the start of Walk 50.

WALK 50
Levada da Calheta – Ponta do Pargo to Ponta do Pargo

Start	Rua da Capela, Cabo
Finish	Ponta do Pargo
Distance	10km (6¼ miles)
Total ascent	Negligible
Total descent	150m (490ft)
Time	4hr
Terrain	The levada path runs level, mostly across steep forested slopes, but also open slopes. A road leads down through cultivated country at the end.
Maps	Carta Militar 1
Refreshments	Restaurant off-route at Lombada Velha. Bars at Ponta do Pargo.
Transport	Rodoeste bus 80 serves Ponta do Pargo and Cabo from Funchal, Ribeira Brava and Porto Moniz. Rodoeste bus 142 serves Ponta do Pargo from Funchal and Ribeira Brava.

The Levada da Calheta – Ponta do Pargo is one of the longest levadas in Madeira. It can be followed on a very gradual gradient for more than 60km (37 miles). This is more than most walkers cover in a day and as facilities are often sparse, it is best to walk the levada in stages. Starting above Cabo, a very convoluted route can be followed towards Ponta do Pargo.

Start above the village of **Cabo** at the junction of the main ER-101 road and the minor Rua da Capela, around 650m (2130ft). Walk down the minor road and turn left as signposted opposite a rectangular concrete reservoir. The narrow concrete **Levada da Calheta – Ponta do Pargo** is fringed with agapanthus on a gentle slope of tall pines and eucalyptus. The path winds gently and crosses the main **ER-101** road soon after starting. The levada pulls gradually away from the road, turning as it crosses the **Ribeira da Veste** using a footbridge. A grassy track is crossed above Lombada Velha as the levada swings round into another little valley and crosses a dirt road above **Ribeira da Vaca**. ▸

Curve round **Vale Seco** then head round into the next valley. The **Ribeira da Vaca** and a tributary are crossed by making tight turns at the valley head, crossing an overspill. Leave the valley and go through a little cutting on the way into the next valley, drained by the **Ribeiro do Pó Branco**. ▸ Swing round from the valley to cross a footbridge over a track in a deep cutting, passing a circular water store above Serrado. The levada continues, flowing beneath two dirt roads, passing burnt pines and bracken. Turn left into a large valley with steep slopes of bracken and a few burnt pines. Penetrate to the wooded valley head, crossing stepping blocks in one steep-sided ravine and crossing a river overspill in another.

Head out of the ravine but soon swing left into another one, passing eucalyptus and crossing a footbridge over a ravine above a waterfall on the Ribeira dos Moinhos. Continue across a slope of pines and later turn left past a small white building. Head round into another little side-valley to cross another footbridge. Walk out of the valley, turning left, and watch out for a path

Restaurante A Carreta on the main road.

There is plenty of forest below, but the higher slopes have been burnt and have fewer trees.

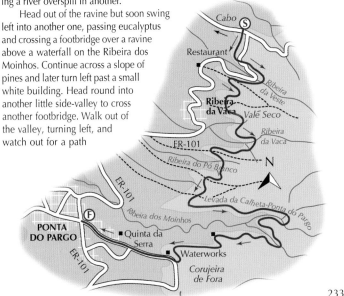

233

A tight bend on the Levada da Calheta – Ponta do Pargo

Accommodation, banks with ATMs, a post office, bars, shops and buses.

on the right down through eucalyptus. This can be followed down to a road junction. If it isn't spotted, the levada passes a keeper's cottage above a **waterworks**. Turn right afterwards to walk down a concrete road to a tarmac road. Turn right to follow the road down to a junction and keep right to pass a tall wall surrounding **Quinta da Serra**. Walk down to the main **ER-101** road in **Ponta do Pargo**, around 500m (1640ft). ◄

WALK 51

Levada da Calheta – Ponta do Pargo to Prazéres

Start	Ponta do Pargo
Finish	Prazéres
Distance	19km (11¾ miles)
Total ascent	140m (460ft)
Total descent	30m (100ft)
Time	6hr 30min
Terrain	The initial ascent is by road, then the levada path is level and easy, crossing cultivated slopes, passing villages and turning round well-wooded valleys.
Maps	Carta Militar 1 and 4
Refreshments	Bars and/or restaurants at Ponta do Pargo, Lombada dos Marinheiros, Lombada dos Cedros, Raposeira, Maloeira and Prazéres.
Transport	Rodoeste bus 80 serves Ponta do Pargo from Funchal, Ribeira Brava and Porto Moniz. Rodoeste bus 142 serves Ponta do Pargo from Funchal and Ribeira Brava. Rodoeste buses 80, 142 and 107 serve Prazéres from Funchal and Ribeira Brava.

The Levada da Calheta – Ponta do Pargo is incredibly convoluted as it contours at a general level of 640m (2100ft) between Ponta do Pargo and Prazéres. It passes through a number of charming little villages where occasional shops and bars are located. Bus services enable the walk to be broken into even shorter sections, while Ponta do Pargo and Prazéres offer accommodation.

Leave **Ponta do Pargo** from a well-signposted crossroads around 500m (1640ft). Follow a minor road signposted 'levada' uphill, swinging right and left to climb past houses on the way out of the village. Pass the tall wall surrounding Quinta da Serra and continue uphill from a junction, on slope of tall pines, to reach a waterworks. The road swings right and a concrete road on the left reaches the **Levada da Calheta – Ponta do Pargo** at 630m (2065ft).

Turn right to follow it, crossing a step-footbridge, walking parallel to the road, then crossing a concrete road at **Lombadinha**. Cross a cultivated slope to go through a tiny rock cutting, reaching a slope of oak, pine and apple while turning round two little valley heads, passing an overspill. Cross a slope of pines, while bracken, brambles and a few hydrangeas grow beside the levada. Cross a track when leaving the valley then cross a road above the village of **Amparo**.

Pass fruit and vegetable plots and cross another slope of pine, as well as oak, chestnut and apple. Pass a house called Casinha do Amparo, then turn round a valley drained by the **Ribeira dos Câmbios** and follow part of a track beside the levada. Turn round into the next little valley, which has a few charred pines and bracken on one side, while the other side bears eucalyptus. Pass a few chestnuts when leaving the valley. The levada is covered as it passes buildings at **Lombo** and crosses a narrow road. Go through a short, narrow cutting and

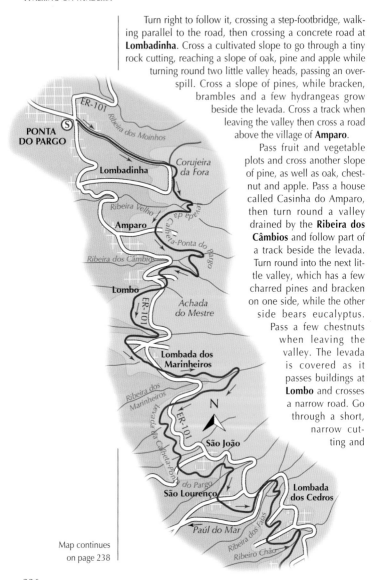

Map continues on page 238

The levada crosses a steep slope on its way to São João

pass some ruins. A picnic site is passed before crossing the **ER-101** road. ▶

A grassy track crosses the levada where the path is flanked by agapanthus and apples. Cross another grassy track and note the view back to the lighthouse at Ponta do Pargo. The next slope has pine and chestnut dotted across it. Turn round a valley, crossing an overspill below a bend on the ER-101 road. There are mixed woods for a short way, then cross a concrete road and swing round a cultivated spur. Go up a concrete road and down a few steps to pass Madeira Native Motion, which offers accommodation and outdoor activities. Turn round a corner along a concrete path. Follow

Tall pine, eucalyptus and bracken grow on the slope.

an earth path across a cultivated slope then the levada is partly covered until it reaches a narrow concrete road. Either walk up to the **Lombada dos Marinheiros**, for a shop and the Bar os Marinheiros, or walk straight across the ER-101 road below the village. ◀ The levada crosses a slope to reach higher, wooded parts of the valley to cross a footbridge over a waterfall on the **Ribeira dos Marinheiros**. Leave the valley and cross the ER-101 road, then the levada is stoutly buttressed. Little loops cross a slope, passing a few tall pines and odd chestnuts before crossing a concrete track. A steep and narrow road is crossed at Casa da Levada, between **São João** and Fajã da Ovelha.

Cross a cultivated slope then climb steps to a concrete road. Walk down a little, then pass a gateway at a house called Golina da Fajã to regain the levada. Cultivated slopes give way to pines round a twin valley head, where the Ribeira de São João is crossed. Cross a slope of bracken and pine to leave the valley and pass houses at **São Lourenço**.

Cross a tarmac road, go through a little cutting, cross a concrete road and pass a water regulator. Follow a wider, deeper stretch of the levada round into the next valley crossing a slope of charred pines. Cross a road that serves **Paúl do Mar** near an unfinished tunnel, and walk up the road a short distance to regain the levada.

It is wooded while walking past **Ribeira das Faias**. The main ER-101 road lies just above while passing small vegetable plots and a few

There is a viewpoint beside the road, looking down the deep Marinheiros valley.

238

trees. ▶ Cross a concrete track and swing round into the next small valley to pass an overspill. Pass a house and reach a tarmac road, turning left uphill then right down steps to regain the levada. Pass well-cultivated terraces and turn round the head of another valley, passing a few tall pines and crossing an overspill on the **Ribeiro Chão**. Leave the valley and swing round a slope to follow a concrete path past fruit and vegetable plots. Cross a concrete road to follow a concrete path to a road and a shop/bar. Turn right, then left to find the levada. The path is tightly enclosed to the next tarmac road and a school at **Raposeira**. ▶ The levada is covered where it leaves the road, then it flows over the top of a main road **tunnel** as it curves round a slope below the church. Agapanthus grows beside the path and mixed woods begin while crossing a road. A wonderful mixture of trees and shrubs are passed on the way round a little valley, crossing a tiny footbridge. On the way to the next little valley tall pines dominate. Cross the **Ribeira da Cova** using a footbridge and follow the path onwards. Cross a minor road above the main road and pass houses at **Maloeira**. ▶ Cross another road and walk past more buildings. Turn into the next valley at Poço Grande, where there are tall pines above. Cross another two footbridges then pass a few chestnut on the way

Shop/bar in Lombada dos Cedros.

Bar Gomes is up this road.

Restaurante Solar da Maloeira is far uphill, and Snack Bar Moinho is nearby downhill.

A well-wooded stretch of the levada near Prazéres

out of the valley. Agapanthus lines the path the whole way round. Cross a tarmac road close to the main road and a bus shelter at **Lombo do Coelho**. Make a tight turn around a little valley full of chestnut, laurel and brambles then follow the levada into another valley full of tall pine, chestnut and bay trees, crossing the Ribeira Seca. There is a greasy overspill, so cross the narrow river just upstream. The levada leads to a road and runs underground at Lombo da Velha.

Walk straight through a crossroads to continue along the road and the levada is seen heading off to the left. Pass vegetable plots and cross an overspill in a valley full of burnt pines. Leave the valley to follow the path past a water regulator where the levada is broader and deeper. A road and the Posto Florestal Prazéres are reached soon afterwards. Turn right down the road to reach a crossroads at the village of **Prazéres**. ◀

Here you will find accommodation, bars, restaurants, buses and a link with Walk 52.

WALK 52

Caminho Real: Prazéres to Paúl do Mar

Start	Prazéres
Finish	Paúl do Mar
Distance	3.5km (2¼ miles)
Total ascent	Negligible
Total descent	640m (2100ft)
Time	1hr 30min
Terrain	A road-walk is followed by steep, cobbled, zigzag steps down into a canyon-like valley to reach the coast.
Maps	Carta Militar 4
Refreshments	Bars and restaurants at Prazéres and Paúl do Mar.
Transport	Rodoeste bus 80 serves Prazéres from Funchal, Ribeira Brava and Porto Moniz. Rodoeste bus 142 serves Prazéres from Funchal and Ribeira Brava. Rodoeste 107 serves Prazéres from Funchal, Ribeira Brava and Raposeira. Rodoeste buses 107 and 115 link Paúl do Mar with Ribeira Brava and Funchal.

A caminho real is literally a 'royal road' and is generally used to describe a route built by the state or a municipal authority. The old cobbled road between Prazéres and Paúl do Mar links two remarkably different villages, one high up surrounded by agricultural acres, the other squeezed between cliffs and the sea. The route is one-way downhill. The challenge is to climb back up again!

Leave **Prazéres** and its striking church by following the Caminho Lombo da Rocha. This runs gently downhill and keeps to the right at junctions with other roads (bars, restaurants and an ATM along the way). The road leads to the Hotel Jardim Atlantico and its little supermarket. ▶ There is a notice for the Caminho Real do Paúl do Mar, or the PR19 trail. Follow a tarmac road downhill and turn right down a flight of concrete steps between apartments to reach a viewpoint overlooking **Jardim do Mar** and **Paúl do Mar**.

Walk down steep cobbled steps with a view across a deep-cut valley to Raposeira, passing an odd fig tree and prickly pears. The path curves left and an old 'danger' sign might be noticed at some stout pines. There is a danger of rockfall, but the path is often fenced where it crosses steep and rocky slopes. Zigzag down the 'rolled' cobbled steps to outflank cliff faces and avoid tangled undergrowth, noting spurges, malfurada and brambles. Cross a concrete bridge and continue down stone steps. Later, when the zigzags are steep and tightly convoluted, hacked from crumbling pumice, look for waterfalls spilling down through the valley, especially after heavy rain.

Cross a bridge spanning the **Ribeira Seca** in a gorge. The path is level then drops again, turning right and

An additional experience is available here, known as the 'Barefoot Walk', walking barefoot across a variety of textured materials. Contact the hotel reception for details.

Waterfalls spill into a precipitous gorge all the way down to the sea at Pául do Mar

Bars, restaurants and limited bus services.

clinging to a crumbling cliff overlooking a concrete-walled harbour. The path swings left and drops steeply to a notice about the PR19 trail. Visit the harbour and admire a waterfall spilling onto the beach, then walk into **Paúl do Mar**. ◄ If a bus isn't available, then either call for a taxi or climb back uphill to Prazéres, which could take twice as long as the descent!

WALK 53

Levada da Calheta – Ponta do Pargo to Lombo dos Faias

Start	Prazéres
Finish	Lombo dos Faias, Calheta
Distance	18km (11¼ miles)
Total ascent	15m (50ft)
Total descent	190m (625ft)
Time	6hr
Terrain	The levada path is level, easy and convoluted as it crosses open slopes and several wooded valleys. The final descent is by road.
Maps	Carta Militar 4
Refreshments	Bars and restaurants at Prazéres.
Transport	Rodoeste bus 80 serves Prazéres from Porto Moniz, Ribeira Brava and Funchal. Rodoeste bus 142 serves Prazéres from Funchal and Ribeira Brava. Rodoeste 107 serves Prazéres from Funchal, Ribeira Brava and Raposeira. All of these are available at the end of the walk.

This stretch of the Levada da Calheta – Ponta do Pargo is surprisingly distant from habitations. Few buildings are passed but there are often views down onto well-settled slopes around Calheta. The levada crosses some open slopes and enters several well-wooded valleys. After passing the Central da Calheta generating station the watercourse becomes the Levada da Calheta – Ponta do Sol. A road is used to reach a bus route.

Start at a crossroads in the village of **Prazéres** and walk up the road signposted for Paúl da Serra to reach the Posto Florestal Prazéres. Turn right to follow the **Levada da Calheta – Ponta do Pargo**, at a general level of 640m (2100ft), away from the village. Agapanthus and hydrangeas line the path on a slope of pines. There is also oak, laurel and eucalyptus, with a brambly ground cover.

*Water is regulated at
a cottage near Lombo
da Ribeira Funda*

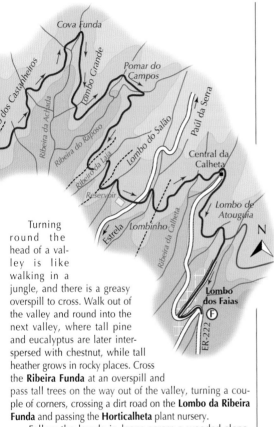

Turning round the head of a valley is like walking in a jungle, and there is a greasy overspill to cross. Walk out of the valley and round into the next valley, where tall pine and eucalyptus are later interspersed with chestnut, while tall heather grows in rocky places. Cross the **Ribeira Funda** at an overspill and pass tall trees on the way out of the valley, turning a couple of corners, crossing a dirt road on the **Lombo da Ribeira Funda** and passing the **Horticalheta** plant nursery.

Follow the levada in loops across a wooded slope, crossing an overspill, then pass a waterworks. The channel is briefly covered at a levada keeper's cottage, then it becomes wider and deeper further upstream. Pass pine and eucalyptus then cross an overspill and a dirt road. Use a footbridge to cross a small ravine. Pass some fenced fruit plots followed by tall pine and eucalyptus. The levada continues making loops, passing a couple of overspills. There is a short, narrow cutting and you will cross a dirt road. ▶ Cross another dirt road on the **Lombo dos Castanheiros** and swing round into a

Old terraces lie below the levada and the grass beneath the trees is used for grazing.

245

big valley. Views down the lower slopes take in hundreds of houses sprawling around Calheta.

After entering the valley, pass an overhang and an overspill, then turn a corner to pass a small tin hut. ◄ The path narrows so take care, later turning round the head of the valley, where the **Ribeira da Achada** has a rocky bed and a big overspill. There is a mixture of laurel, tree heather and candleberry, giving way to eucalyptus and tall pine. The path narrows on a steep and rocky slope but it isn't too exposed. There is a pronounced turn round the **Lombo Grande** into the next valley. Pass another tin hut among some burnt trees, while a little side-valley features tufts of heather. Continue past a fine variety of trees and shrubs, turning round the head of the valley to cross an overspill, followed by another one on the **Ribeira do Raposo**.

There is yet another tin hut beside the levada on the way out of the valley. ◄ The levada swings out of the valley, passing signs for Lombo Estrela and Lombo Salão on a dirt road. Go through a little cutting and stay among tall trees. Walk round a couple of smaller valleys, crossing a dirt road between them, then pass a concrete reservoir. Follow

Watch for laurel among the eucalyptus and pine.

Eucalyptus is dominant at first followed by tall pine.

The Levada da Calheta – Ponta do Pargo is broad and deep as it is followed towards the Central da Calheta

a concrete path and the channel is wider, deeper and covered in big slabs. Pass a levada keeper's cottage and reach a road. ▶

Cross the road to find the levada flowing through a big concrete trough. Sometimes it is covered with slabs and sometimes it is open as it turns round a small, wooded valley full of eucalyptus and pine. Steps lead up and down while crossing an old, grassy, cobbled road on Lombo Brasil. Follow the concrete trough across the slope, sometimes on a concrete path or with fencing alongside. The slope is steep and grassy with a few trees. There is a tight little turn round a side valley to cross a bridge, then the levada runs among tall pines, with a few eucalyptus and mimosa.

Climb a flight of steps and cross a dam on the **Ribeira da Calheta**, then walk past the **Central da Calheta** generating station and set off along its cobbled access road. ▶ The levada heads gradually left with a wide and deep channel. From here on, it is the Levada da Calheta – Ponta do Sol. Walk carefully along the top of a wall between the levada and the road, then follow an earth path into mixed woods with agapanthus growing alongside. Cross an overgrown cobbled track on Lombo Doutor and swing round into a little valley. Pass pines and a few cultivation terraces to reach buildings and a cobbled road at **Lombo Atouguia**. Unless continuing further, turn right to follow a road down to **Lombo dos Faias**, turning left to reach the main ER-222 road where it crosses a river, with buses available.

This very steep and patchy road offers a rapid descent to Estrela da Calheta if needed. Uphill, it leads to Rabaçal, Walk 42 and Walk 43.

A short-cut down to the main road is possible.

WALK 54
Levada da Calheta – Ponta do Sol to Ponta do Sol

Start	Lombo dos Faias, Calheta
Finish	Ponta do Sol
Distance	20.5km (12¾ miles)
Total ascent	180m (590ft)
Total descent	640m (2100ft)
Time	8hr
Terrain	The levada path is mostly level and easy, crossing wooded valleys and cultivated slopes, but is exposed around the Madalena valley. A steep descent on roads at the end.
Maps	Carta Militar 4, 5 and 8
Refreshments	Bar above Carvalhal. Plenty of choice at Ponta do Sol.
Transport	Rodoeste buses 80, 107, 115 and 142 serve the main road above Calheta from Funchal and Ribeira Brava. All the above are available at the end of the walk, plus Rodoeste bus 4 to Ribeira Brava and Funchal. Taxis at Ponta do Sol.

The eastern part of the Levada da Calheta – Ponta do Sol runs to a point high above Ponta do Sol. It passes little farming communities but is well above the villages that sprawl along the main road. The levada loops in and out of several little valleys and also works its way round the magnificent Madalena valley. The final descent is along steep roads to the coast at Ponta do Sol.

Start on the **ER-222** road above Calheta, where a road is signposted for the Central da Calheta generating station, and 'levada', around 460m (1510ft). Walk up the road, but turn right up another road to climb above **Lombo dos Faias**, following a cobbled road onto a cultivated shoulder at Lombo do Atouguia. Turn right along the **Levada da Calheta – Ponta do Sol**, around 640m (2100ft). Head into a little well-wooded valley and cross a footbridge over the **Ribeira do Luis**. Walk out of the valley, and you will notice little storage sheds dotted all over the terraces. Cross a footbridge over a wooded gully on the way round into the next well-wooded valley.

Cross a footbridge over the **Ribeira das Faias**, then pass pine and chestnut on the way out of the valley. Walk through a shallow cutting lined with agapanthus, cross a road at Casa da Relva and swing round into the next little valley at Faias, which is well cultivated. Cross a tarmac road and continue along the path. ▶ Reach a picnic site and viewpoint, then

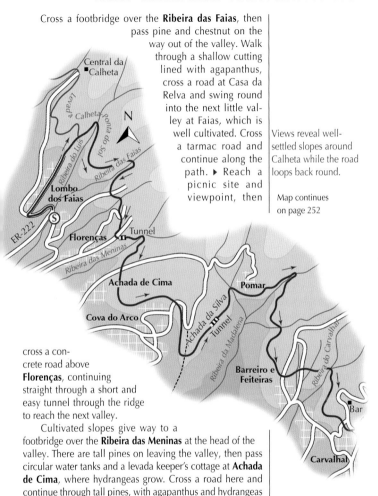

Views reveal well-settled slopes around Calheta while the road loops back round.

Map continues on page 252

cross a concrete road above **Florenças**, continuing straight through a short and easy tunnel through the ridge to reach the next valley.

Cultivated slopes give way to a footbridge over the **Ribeira das Meninas** at the head of the valley. There are tall pines on leaving the valley, then pass circular water tanks and a levada keeper's cottage at **Achada de Cima**, where hydrangeas grow. Cross a road here and continue through tall pines, with agapanthus and hydrangeas beside the levada. ▶ Pass a water regulator and cross a steep, cobbled road, then continue along a slab-covered stretch of the levada as it passes through a small cutting. The channel crosses a cliff face where the parapet is narrow and fencing is damaged. Slabs cover the levada and some are broken or

Trees thin out to give a grand view over the well-settled hollow of Arco da Calheta.

The levada crosses a slope above Cova do Arco

missing. An easier path continues past tall eucalyptus and pine with charred trunks. Turn through a little cutting where the levada goes under an overgrown, cobbled track and is covered with slabs; there is a glimpse down to Madalena do Mar before turning left at **Achada da Silva**.

Enter the Madalena valley, cross a slope of eucalyptus and mimosa, then follow a narrow parapet path with damaged fencing. Rock overhangs the levada and there is a small, curved **tunnel** with a good path and good headroom. The channel is covered where the levada has cliffs above and below. Beware of rockfalls. Turn round a rugged side-valley with rock walls, mixed woods, laurel and heather. Drop down a path with steps and cross a concrete footbridge, then climb steps to avoid a narrow, slippery parapet at the head of the valley.

Walk back into the main valley across slopes of fruit and vegetables, passing farm buildings and a concrete road at **Pomar**. The head of the Madalena valley is wilder, with an undercut dripping cliff and narrow parapet in places. The path is fenced, but not particularly exposed. There are plenty of laurels, then cross a footbridge over the bouldery gorge of the **Ribeira da Madalena**. ▸ Walk away from the head of the valley passing cliffs covered in pine and eucalyptus. The path is exposed for a bit.

There are lovely ferns in this dark and damp recess.

Turn into a side-valley full of eucalyptus and pine, and cross a footbridge over a deep, narrow, ferny gorge. Leave the side-valley and return to the main Madalena valley, where the levada is covered in slabs and earth. It is exposed for a bit, then less exposed as heather, agapanthus, broom and odd pines rise alongside. Turn left to walk among tall pines and the levada is open again on the way downstream. Gentle cultivated slopes are passed at **Barreiro e Feiteiras**. Cross a road, then you'll notice a house sits on the levada, so keep to the garden wall on the downhill side, climbing steps to rejoin the flow.

Walk round a large cultivated hollow and cross another road, passing houses and following a concrete path to cross a concrete road. A narrow path leads to a tight turn across an overspill at the head of the valley. Cross a step-footbridge over the **Ribeira do Carvalhal**. ▸ Pass high above a church

The slope bears pines on leaving the valley, but there are other trees.

The levada as it passes above the village of Carvalhal

and cross a track, then at **Carvalhal**, in the next cultivated hollow, the levada runs beneath a vegetable plot, a concrete road and slabs to pass a house. Follow the path down to avoid a narrow parapet and climb steps to continue. There is a footbridge over a concrete road, then other parts of the channel are under concrete. Cross the **ER-209** road. ◄ Continue past a circular water tank. A concrete path continues and two roads are crossed. The levada swings into a little valley full of pine and eucalyptus and crosses an overspill. On leaving the valley there is a view for a while. Cross a road and another step-footbridge. Pass vegetable plots and cross another steep road, then walk into the Santiago valley. Pass eucalyptus, pine and mimosa to make a tight turn across an overspill on the **Ribeira de Santiago**. The woods are quite dense on leaving the valley and many parts are dominated by eucalyptus. Cross a dirt road and a road on the **Lombo de São João**, above greenhouses. The next valley has a mixture of chestnut and eucalyptus. Turn round its head to cross an overspill on the **Ribeiro de São**

The Snack Bar Moisés is uphill.

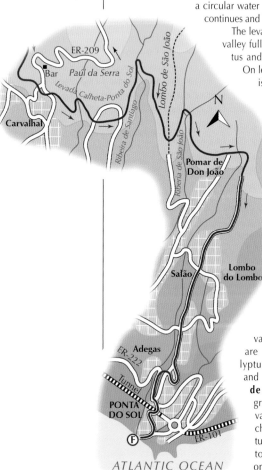

252

João. ▶ Greenhouses are seen below at **Pomar de Don João**. Cross a concrete road to reach a steep road, the Caminho do Pomar de Don João, then pass a square concrete tank. A dirt road, the Caminho da Fonte Coxo, runs beside the levada, with agapanthus alongside. Head downhill and turn right at a house, down a concrete and cobbled road, the Caminho do Castanheiro.

Pass pine, eucalyptus, chestnut and mimosa on the way out of the valley.

The road runs along a pine-covered crest, passing a reservoir to descend with a levada alongside. Follow the road downhill then switch to a steeper concrete road on the right. This leads down to a junction and picnic site, where the steepest concrete road, still the Caminho do Castanheiro, should be followed straight downhill, using steps built into it. Go straight down steps, through a road junction at **Salão** and pass a church. Continue straight down the steepest tarmac road, still the Caminho do Castanheiro, on a slope covered in bananas. Pass the Bar Ingriota at a crossroads and keep right. Watch for signs reading Caminho das Terças, which reveals useful short-cuts when other roads make really wide bends. Pass near the Bar São Caetano on the way down to the **ER-222** road. Continue down steep roads and flights of steps into **Ponta do Sol**.

PONTA DO SOL

Anyone who follows the whole of the Levada da Calheta – Ponta do Pargo and Levada da Calheta – Ponta do Sol, detouring off-route for buses or accommodation, will walk 73km (45½ miles) to this bustling little town. Other levadas could be linked, albeit with gaps between them, to continue to Ribeira Brava, Funchal and even Caniçal. Ponta do Sol sits in a steep-sided, sun-trap valley. It offers hotels, banks with ATMs, a post office, a shopping centre, bars, restaurants, buses and taxis.

WALK 55

*Levada Nova and Levada do
Moinho from Ponta do Sol*

Start	Ponta do Sol or Jangão
Finish	Lombada or Ponta do Sol
Distance	8.5km or 13.5km (5¼ or 8½ miles)
Total ascent	0m or 400m (0ft or 1310ft)
Total descent	100m or 400m (330ft or 1310ft)
Time	3hr or 4hr 30min
Terrain	Steps and steep roads are used for the optional ascent and descent. The Levada Nova crosses cliffs, is often very exposed and has a tunnel (for which you will need a torch). The Levada do Moinho crosses very steep slopes, but is often well-vegetated.
Maps	Carta Militar 5 and 8
Refreshments	Plenty of choice at Ponta do Sol. Small bar at Lombada.
Transport	Rodoeste buses 4, 8, 107, 115 and 142 serve Ponta do Sol from Ribeira Brava and Funchal. Taxis at Ponta do Sol.

Two splendid levadas pick parallel courses across the steep and rocky flanks of a valley above Ponta do Sol. They run close together, but are separated by cliffs or excessively steep slopes, but there is an opportunity to link one with the other in the same walk. Either climb from Ponta do Sol to pick up the courses of these levadas or use a taxi to start as high as Jangão. The Levada do Moinho is very old, and when local people feared that the construction of the Levada Nova would rob them of water, they protested. In 1962 there were violent clashes over water rights, resulting in arrests, injuries and one death.

Leave **Ponta do Sol** by climbing steps behind the church, Rua Santo António, then follow the main road uphill as if for Funchal. Swing sharply right after passing a cliff lift to climb a steep road called the Caminho do Passo. Climb steps onto a headland for a fine view of the cliff coast beyond Ribeira Brava. Keep climbing a narrow concrete road up to a crossroads at a bend on the main **ER-222** road. Cross with care to walk straight up the quiet Caminho do Pico do Melro. A little church stands to the right, but walk straight uphill past houses. The road levels out and descends gently to a junction.

Turn left up a concrete road, which later descends. Once it starts climbing again, turn left along a narrow concrete path, then turn right up a narrow flight of steps. The steps are equipped with lights and climb past cultivated plots, reaching a concrete road. Turn left to climb to a car park, tree-shaded square, church and school at **Lombada**. ▸ Walk towards a small shop/bar and turn left up the steep concrete Travessa das Pedras. Continue up a tarmac road with fine views over the Ponta do Sol valley, trying to pick out the courses of the levadas that will be followed later. When the road drifts right, away from the edge, climb a concrete path and steps to reach a huddle of houses at **Jangão**. ▸

Turn left along the **Levada Nova**, which is covered with slabs until it leaves the houses and enters the awesome Ponta do Sol valley beyond. The path is exposed, though other parts are safer and more

The school building dates from the early settlement of Madeira.

Using a taxi saves all the distance and ascent so far.

255

A waterfall drops from the Levada Nova to the Levada do Moinho

Take in the view down the valley from the church at Lombada to the church at Ponta do Sol.

vegetated. Watch your head when the levada curves to the left under a rocky cutting. ◄ There are stretches of fencing alongside the path. A rather wet and slippery stretch of path is avoided by crossing a metal footbridge. Exposed stretches of path are generally fenced, giving way to tree cover later, including laurel and candleberry and chestnut.

Turn round a corner into a rocky hollow to find a **tunnel** where a torch is needed. The entrance is quite low but once inside there is good headroom and a good path. Exit into an awesome rocky gorge containing **waterfalls**. Go through a rock arch and pass behind the falls, where slabs laid over the levada are slippery and there is a constant shower of drips. Wear waterproofs or use an umbrella. An exposed, but fenced path leads out of the gorge, then the way is more vegetated. Note a path down to the left, but follow the levada onwards, passing a water regulator. An impasse is reached where water is carried across the valley of the **Ribeira da Ponta do Sol** in suspended plastic pipes.

Retrace your steps along the Levada Nova, passing the water regulator, then walk down 130 stone steps to reach the **Levada do Moinho**. Turn right to follow the levada, then cross the bouldery bed of the **Ribeira da Ponta do Sol**. A track leads to a picnic site, where a waterfall can be seen, feeding water from the Levada Nova to the Levada do Moinho.

Retrace steps to the Levada do Moinho and follow it downstream from the stone steps, passing bay trees and turning round into a dark side-valley. The levada crosses stepping stones over a river below waterfalls.

The path is fenced where it crosses a rock-face, then the channel is obscured by flowery scrub, or the water passes beneath a couple of huge boulders. There are good views down a wooded part of the valley. Fencing occurs from time to time and the path is fenced around a little side-valley. The path is fenced where it runs almost vertically above the Ribeira da Ponta do Sol, picking up speed as it turns a left-hand bend. This is generally a fast-flowing levada anyway, crossing a steep, wooded slope.

A shelter protects walkers passing a dripping cliff. There is a view all the way to Ponta do Sol while crossing steep terraces. The terraces are lost as the fenced path slices across steep slopes and cliff faces, though there is a splendid view back to the head of the valley. A concrete path runs beneath a chunky overhang, then there is a view from the church at Lombada all the way down to Ponta do Sol. The path cuts across steep, cultivated terraces and a tangled slope, reaching the church at **Lombada**. From here you can either retrace your steps all the way back down to Ponta do Sol, or retire to the bar and call for a taxi.

A footbridge avoids a slippery part of the Levada do Moinho

WALK 56
Levada Nova: Jangão to Ribeira Brava

Start	Jangão
Finish	Ribeira Brava
Distance	11km (6¾ miles)
Total ascent	15m (50ft)
Total descent	415m (1360ft)
Time	3hr 30min
Terrain	The levada has a level, easy path across cultivated and wooded slopes. Steep roads and flights of steps run down to the coast.
Maps	Carta Militar 5 and 8
Refreshments	Bar at Jangão. Café at Tábua. Plenty of choice at Ribeira Brava.
Transport	Plenty of Rodoeste bus services between Funchal, Ribeira Brava and Ponta do Sol. Some buses are termed 'Via Rapida', covering the distance much quicker than other buses. Taxis at Ponta do Sol and Ribeira Brava.

The Levada Nova loops through lovely valleys full of cultivation terraces high above Ponta do Sol and Ribeira Brava, running at a general level of 400m (1310ft). A lengthy traverse around a large valley passes the remote little village of Tábua. Towards the end, fine views are available from steep roads and flights of old steps, leading down to the coast at Ribeira Brava.

To start this walk, either climb from Ponta do Sol to Jangão (see Walk 55), or use a taxi to save a climb of 400m (1310ft) over 5km (3 miles). Make sure the taxi driver follows the **Levada Nova** signposts to where the road crosses the levada. Turn right to start walking, bearing in mind that the channel soon becomes buried beneath houses in **Jangão**. Go down a flight of steps to reach the old part of the village where there is a very anonymous shop/bar at a junction. Walk gently up the Caminho do Jangão, passing old and disued buildings. The levada is seen down on the right of the road, but don't try to reach it until a flight of steps leads down to it, then follow it round the head of the valley, passing an overspill.

Cross a cultivated slope and swing sharply into the next valley, crossing a narrow concrete path and finally leaving the village. The levada crosses a concrete path as it swings left into a rugged valley. Follow the path across overgrown cultivation terraces and go through a short tunnel. Turn round the head of the valley, crossing a metal footbridge near a waterfall on the **Ribeira da Caixa**. Parts of the levada are covered in slabs while crossing overgrown and cultivated terraces. Walk along a short wall and cross a slope of tall pines where agapanthus and brambles flank the levada. Leave the valley and cross a tarmac road. Continue along a concrete path then leave the levada briefly where it flows under a house. Head up to the left to join a concrete road, then walk down a little and turn left to pick up the watercourse again.

The levada passes a couple of houses and enters the big Tábua valley, passing a few pine and mimosa. Parts of the levada are covered in slabs, and you will notice the old street lights running alongside, leading to a solitary house on a spur. An open slope is followed by a small, shady wood in a side-valley. Swing round a rocky corner back into the main valley.

A few pines stand on a slope, with more round a rocky corner. Turn yet another rocky corner to enter a side-valley full of eucalyptus and continue across a cut in a rocky slope where there are

Map continues on page 261

The footbridge over the Ribeira da Caixa

The Café Sitio da Ribeira lies well above the church in Tábua, reached by following signs.

brambles and malfurada bushes. Enter another little side-valley and cross an overspill at its head. Leave the valley and cross a few terraces, then there is a metal footbridge over a river. A short walk leads to the slippery bed of the Ribeira da Tábua, where it is better to cross using a road bridge just upstream. Cross a tarmac road below the little church in the village of **Tábua**. ◄

Continue downstream beside the levada where tall pines used to limit the views, until they were destroyed by a fire. There are some short, exposed stretches on the levada and big slabs cover the channel at a corner where there is a rock cutting. Brambles and agapanthus flank the path but there is another exposed stretch on the way to a short **tunnel**. The path inside is wide, but also uneven with low headroom. Emerge to walk along a concrete wall and cross a road.

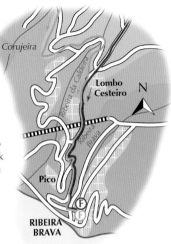

A few exposed stretches are passed and a rocky edge is covered in mimosa, brambles and prickly pears. Enjoy the view before leaving the Tábua valley, crossing a gentle ridge. Walk past terraces and vegetable plots, then climb a set of large steps rising to the left. Walk up to a road and turn right to walk down it for a while. The levada is seen again to the left, so follow it onwards. Pass more vegetable plots and houses, then follow an exposed, fenced path along the top of a concrete wall. Cross the road to continue and also cross the **Ribeira da Caldeira** and use a flight of steps.

The levada is narrow in its final stages with an earth or concrete path as it crosses terraces. A sign at a concrete road announces the end, so turn right downhill and continue down steep steps that

Steep flights of steps on the long descent to Ribeira Brava

wind to a road. Cross over and go down hundreds more steps on the Caminho do Lombo Cesteiro. Turn left at the bottom down a concrete road to reach the edge of a huge valley. There is a safety rail alongside and splendid views over the edge. Briefly walk on tarmac further down, but keep straight onwards. The road bends right, away from the edge, but you should keep left at a junction along the Caminho da Cruz to get back to the edge of the valley. ◄

Right leads to the Hotel do Campo.

The concrete road zigzags and has steps built into it. In fact, the road becomes a flight of steps before landing on a hairpin bend on the ER-222 road. Walk down the road a short way then down another zigzag flight of 350 steps. Cross a road bridge at the bottom to reach bustling **Ribeira Brava**.

RIBEIRA BRAVA

The old part of Ribeira Brava, with its narrow cobbled streets, lies close to a cobbly beach. The centrepiece of the little town is its church and the square in front of it. In recent years the town has expanded well inland, limited by the narrowness of the canyon-like valley it occupies. There are hotels, banks with ATMs, a post office, shops, bars and restaurants. Buses depart near the church and tickets can be bought from a kiosk. There are also taxis nearby and on the seafront. The Tourist Information Office is in the stout, stone Forte de São Bento (tel 291 951675).

WALK 57

Lombo do Mouro to Ribeira Brava

Start	Lombo do Mouro
Finish	Ribeira Brava
Distance	10km (6¼ miles)
Total ascent	Negligible
Total descent	1300m (4265ft)
Time	3hr 30min
Terrain	The levada path is rough and stony as it crosses steep slopes. Later it runs through forest and gives way to a broad track. Steep roads and steps lead down to the coast.
Maps	Carta Militar 5 and 8
Refreshments	Plenty of choice at Ribeira Brava.
Transport	Taxi to Lombo do Mouro. Plenty of Rodoeste bus services between Funchal, Ribeira Brava and Ponta do Sol. Some 'Via Rapida' buses cover the distance much quicker than other buses. Taxis at Ribeira Brava.

There are no buses from the Boca da Encumeada to Lombo do Mouro, and as this is a linear walk, a taxi is needed for access. However, bear in mind that the ER-110 road is often 'closed' due to rock-fall, and some taxi drivers won't use it, even if other motorists are willing to take a chance. Starting high on the road, a rugged path follows a fast-flowing levada downstream, with a track continuing down through dense eucalyptus. The route follows steep roads and winding flights of steps to reach the sea at Ribeira Brava.

▶ Start at a bend high on the ER-110 road at **Lombo do Mouro**, at around 1300m (4265ft). A short, steep road drops to a building, then a rugged path with uneven steps and wooden fencing zigzags steeply downhill to land beside the narrow **Levada do Lombo do Mouro**. The slope is rough and rocky, covered in burnt broom and heather. Turn right to follow the path downstream from the isolated house of **Casa do Lombo do Mouro**. The levada runs more or less level, but is overgrown as it cuts across the head of a steep-sided

For map, see Walk 56.

Looking down on the Residencial Encumeada complex from the road leading up to Lombo do Mouro

valley, susceptible to rock-falls. Two stretches of the levada were damaged in recent storms and now run through black plastic pipes.

The path becomes easier as it continues gently downhill, flanked by bracken and the charred remains of former heather cover. Swing out of a valley head and cut across a rugged slope. The water picks up speed on an incline as it rushes downhill. ◄ Pass a cave cut from the rock, and enjoy fine views down the valley to Serra de Água as well as to the high mountains beyond. Turn a corner round **Pico do Folhado** to go through a small rock cutting on a ridge. Descend a grassy path on a slope of bracken past charred chestnuts.

Pumice and other stones rain down on the path from the cliff above, so take care.

The levada reaches a valley below **Pico Queimado** that is densely wooded with eucalyptus. Watch out for fallen tree trunks that might be awkward to pass. Later, the trees step back a bit and bracken covers a gentle gap on the ridge near **Pico da Giesta**. Continue downstream and pass through a crumbling cutting. Exit left onto a track and turn right to follow it, noticing the levada on a couple of occasions on the left. You might choose to follow it, but don't be tempted if the surroundings look impenetrable. The track runs down to a road bend beside a large green **water tank**.

Turn left along the road, then turn right down a steep concrete road. Walk straight along a tarmac road that follows

An overgrown part of the levada as seen from a forest track

an edge overlooking a steep-sided valley above Ribeira Brava. The road runs downhill, but when it swings to the right, leave it and head down a steep and narrow concrete road. A few houses stand on the top part of the road but the middle part is flanked by mimosa and pine. Cross a tarmac road and walk down another steep concrete road, crossing the Levada Nova (refer to Walk 36).

Steep steps wind down to a road. Cross over and go down hundreds more steps on the Caminho do Lombo Cesteiro. Turn left at the bottom down a concrete road to reach the edge of a huge valley. There is a safety rail alongside and splendid views over the edge. Briefly walk on tarmac further down, but keep straight onwards. The road bends right, away from the edge, but you should keep left at a junction along the Caminho da Cruz to get back to the edge of the valley. ◄

Right leads to the Hotel do Campo.

The concrete road zigzags and has steps built into it. In fact, the road becomes a flight of steps before landing on a hairpin bend on the ER-222 road. Walk down the road a short way then down another zigzag flight of 350 steps. Cross a road bridge at the bottom to reach bustling **Ribeira Brava**. (For facilities, see Walk 56).

Overlooking Ribeira Brava during the long, steep descent

7 PORTO SANTO

A path follows the rocky ridge of Espigão (Walk 60)

The island of Porto Santo is remarkably different to Madeira, and while it has steep, rugged slopes and sheer cliffs, it also has plenty of gentle slopes and therefore offers easier walking. The size of the island naturally limits the amount of walking you can do, but while a keen walker could dash round it in a weekend, others might take up to a week. The things that immediately strike visitors as being different from Madeira include a rather arid and sparsely vegetated landscape, gentler contours, less hurried lifestyle, and an amazing, long, golden beach.

Walkers can either base themselves in the only real town, Vila Baleira, or in one of the hotels at Cabeço da Ponta.

Bus services are limited, so if using them, be sure to study the timetables carefully. Taxis are also available and these can be used to get quickly and easily to the start of all the walks. The island is divided into three parts by two large-scale developments. The airport runs almost coast-to-coast, and so does a large golf course. As a result, three circular walks more or less suggest themselves in the east, middle and west of the island. Any or all of these walks can be extended along the sandy beach towards the end of each day.

Organising ferries or flights to Porto Santo is simple. Flights can be booked at the airport on Madeira, or with Sevenair, fly.sevenair.com. Ferries can be booked

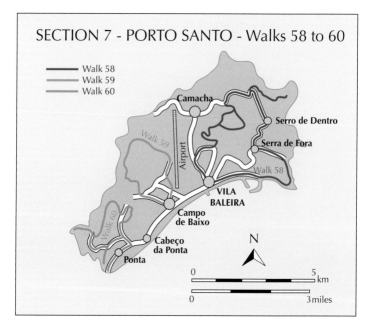

SECTION 7 - PORTO SANTO - Walks 58 to 60

in Funchal, or with Porto Santo Line, www.portosantoline.pt. Either deal directly with the flight or ferry operators, or use any travel agent in Funchal. You can arrange accommodation on Porto Santo at the same time as booking a ferry crossing, and this may work out cheaper than trying to book accommodation separately by yourself.

WALK 58

Pico do Castelo, Pico do Facho and Pico Branco

Start	Vila Baleira
Finish	Camacha, Serra de Fora, or Vila Baleira
Distance	12km, 20.5km or 27km (7½, 12¾ or 16¾ miles)
Total ascent	490m or 950m (1610ft or 3115ft)
Total descent	390m or 950m (1280ft or 3115ft)
Time	3hr 30min, 6hr or 8hr
Terrain	Mostly good tracks and paths on forested slopes, open slopes and sea cliffs, as well as road-walking and a rough and rocky coastal track.
Maps	None available
Refreshments	Bars at Camacha (off-route) and Calhau. Plenty of choice at Vila Baleira.
Transport	Moinho bus 1 serves Camacha from Vila Baleira. Moinho bus 2 serves Serra de Fora from Vila Baleira.

The northern and eastern parts of Porto Santo include the highest hills, as well as impressive sea cliffs and headlands. Many slopes are dry and treeless, but there have been laudable attempts to reforest some parts. The full walk is long and takes all day, but it is possible to finish early at Camacha or Serra de Fora, if bus timetables suit, or with the aid of a taxi.

Leave **Vila Baleira** by following the main road straight inland. Turn left at the first roundabout and right at the second, then turn right up a cobbled road at **Dragoal** as signposted for Pico Castelo (shop/bar). Follow the road across an old levada and turn sharp left on a forested slope. Turn right at a junction to walk up to the Miradouro Pico Castelo, which is a viewpoint and picnic site with a cannon.

Just before the viewpoint, turn left up a path signposted for Pico Castelo and Moledo, via the PR2 trail. Paths and stone steps zigzag uphill to pass a building and reach another signposted junction. Turn left to zigzag further up more than 300 stone steps on the steep forested slope, passing terraces

269

PICO CASTELO

From the 15th century, this steep-sided hill was a natural retreat. French and Algerian pirates raided Porto Santo and the top of Pico Castelo was fortified. There is a level summit platform and a building with a garden alongside. In clear conditions views extend beyond Vila Baleira, Camacha and the airport to southernmost Porto Santo, with the Ilhas Desertas, Ponta de São Lourenço and the whaleback crest of Madeira prominent.

There is a bust of the Regente Florestal António Schiappa de Azevedo, who was responsible for reforesting Porto Santo's barren hills.

full of interesting plants. A stone water tank is passed on the way to a fine viewpoint. ◀ A few more steps lead to the summit of **Pico Castelo** at 487m (1598ft).

Go down the only other stone steps off the summit, on steep forested slopes overlooking Camacha. Over 200 stone steps zigzag down to stone seats. Just below is a forest track, which leads down to a broad, cobbled road. Turn right up this road to reach a gateway and another signpost for the PR2. The sign gives two options, but an ascent of **Pico do Facho** presents a third option.

Ascent of Pico do Facho

Follow the dirt road straight up through a cutting. The road is concrete as it bends left on the higher forested slopes. Watch for a few steps on the right, leading onto a path climbing between the trees to reach a small building and a tall communication mast. Go behind the building to scramble up bare rock to a trig point on Pico do Facho at 516m (1693ft). ◀ Walk back down to the gateway.

This is Porto Santo's highest point, offering views all round the island.

Long option

Face the gateway, and there is a signpost to the right for 'Moledo (O)'. A path climbs parallel to the dirt road but quickly drifts away from it, becoming a pleasant, grassy path contouring round the slopes of Pico do Facho. It stays just below the forest, undulates gently and zigzags up through a small gateway. Views include Pico Juliana, Pico Branco, Pico do Concelho and Pico do Maçarico. In spring, flowers cover old terraces high above the village of Serra de Dentro. The path enters the forest and winds round a slope to reach a gap between Pico do Facho and Pico Juliana. There is an option to climb **Pico Juliana**.

Short option

Face the gateway, and there is a signpost to the left for 'Moledo (E)'. It starts as a narrow but obvious forest path zigzagging uphill a little, then undulating across the steep slopes of Pico do Facho. It occasionally crosses steep, grassy, flowery slopes and climbs a few log steps. A gap is reached between Pico do Facho and Pico Juliana, where both alternatives meet. Follow a low
stone wall along a

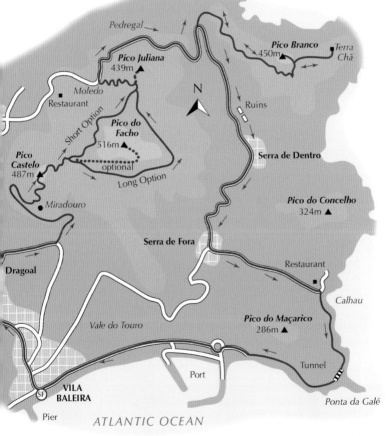

forested crest, stepping down to a track near a gap. There is an option to climb Pico Juliana.

Ascent of Pico Juliana

Follow a path steeply uphill beside a drystone wall on a forested slope. Once above the forest the path is difficult to trace on a rocky, stony slope. Keep climbing and cross a short drystone wall among a few pines. The rocky crest leads to the rocky summit of Pico Juliana, at 439m (1440ft). The highest point is a pillar of rock. Retrace your steps very carefully back down to the track.

The track zigzags down to a road at **Moledo**. ◀ Those who wish to continue further should turn right to follow the road round the lower slopes of Pico Juliana.

Cross bare and open slopes, passing a picnic site and viewpoint. There are ruined farms at **Pedregal**, then the road loops downhill in sight of a small quarry. A notice on the left announces the Vereda do Pico Branco e Terra Chã, or PR1 trail, one of the most dramatic on the island. Climb between short stretches of fencing, turning right as signposted at another stretch of fencing. The path climbs gradually across a steep and stony slope. There are wooden steps and splendid

Walkers who wish to finish early can turn left and follow the road to Camacha (bar/restaurants, museum and bus to Vila Baleira).

The rough and rocky ridge of Pico Branco leads the eye to a small stone building at Terra Chã

views back to Pico Juliana. Walk down fenced steps to turn round a rocky ravine below basalt columns. The path climbs gently across another rugged slope, crossing old terraces. There is plenty of fencing as the path zigzags steeply uphill, sometimes on bare rock, with hundreds of steps. Cross a rocky ridge to reach a steep slope of pine and cypress where the path has been hacked from bare rock above an exceptionally rugged coast.

Turn left at a junction to climb stone steps and a zigzag path up a rocky, wooded slope to the flat summit of **Pico Branco**, crowned by a trig point at 450m (1476ft). Walk back downhill, then walk along the other path, down and up steps, then down and up again. Follow a crunchy red pumice path to a small building at **Terra Chã**, and enjoy splendid views of sea cliffs. ▸ Retrace your steps back down to the road.

More distant views include the Ilhas Desertas and the Ponta de São Lourenço on Madeira.

Follow the road down past the village of **Serra de Dentro**, which is partly in ruins. Notice gullies riven down hillsides. Trees have been planted to stabilise the slopes and dams have been built across rivers. A few buildings at the bottom of the road are inhabited, and Casa da Serra is open to visitors. ▸ Follow the road up a slope to pass a recycling centre on a gap then walk down to **Serra de Fora**, where there are occasional buses to Vila Baleira.

There are restored buildings and opportunities to taste traditional food and drink.

A glimpse of the sea from the road-walk at Serra de Dentro

The rugged cliff coastline at Ponta da Galé

A sign warns of rockfalls and this is a constant problem along the coastal track.

A fine view along the coast takes in the Port, Vila Baleira and the long, sandy beach to Calheta.

Follow a road signposted for Porto dos Frades, which leads down to a rugged cove at Calhau, passing the Porto dos Frades bar/restaurant. Turn right and follow a track across a stream-bed where tamarisk bushes grow. ◄ Pass through an area of calcareous sandstone, then the track enters a big **tunnel** through **Ponta da Galé**, where the island of Ilhéu de Cima can be studied from both sides. Tread carefully beyond the tunnel as the cliffs are unstable and rock-falls are common. ◄ After picking a way along a very rock-strewn path, follow a dirt road to a tarmac road beside a go-kart track and walk past the harbour. When the ferry arrives and departs, a bus or taxi can be used to return to **Vila Baleira**, otherwise follow either the beach or the road back to town.

WALK 59

Campo de Baixo, Bárbara Gomes and Eiras

Start/finish	Campo de Baixo
Distance	9.5km (6 miles)
Total ascent/descent	300m (985ft)
Time	3hr
Terrain	Road-walking at the start and finish, otherwise good tracks and paths on gentle scrubby slopes.
Maps	None available
Refreshments	Bars and restaurants at Campo de Baixo.
Transport	Moinho bus 4 serves Campo de Baixo from Vila Baleira.

The middle part of Porto Santo contains only a few low, gently rolling hills, with a savage cliff coastline to one side and a glorious sandy beach to the other. The area is hemmed in by two large developments that run almost coast-to-coast across the island – the airport and Porto Santo Golf. A curious feature of this walk is the proximity of old windmills with modern wind turbines.

Start at the Zarco Shopping centre at **Campo de Baixo**. ▶ Walk inland by road along the Estrada Dr Francisco Rodrigues Jardim and keep right, in effect straight ahead, along the Estrada José Joaquim Pestana Vasconcelos. Continue straight along the road signposted for Campo de Cima which has a limekiln *(forno da cal)* on the left. Cross a well-vegetated river and follow the road uphill. Go straight past a roundabout. ▶ Go straight up a dirt road to pass small fruit and vegetable plots. Turn right along a road at the top to reach a complex junction at the end of the Estrada Benvinda Ascensão Oliveira. Simply walk straight ahead along a broad, level dirt road to reach the airport fence.

Fork left at the fence to pass one last house and keep walking along the most obvious track to pass tiny walled plots. Notice a few tiny, stone-walled enclosures full of untended figs and vines. Climb straight uphill and ignore any tracks left or right. To the left, part of the hillside is covered in solar panels. Reach a mast and buildings on top of **Bárbara Gomes**, at 227m (745ft). This stands in the middle of Porto

Bank with ATM, bars, restaurants, shops.

The Quinta das Palmeiras mini-zoo and old windmills lie far away to the left.

Note the abundance of snail shells scattered everywhere, seldom seen on Madeira. Calcareous sandstone fills the middle of Porto Santo, providing snails with calcium for their shells.

Santo offering views all round the island. ◄ Walk straight down towards the cliff coast, crossing arid, stony scrub, landing on a track between a solitary farm and a stone-crushing plant. Turn left to follow the track roughly parallel to the cliffs, keeping well away from the stoneworks. Climb to a building, masts and a trig point on top of **Eiras**, at 176m (577ft). Pass around a fenced enclosure on the summit and continue along the track, but don't go near the amazingly green **golf course**. Swing left along obvious tracks, passing alongside a drystone wall, then climbing towards three **wind turbines** on a low hill.

Pass between the turbines then head right a little to follow a track down to the nearest house. Walk down the road, the Rua dos Caçadores, and turn right at the bottom. Turn left at another road junction, then right at a junction shortly afterwards. Go straight through a roundabout and maybe a couple of small bars might be open. The road can be followed back to Campo de Baixo, but it is worth varying the route slightly.

Turn left up the Rua Bispo D Francisco Santana, then turn right at the top, where an open crest has been spared building development. There are two small **windmills** to see. Keep right of the second one to follow a road, dirt road and another road straight downhill at Beco de Viola. Turn right at the bottom, then left to return to **Campo de Baixo**.

Beach extension

Those who want to extend the walk onto Porto Santo's wonderful sandy beach can go along the nearby Estrada do Forno da Cal. If staying at Vila Baleira, turn left along the beach. If staying at Cabeço da Ponta, turn right along the beach. Either way adds a pleasant and easy 2km (1¼ miles) to the walk.

Climbing from the airport fence towards Bárbara Gomes

Porto Santo Golf, seen on the way down Pico de Ana Ferreira

WALK 60

*Ponta, Pico de Ana Ferreira, Pico
do Espigão and Calheta*

Start	Ponta
Finish	Calheta
Distance	14km (8¾ miles)
Total ascent	450m (1475ft)
Total descent	450m (1475ft)
Time	5hr
Terrain	Road-walking at the start and finish, otherwise rugged slopes, vague paths and good tracks.
Maps	None available
Refreshments	Bar at Calheta.
Transport	Moinho bus 4 serves Ponta and Calheta from Vila Baleira.

The south and western parts of Porto Santo include a couple of rugged hills, an impressive cliff coast and an amazing sandy beach unlike anything seen in Madeira. This walk includes spur routes to notable viewpoints and passes barren and eroded slopes that have been reforested. There is an option at Calheta to walk the entire golden sandy beach to Vila Baleira.

Start at a junction near **Ponta**, following the road called Estrada Comendador José de Castro Vasconcelos, signposted for Porto Santo Golf. When a **water treatment station** is reached, turn right up a steep and rugged forest track. Follow the track as it bends right and left, then walk straight across the slope to pass a low dry-stone wall. Leave the forest below the rocky summit of **Pico de Ana Ferreira**, at around 200m (655ft). Walk along a level track before heading downhill by keeping left at a couple of junctions. Emerge onto a road near **Porto Santo Golf** and turn left to walk away from it. Before the crest of the road is reached, turn right along a track, then right again to pass some brown hummocks. After passing some wooden stakes turn left and climb straight uphill until the track ends. A path runs beside a rocky ridge, a resistant basalt dyke, to reach a trig point at 270m (886ft) on the rocky top of Pico do Espigão. Enjoy views all round Porto Santo.

Pines and prickly pears have been planted to revegetate the rugged, eroded slopes.

Follow the rocky crest further, reaching a tall tower bearing a radome. Swing right to pick up and follow a vague path down to a dirt road, then turn right to walk to an exotic picnic site at **Morenas**. ◄

Follow the track further and look to the right to see a cliff face featuring a complex arrangement of igneous dykes. Reach a parking space and fenced viewpoint at **Ponta da Canaveira** and study the offshore Ilhéu de Ferro. When heavy waves batter it, plumes of spray spout from a blowhole.

A bronze bust of the artist Francisco José Peile da Costa Maya stands at the viewpoint.

Retrace your steps back to Morenas and continue gently up the dirt road. Pines grow on both sides of the road for a while during a descent then a prominent junction of dirt and tarmac roads is reached. Turn right as signposted for a **miradouro**. The dirt road reaches a car park and the **Miradouro das Flores**. ◄ Views embrace Porto Santo, the

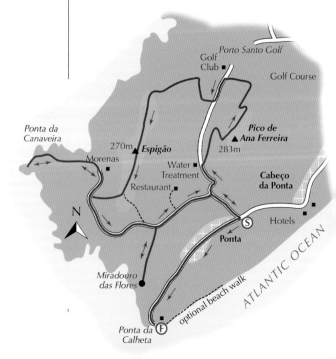

Ilhéu de Baixo, seen from Ponta da Calheta

rugged Ilhéu de Baixo and the distant Madeira. Calheta is seen below, but the slopes are too dangerous to allow a direct descent.

Walk back to the junction and turn right to descend a tarmac road. A track on the left leads to a restaurant, otherwise keep walking down the road to return to the junction where the walk began near **Ponta**. Turning right, follow the road to its end at **Calheta** where there is a bar/restaurant. ▶

This is a fine place to enjoy food and drink while observing currents in conflict around Ilhéu de Baixo, but keep an eye on the time if catching a bus.

Beach extension

An excellent extension, up to 6km (3¾ miles) in length, involves walking along the glorious golden beach. There is nothing like this on Madeira, so make the most of it! Calcareous sandstone outcrops on the shore at first, giving way to a wonderful strand. Walk either to the hotels at Cabeço da Ponta or come ashore at the pier at Vila Baleira.

CRUISE TO THE ILHAS DESERTAS

The landing place on Deserta Grande is a bouldery area formed by a landslip in 1894

Those who wander round the harbour at Funchal notice all kinds of sea-trips advertised, including day-trips to the Ilhas Desertas. The 'Desert Islands' feature in views from eastern Madeira, but seem distant and unapproachable. If you have an interest in marine wildlife and sea-birds, then a cruise will be most informative, but take one that includes a landing on Deserta Grande. Cruises to the Ilhas Desertas are of course weather-dependent and last all day, typically from 9am–5pm, with most of the time spent sailing there and back. The journey is greatly enhanced if local wildlife experts are on board. Half-a-dozen species of dolphin frequent the region, plus even more species of whale, along with loggerhead turtles and a variety of birds. Sailings pass the Reserva Natural Parcial

do Garajou on leaving Madeira and a local expert will be aware of any recent sightings.

Drawing close to the Ilhas Desertas, they appear impregnable, being flanked by cliffs on all approaches. They are, from north to south, little Ilhéu Chão, big Deserta Grande, and middle-sized Bugio. The islands were once frequented by pirates, but any attempts to establish settlements were thwarted by a lack of water. In 1894 a colossal landslip on the western flank of Deserta Grande formed a bouldery peninsula called Fajã Grande, creating a natural harbour suitable for landing. Usually, lunch is served on board, while swimming and snorkelling are popular. A dinghy ferries people ashore for a brief visit. Anyone visiting with their own craft can moor for

Rare monk seals have a breeding colony and can occasionally be spotted. Apart from this local population, monk seals are found only in the Mediterranean. Rare Fea's petrels breed at the southern end of Bugio, while Zino's, Bulwer's and Madeiran storm petrels are also seen. Manx, Cory's and little shearwaters are present, along with roseate and common terns. Yellow-legged gulls are very likely to be seen. A herd of wild goats were introduced by humans, and the islands teem with little lizards. A rare species of spider lives on the top of Deserta Grande, along with a rare plant known as rock cabbage.

There are smaller members of the Madeira Islands group. The remote Ilhas Selvagens can't even be seen from Madeira and lie closer to Tenerife. Trips to these islands are not available from Madeira and, in any case, even among the scientific community there is apparently a long waiting-list for access.

a period of 48 hours without needing special permission.

The islands and the nearby sea are designated as a Reserva Natural Parcial and Reserva Natural Integral, and access is strictly controlled. Day-trip landings rarely include more than an hour ashore, and access is limited to a short circular trail within sight of the warden's base. This offers an opportunity to see a few plants on arid, stony slopes, but little else. Stone steps climb up a cliff face, giving access to the high crest of the island, at 479m (1572ft), and the rolling plateau of Pedregal, but this is available only to visitors who book specific tours that include an overnight stop on the island. Information can be obtained from displays at the base. There are no real facilities for visitors, and even the drinking water has to be delivered by the Portuguese navy.

N

▲ 444m
Pedregal

Deserta Grande

ATLANTIC
OCEAN

▲ 479m

Warden's Base ■

Fajã Grande

APPENDIX A

Route summary table

Walk	Start	Finish	Distance	Ascent/Descent	Time	Page
Walk 1	Monte	Camacha	15.5km (9¾ miles)	330m/130m	5hr	39
Walk 2	Camacha	Quatro Estradas	17km (10½ miles)	150m/100m	5hr 30min	46
Walk 3	São João de Latrão	Camacha	10km (6¼ miles)	120m/100m	3hr 15min	50
Walk 4	Camacha	Santo da Serra	19.5km (12 miles)	120m/140m	6hr 15min	52
Walk 5	Santo da Serra	Santo da Serra	13.5km (8½ miles)	180m/180m	4hr	56
Walk 6	Baia d'Abra	Baia d'Abra	7.5km (4¾ miles)	450m/450m	2hr 30min	59
Walk 7	Maroços	Caniçal	11.5km or 18km (7¼ or 11¼ miles)	50m/210m	4hr or 6hr 30min	62
Walk 8	Santo da Serra	Portela	7km (4¼ miles)	150m/160m	2hr 30min	67
Walk 9	Portela	Maroços	9km (5½ miles)	150m/580m	4hr	70
Walk 10	Porto da Cruz	Ribeira Seca	10km (6¼ miles)	400m/250m	4hr	72
Walk 11	Moinhos	Moinhos	5.5km (3½ miles)	550m/550m	3hr	79
Walk 12	Portela	Ribeiro Frio	11km (6¾ miles)	190m/10m	4hr	82
Walk 13	Poiso	Porto da Cruz	13km (8 miles)	100m/1500m	4hr	86
Walk 14	Fajã da Nogueira	Fajã da Nogueira	9.5km or 18km (6 or 11¾ miles)	390m or 640m/390m or 640m	4hr or 7hr	89
Walk 15	Poiso	Santana	18.5km (11½ miles)	630m/1630m	7hr	93
Walk 16	Poço da Neve	Monte	9km (5½ miles)	50m/1140m	3hr	99
Walk 17	Poço da Neve	Barreira	8km (5 miles)	50m/1040m	2hr 30min	103
Walk 18	Curral das Freiras	Funchal	15km (9¼ miles)	15m/400m	5hr	107
Walk 19	Lombada	Funchal	6.5km or 11km (4 or 6¾ miles)	35m/25m	2hr 15min or 4hr	114
Walk 20	Boca da Encumeada	Achada do Teixeira	13.5km (8½ miles)	1480m/900m	7hr	121

Walk	Start	Finish	Distance	Ascent/Descent	Time	Page
Walk 21	Boca da Encumeada	Curral das Freiras	15km (9¼ miles)	680m/1040m	5hr	125
Walk 22	Pico do Areeiro	Pico do Areeiro	7.5km (4¾ miles)	400m/400m	3hr	129
Walk 23	Pico do Areeiro	Pico do Areeiro	12km (7½ miles)	1300m/1220m	6hr	132
Walk 24	Pico Ruivo	Ilha	8.5km (5¼ miles)	30m/1530m	3hr 30min	136
Walk 25	Pico Ruivo	Santana	10.5km (6½ miles)	50m/1490m	3hr 30min	140
Walk 26	Pico das Pedras or Queimadas	Pico das Pedras or Queimadas	16km or 20km (10 or 12½ miles)	100m/330m	6hr or 7hr	142
Walk 27	Quebradas	Quebradas	10km (6¼ miles)	150m/150m	3hr 30min	146
Walk 28	Pico do Tanoeiro	São Jorge	5.5km or 6km (3½ miles or 3¾ miles)	300m/330m	2hr or 2hr 30min	148
Walk 29	Boca da Encumeada	Boca da Encumeada	17.5km (10¾ miles)	1100m/1100m	6hr	151
Walk 30	Colmeal	Colmeal	14km (8¾ miles)	1450m/1450m	6hr	156
Walk 31	Fajã dos Cardos	Fajã do Penedo	13km (8 miles)	950m/1400m	5hr	160
Walk 32	Boca da Encumeada	Colmeal	9.5km (6 miles)	740m/1110m	5hr	163
Walk 33	Boca da Encumeada	Marco e Fonte	15km (9¼ miles)	600m/700m	6hr	170
Walk 34	Marco e Fonte	Curral das Freiras	10.5km (6½ miles)	660m/920	4hr	174
Walk 35	Cabo Podão	Lombo Chão or Curral das Freiras	4.5km or 9km (2¾ or 5½ miles)	260m or 590m/600m or 730m	1hr 45min or 3hr 15min	177
Walk 36	Marco e Fonte	Fontes	8km (5 miles)	520m/480m	3hr 30min	180
Walk 37	Boca da Corrida	Boca da Corrida	5.5km (3½ miles)	300m/300m	2hr	183
Walk 38	Fontes	Fontes	8.5km (5¼ miles)	380m/380m	3hr	185
Walk 39	Fajã da Ribeira	Boa Morte	6.5km (4 miles)	500m/20m	2hr 30min	187
Walk 40	Boa Morte	Estreito de Câmara de Lobos	17.5km (10¾ miles)	30m/20m	5hr 30min	190

Walk	Start	Finish	Distance	Ascent/Descent	Time	Page
Walk 41	Estanquinhos	Estanquinhos	13.5km (8½ miles)	300m/300m	4hr	196
Walk 42	Rabaçal	Rabaçal	13km (8 miles)	300m/300m	4hr	199
Walk 43	Rabaçal	Cristo Rei	5.5km (3½ miles)	50m/10m	2hr	201
Walk 44	Cristo Rei	Cristo Rei	9km (5½ miles)	315m/315m	3hr	203
Walk 45	Boca da Encumeada	Boca da Encumeada	18km (11¼ miles)	500m/500m	8hr	206
Walk 46	Vão da Fanal	Ribeira da Janela	12km (7½ miles)	0m/1200m	4hr 30min	211
Walk 47	Fonte do Bispo	Lamaceiros or Porto Moniz	14km, 17km or 18.5km (8¾, 10½ or 11½ miles)	15m/850m or 1250m	7hr, 8hr or 9hr 30min	215
Walk 48	Farol at Ponta do Pargo	Fonte do Bispo	10.5km (6½ miles)	1210m/10m	3hr 30min	225
Walk 49	Tornadouro	Ribeira da Cruz	10.5km (6½ miles)	400m/130m	3hr 30min or 4hr	228
Walk 50	Cabo	Ponta do Pargo	10km (6¼ miles)	0m/150m	4hr	232
Walk 51	Ponta do Pargo	Prazéres	19km (11¾ miles)	140m/30m	6hr 30min	235
Walk 52	Prazéres	Paúl do Mar	3.5km (2¼ miles)	0m/640m	1hr 30min	240
Walk 53	Prazéres	Lombo dos Faias	18km (11¼ miles)	15m/190m	6hr	243
Walk 54	Lombo dos Faias	Ponta do Sol	20.5km (12¾ miles)	180m/640m	8hr	248
Walk 55	Ponta do Sol or Jangão	Lombada or Ponta do Sol	8.5km or 13.5km (5¼ or 8½ miles)	0m or 400m/100m or 400m	3hr or 4hr 30min	254
Walk 56	Jangão	Ribeira Brava	11km (6¾ miles)	15m/415m	3hr 30min	258
Walk 57	Lombo do Mouro	Ribeira Brava	10km (6¼ miles)	0m/1300m	3hr 30min	263
Walk 58	Vila Baleira	Camacha, Serra de Fora or Vila Baleira	12km, 20.5km or 27km (7½, 12¾ or 16¾ miles)	490m or 950m/390m or 950m	3hr 30min, 6hr or 8hr	269
Walk 59	Campo de Baixo	Campo de Baixo	9.5km (6 miles)	300m/300m	3hr	275
Walk 60	Ponta	Calheta	14km (8¾ miles)	450m/450m	5hr	279

APPENDIX B
Language notes

Days of the week

Portuguese	English
Domingo	Sunday
Segunda-feira	Monday
Terça-feira	Tuesday
Quarta-feira	Wednesday
Quinta-feira	Thursday
Sexta-feira	Friday
Sábado	Saturday
2a-6a feira	weekdays

Transport and timetables

Portuguese	English
Bus/Autocarro	bus
Paragem	bus stop
Carreira	route number
Chegadas	arrivals
Destino	destination
Duração da viagem	journey time
Feriados	holidays
Horários	timetables
Inicia no…	departs from…
Não se efectuam viagens no…	doesn't run on…
Não se realiza a…	doesn't run on…
Partidas	departures
Percurso	route
Regresso	return
Serviço	service
Só à 6a feira	Fridays only
Só no periodo escolar	schooldays only
Só no periodo não escolar	school holidays only
Todos os dias	every day

Food and drink

Portuguese	English
Açorda	bread soup
Açúcar	sugar
Arroz	rice
Atum	tuna
Azeite	olive oil
Azeitonas	olives
Bacalhau	salted cod
Batata	potato
Batatas fritas	chips
Bebida	drink
Bolo do Caco	bread (may contain meat!)
Bolo do Mel	honey (actually molasses) cake
Café (com leite)	black coffee (white)
Caldeirada	fish stew
Caldo verde	cabbage soup
Carne	meat
Caseiro	home-made
Cebolla	onion
Cerveja	beer
Chã (com leite)	black tea (white)
Dourada	golden bream
Ensopada	stew
Espada	black scabbard fish
Espetada	spicy skewered beef
Farinha	flour
Frango	chicken
Gelado	ice-cream
Gelo	ice
Laranja	orange

Portuguese	English
Legumes	vegetables
Leite	milk
Maça	apple
Manteiga	butter
Maracúja	passion fruit
Marisco	seafood
Milho	corn
Ovos	eggs
Peixe	fish
Pequeno almoço	breakfast
Pimento	pepper
Porco	pork
Prato do dia	dish of the day
Queijo	cheese
Sal	salt
Salada	salad
Sobremesa	dessert
Sopa (de tomate e cebolla)	soup (tomato and onion)
Sumo	juice
Vino (branco/tinto)	wine (white/red)

Topographical glossary

Portuguese	English
Achada	plateau
Água	water
Alto	high
Baia	bay
Baixo	low
Boca	col/gap/saddle
Brava	wild
Cabeço	head/headland
Cabo	cape/headland
Caldeirão	cauldron/hollow
Calheta	creek/rivermouth
Caminho	road/path
Campo	field/plain

Portuguese	English
Chão	flat area
Cova	cave/hollow
Cruz	cross
Cruzinhas	crossroads
Curral	corral
da/de/do/das/dos	of the
Eira	threshing floor
Fajã	landslip
Fonte	spring/fountain
Gordo	fat
Grande	big/large
Igreja	church
Levada	watercourse
Lombada	long ridge
Lombo	ridge/crest
Miradouro	viewpoint
Monte	mountain
Nova	new
Paúl	marsh
Penha	cliff/rocky
Pequena	little/small
Pico	peak
Ponta	point
Porto	port/harbour
Posto Florestal	forestry post
Praia	beach
Quebrada	steep slope
Queimada	burnt
Quinta	farm/mansion
Ribeira/Ribeiro	river
Rocha	rock
Santo/São	saint
Seixal	cobbly
Serra	mountain range
Torre	tower
Vale	valley
Velha	old
Vereda	path

APPENDIX C
Useful contacts

Travel and transport

Flights
Scheduled, charter and budget flights are available from many British and European airports direct to Madeira. Check the airport website for full details of operators and routes.Direct flights to Porto Santo from Britain and Europe are few, but the island can be reached by a 15-minute flight with Sevenair from Madeira.

Madeira Airport
www.aeroportomadeira.pt

Porto Santo Airport
www.aeroportoportosanto.pt

Buses and timetables
Either collect timetables from individual bus companies or check details of services online. 'The Unofficial Madeira Bus Guide' contains useful summaries of timetables.

Unofficial Madeira Bus Guide
www.tjwalking-madeira.com/buspurchase.html

Horários do Funchal
(urban and interurban)
www.horariosdofunchal.pt

SAM (Eastern Madeira)
www.sam.pt

Rodoeste (Western Madeira)
www.rodoeste.pt

Porto Santo Line
The Porto Santo Line ferry, the Lobo Marinho, runs daily between Madeira and Porto Santo. Each crossing takes about 2hr 15min. The company can also arrange accommodation (www.portosantoline.pt).

Madeira Islands Tourism
Tourist Information Office, Avenida Arriaga 16, Funchal, tel 291 211902. Open from 9am–8pm Monday to Friday and 9am–6pm at weekends (www.visitmadeira.pt/en-gb/homepage). English-speaking staff can help with queries about accommodation, transport, tours and visitor attractions. Smaller tourist information offices can also be found around Madeira.

Airport – tel 291–524933

Ribeira Brava – tel 291–951675

Porto Moniz – tel 291–853075

Santana – tel 291–575162

Vila Baleira, Porto Santo –
tel 291–985244

Protected Areas
Much of the high mountainous area of Madeira is protected as the Parque Natural da Madeira. The rugged eastern end of the island is protected as the Reserva Natural da Ponta de São Lourenço. The native vegetation is being restored in an area north of Funchal, forming the Parque Ecológico do Funchal. A marine reserve is located east of Funchal: the Reserva Natural Parcial do Garajau. The whole of the Ilhas Desertas is protected by two reserves: the Reserva Natural Parcial and the Reserva Natural Integral. For details of protected areas around Madeira see https://ifcn.madeira.gov.pt/. An interesting visitor centre at Porto Moniz, Centro Ciência Vivo, focuses on the *laurisilva*.

NOTES

NOTES

NOTES

LISTING OF CICERONE GUIDES